Peter Woodward is Emeritus Professor of Politics at the University of Reading. He is a leading expert on politics and international relations in Africa with special reference to Sudan and the Horn of Africa. He has been Visiting Professor at the University of Natal (Durban) and at the American University of Cairo. He is consulted by the British Foreign and Commonwealth Office and the US State Department, and has broadcast frequently on the BBC World Service.

PETER WOODWARD

CRISIS IN THE HORN OF AFRICA

POLITICS, PIRACY AND THE THREAT OF TERROR

I.B. TAURIS

LONDON · NEW YORK

Published in 2013 by I.B.Tauris & Co Ltd
6 Salem Road, London W2 4BU
175 Fifth Avenue, New York NY 10010
www.ibtauris.com

Distributed in the United States and Canada Exclusively by Palgrave Macmillan
175 Fifth Avenue, New York NY 10010

ISBN: 978 1 78076 220 3 (HB)
ISBN: 978 1 78076 221 0 (PB)

A full CIP record for this book is available from the British Library
A full CIP record is available from the Library of Congress

Library of Congress Catalog Card Number: available

Typeset in Minion Pro by Ellipsis Digital Limited, Glasgow
Printed and bound in Great Britain by T.J. International, Padstow, Cornwall

MIX
Paper from
responsible sources
FSC
www.fsc.org FSC® C013056

CONTENTS

ACKNOWLEDGEMENTS

My thanks to Lester Crook who has encouraged me over the past 20 years. Also to friends and colleagues at numerous seminars and conferences who have made suggestions with regard to various papers, many of which have found their way into this book. Special thanks are due to the Leverhulme Trust through Reading University's 'Liberal Way of War' Programme, imaginatively conceived by Alan Cromartie, which funded travels in Africa and the USA during the course of the writing. Finally thanks to my band of grandchildren who have grown in number and stature since the book started, and who have been a welcome diversion: Emily and Ben Fleming; and Sam, Isla and Joe Woodward.

Peter Woodward, Reading

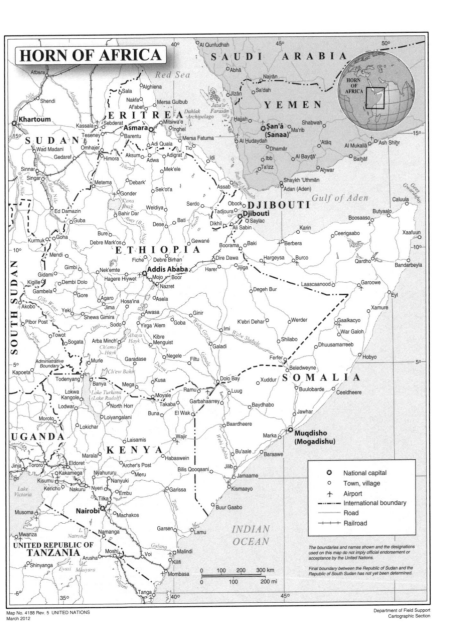

Map: The Horn of Africa.

CHAPTER 1

Introduction

'Crisis in the Horn of Africa' tends to invite the obvious response: 'So what's new?' An analysis published in 2009 began, 'The most dangerous corner of Africa is its north-eastern Horn, where instability reigns and terrorism thrives on the antagonisms of its governments'.[1] It could have been written at just about any time since the end of the Cold War, and before it as well. However, the end of the Cold War is not a bad place to start because it was seen as opening up a new era in which the liberal West, led by the USA, had proved itself victorious and would now be in a position to shape the future of the world: the notorious 'end of history' moment. Two systems had struggled, and behind them academics had pondered the respective merits of two broad ideological camps: variants of Marxism through Leninism and Maoism on the one hand, and 'modernization theory', perceived as liberal approaches to politics and economics, on the other. In true Hegelian spirit a new era of synthesis had taken place, in that the victorious West would emerge from the traumas of conflict to carry its values into the re-shaping of the rest of the world.

But what was that world really like? The Cold War was over, but there were many other armed conflicts around the world, some spawned in part at least by the Cold War itself. For a while there was talk at the highest level in Washington, the capital of the world's one remaining superpower, of a New World Order. However, as the 1990s wore on it seemed that some wars at least continued resisting any such new order; from time to time new wars broke out in the Third World, as 'developing' countries were still often referred to collectively, and even in Europe itself in the case of the new wave of Balkan wars. This gave rise to talk of a coming global anarchy in some quarters suggesting situations of 'permanent emergency', and of the necessity and right of the international community to decide to intervene. Thus the liberal victors of the Cold War sought to grapple with the reality of new and continuing conflicts: what should be done, when, for what objectives, by whom and by what methods? It added up to issues of liberal/human-itarian interventionism which were to challenge the prevailing under-standing of national sovereignty. Initially it was presented mainly in 'liberal' terms: many peoples suffered at the hands of their govern-ments which was bad in itself and justified a humanitarian response, whether or not the governments involved sought it. But humanitarian intervention was not enough, as governments might repeat their bad ways, and reform in the direction of improved policies and practices was required which could justify greater involvement. Democratic tran-sitions could have the dual effect of improving governments, through accountability and empowerment of populations, and reducing inter-national conflicts, since it was an oft-repeated mantra that democra-cies do not go to war with one another. In addition, the perpetrators of violence, including state violence, were themselves to be made more accountable.

11 September 2001 was to add to the claim that liberal states faced serious new and growing threats, and that intervention, including outright invasion, would not only liberate the peoples of at least some countries, but make the world safer for liberal democracies as a whole. It was to herald what was seen by some as a potential revolution in international relations, including a consolidation of the power of the Western liberal democracies led by the USA. One high-profile leader

in this direction was Britain's Tony Blair. From his Chicago speech in 1999 on the 'Doctrine of the International Community' questioning the sanctity of national sovereignty, through to his later justifications of Britain's role in the invasions of Afghanistan and then Iraq, he was to contribute to debates about 'the right to protect,' often abbreviated to R2P.

The Horn was one of the more obvious areas of the world in which to address these issues given its levels of conflict and suffering of every kind: it was certainly a region that was well qualified to meet Blair's view that Africa was 'a scar on the conscience of the world'. These issues in turn needed careful analysis, both theoretically and empirically, if effective decisions were to be taken, and there has been a great deal of analysis of various aspects of conflicts and crises, some of which has spawned sub-disciplines and associated research in a number of universities and think tanks. The London School of Economics (LSE) even established a Crisis States Research Centre in which the Horn has featured.

One of the first new or revived areas of study to carve out a niche, with the Horn playing a central role, was that of famine. There is, of course, nothing new about famine, but it was hoped – perhaps expected – that with the rapid growth of the global economy after the end of World War II famine would have been left behind. There was famine in Africa's Western Sahel in the 1970s, but it was in the Horn that it caught international media attention in the mid 1980s and 'famine studies' really took off. Some of it was concerned with definitions of famine and *Famine that Kills*, the title of a notable book on Western Sudan of that period; some with 'coping mechanisms' by which local communities could be assisted rather than made 'aid dependent'; and some with early warning systems and pre-emptive action.[2] Realization in 2011 that hunger, if not full blown famine, continues to hang over large areas of the Horn a quarter of a century later, from Somalia in the east to Darfur in the west, is a reminder that food crises have not been eradicated. Such crises in turn raise more issues of humanitarian intervention. When, where and how should intervention take place in famine and near-famine conditions, and are there any political circumstances which should influence such decisions?

In a wider context it seemed to many writers that food provision was part of economic development. Economic development as a subject had also been around for decades, encouraged by the attainment of political independence by so many of the world's poorer countries after World War II. Various theories were taught, some of which had political implications linked to the Cold War and the possibilities of new sources of aid. The end of the Cold War and the apparent victory of Western capitalism gave impetus to the Washington Consensus and what has been called the 'three decades of market triumphalism'. It was to feed into new thinking about marketization and economic development, not least in international organizations such as the World Bank and the IMF, and this affected the Horn as everywhere else.[3] It was an aspect of the new globalization centred around the growth of ever more powerful international corporations. Like much of the rest of Africa, the new globalization in the Horn was to be mainly another chapter in the scramble for minerals, and later for agricultural land, including Sudan's emergence as sub-Saharan Africa's third largest oil producer after Nigeria and Angola. However, ideas on economic development were in turn questioned by issues of global warming that sought to at least amend the unfettered 'free market' in the direction of sustainable growth, and by the global financial crisis of 2008 which brought the state back in to save the financial markets from themselves. In the Horn it seemed possible that global warming played some part in food shortages, while the state – or lack of it – in one way or another had always been linked to economic development. While market economics has been the dominant paradigm of the past two decades, the rise of Asia in particular has given rise to analyses of the 'developmental state', in which state intervention has been as much a feature of the direction of economic growth as has simply opening up to the shifting winds of free-market globalization. As ever, 'development economics', like all economics, is less an exact science than an ever-changing understanding of shifting economic, social and political realities.

Issues of economic development have been closely linked to debates about aid. The humanitarian case *in extremis* is hard to deny, but much more controversial has been long-term aid and the danger of it fostering dependency. Likewise, there are critics who have linked aid to foreign policy: it is hard to deny some relationship when the figures suggest a close correlation in the Cold War, although subsequently the connection has been less obvious. The question has also been raised of distinguishing 'relief' aid, and 'development' aid, with the claim that the latter can assist the long-term alleviation of the former. Both forms of aid have also been associated with closer relations between donor states and international non-governmental organizations (INGOs), raising questions about the independence of the latter and possible construction of 'welfare colonialism'.[4]

Another area of studies has been concerned with conflict. Africa's numerous wars have been variously explained.[5] In the early years it was often about nationalist struggles: while much de-colonization proceeded by negotiation, there were a number of significant armed struggles. Probably the most notable in the Horn was that of Eritrea: not against a European colonial power but against imperial Ethiopia to which it had been attached by the UN in 1952. But there have also been 'sub-nationalisms' within imperially defined states, such as those of southern Sudan and later Somaliland, which have raised the possibility of the division of an existing state; as indeed has happened in Ethiopia and Sudan. Much has also been written about other ideological dimensions of armed struggles, including various strands of socialism such as have been seen in Ethiopia, or religion as in Sudan's north–south wars. More recently ethnicity has become associated with conflicts. Almost all of ᴜᴖᴄ conflicts of the Horn can be described as having an ethnic dimension, but often as part of a larger, more complex explanation. Perhaps the closest to ethnicity as 'the answer' has been the role of clan and sub-clan groups in analyses of the years of conflict in Somalia. However, such sources of conflict may not represent historic or primordial rivalries so much as more recent constructs, and mobilization arising from economic disparities, and especially the state's role in creating and sustaining such disparities: conflict may breed ethnicity as much as result from it.[6] This has given rise in recent years to a substantial body of literature which itself opens up questions of 'greed or grievance' in relation to conflicts that are deemed to have an economic motivation. In recent years issues pertaining to minerals and land in the Horn have magnified this aspect of the literature on its several conflicts.

Conflicts have become the best-known sources of refugees. In reality people cross Africa's porous borders for numerous reasons, but conflict bestows a particular status as an internationally recognized refugee, entitled to support from the United Nations High Commission for Refugees (UNHCR). Its numerous conflicts have meant that the Horn has had the highest concentration of refugees in Africa, if not in the world, for decades. And if and when conflict has ended then issues of refugee resettlement have arisen. These situations have in turn contributed to the growth of another sub-discipline, 'refugee studies', which has long had an established home in Oxford University in particular.[7] More recently there has been recognition that many victims of conflict may seek refuge in their own countries rather than crossing borders. This has given rise to the internationally recognized category of Internally Displaced Persons (IDPs), who require assistance both during and after conflicts. In the Horn, the Darfur conflict after 2003 gave fresh coverage of IDP issues.

In parallel with the discussion of conflict, a body of literature on conflict resolution has developed. What kinds of conditions make a negotiated conclusion of a conflict more or less likely? How should

negotiations be started, sustained and concluded? Faced with sometimes decades of apparently intractable conflict various parties, often
from the international community, have endeavoured to become
involved. Such activities contribute to the growth of both theorists and
practitioners, and once more a specialized literature has emerged. Just
about every conflict in the Horn has seen attempts at conflict resolution at one time or another, with varying degrees of success.[8] Emerging
from conflict resolution has also been the recent theme of post-conflict
studies, rightly seen as a necessary part of attempting to prevent the
reopening of conflict.

In the wake of the Cold War in particular many politicians have
proclaimed the need for 'good governance'. This rather eighteenth-
century term, deployed in some political theory literature in the past,
has now taken on a new life of its own. For the past 20 years there has
been a rapidly growing body of academic literature, for which the aid
industry, both governmental and non-governmental, has shown an
active enthusiasm. Various ingredients have been put forward including:
forms of governmental accountability, such as the holding of free and
fair elections; freedom of thought and expression, including a free
media; an independent judiciary; the recognition of human rights;
building civil society; gender equality; decentralization of government;
improved performance of executive and bureaucratic tasks, including
reduction of corruption; and enhanced responsibility of the state for
the provision of basic services. Increasingly, progress on governance
was seen as part of the conditionality of international aid, sometimes
to be used rather crudely in packages of sticks and carrots for recipients. In the post-Cold War Horn, debates about good governance have
arisen with regard to democratization and decentralization in Ethiopia
in particular, while Sudan and Eritrea have often been criticized for
their poor governance records.

In the same period it has become more apparent that, while good
governance may be a desirable objective, there is a threat not just of

'bad' government but of no government at all. The literature has again been growing for some three decades with reference to 'quasi states', 'failed states' and 'state collapse'. Sometimes it is seen in black-and-white terms, as in Somalia where the collapse of the internationally recognized state in 1991 has been seen as a major factor in the later emergence of piracy amongst other things. Elsewhere state malfunctioning may be presented as a matter of degree, perhaps with greater 'statehood' in core areas, but elements of 'failure' in more outlying or peripheral areas. Sudan has been an obvious case of this kind, although Ethiopia shows some characteristics as well. Thinking about state crises beyond the agenda normally associated with good governance, including questions of basic security, has arisen and may give rise to some difficult political and moral judgements as international engagement with Somalia has shown.

Even piracy has managed to go down the path of specialization. In 2011 a colloquium on 'piracy studies' was held, most appropriately at Greenwich University in London which is housed in the former Royal Naval College.

Many of these specialisms have given rise to books in which chapters drawn from the Horn are included. They are, however, often presented in terms of the particular specialism rather than concerned with their inter-connections in the broader context of whole states or regions. There is a danger of 'single-issue management' and particular specialisms reflecting the 'flavour of the month' with the media, NGOs, the public and politicians, which can turn into in academic fashions and fads with implications for research funding. At the state level there are works published which may embrace aspects of several or even all of these specialisms, however, the problem with this is treating states in Africa in isolation from one another. So many aspects of what are often comparatively weak and porous states have important regional inter-connections, even if the particular problems and issues appear to be grounded in a specific country.

This immediately brings in the literature of international relations. For much of the post-World War II period the subject seemed dominated by the Cold War, and certainly the Cold War intruded significantly on the Horn. Ethiopia, Somalia and Sudan were all allied with both superpowers at different times (as was neighbouring Egypt) which was a unique record in the world politics of that era. The reason was essentially the Horn's geo-strategic position on the Red Sea, the Arabian Sea and the Indian Ocean, together with its proximity to the oil-producing Gulf region. The switching of sides was not just a matter of superpower choices, but largely reflected developments in domestic politics, including switches precipitated by regime changes in the states of the Horn. Such were their regional animosities that a change from one superpower to another in one country could lead to a corresponding switch in another. Probably the clearest example was in the late 1970s when, following the advent of military rule in 1974, Ethiopia's switch from the USA to the USSR was followed by Somalia's move in the opposite direction.

However, the post-Cold War era brought questions about a new order in international relations. One theme that was to emerge was the perceived growing importance of regionalism, perhaps even amounting to regional security complexes, an approach that soon developed theoretically as well as empirically, including Africa.[9] It was not long before this approach was being addressed to the inter-state relations of the Horn. Regionalism is always in flux as situations change both in relations within regions, and as external factors have an influence upon them. There is a sense of an historic Horn, especially centred on Ethiopia, or Abyssinia as it was generally known before World War II. Ethiopia projected an ancient history based on the highlands with its settled agriculture, sometimes loosely referred to as of a feudal character. In that context. statebuilding had developed into a monarchy supported by local lords (*ras*) and the ancient Coptic Christian church. Around the highlands were various societies, including large pastoral communities, amongst which to the east and the north – in modern-day Somalia, Eritrea and Sudan – Islam was the predominant religion. Relations between the Coptic Christians and the Muslims were to prove contentious, with tradition focusing especially on the sixteenth-century figure Imam Ahmed Gran who led an unsuccessful attempted invasion of Abyssinia from the Somali plains. That in turn had been linked to the wider ambitions of the Ottomans, while Abyssinia was aided by the Portuguese, both superpowers of the time. For centuries afterwards Abyssinia/Ethiopia was to present itself as a Christian bulwark in a sea of hostile Muslims. In the nineteenth century it not only resisted European imperialism by defeating Italy at Adowa in 1896, but also embarked on its own empire-building, spreading its control over surrounding lowlands and their Muslim inhabitants.

However, the Horn as a geo-political feature of more modern international politics has been largely due to later developments in Europe. It was the late nineteenth-century imperial rivalries of Britain, France and Italy which were to register the Horn's geo-politics on the map of Africa. As these powers disengaged after World War II, contributing much to the boundaries left behind, new problems were to emerge that helped to define the Horn as an area of conflict in particular. Ethiopia had managed to incorporate large areas occupied by Somalis in the south-east as well as Eritrea in the north, and both borders were to be contested. The Eritrean conflict in particular was to involve Sudan, while Ethiopia in turn was involved in conflict in southern Sudan. Thus by the 1960s, literature on the Horn embraced a growing area. Some even referred to the 'Greater Horn' a concept that seemed to gain traction from 1986 when a new regional organization was formed; the Inter-Governmental Authority for Drought and Development (IGADD – though 'Drought' was later dropped from its title so that it was commonly known as IGAD) comprising Ethiopia, Sudan, Somalia, Djibouti, Kenya and Uganda, as well as Eritrea following its independence in 1993. But any regional organization faces the internal politics, problems and consequent interests of its constituent members, as well as the international environment in which it seeks to operate.

For the Horn that environment is both that of the states immediately surrounding it and that of the wider international community. In the era of the Cold War the latter had largely been the rivalry of the superpowers reflecting their geo-strategic rivalry, with the Horn often raised during the Second Cold War of the early 1980s as geographically part of the 'arc of crisis' that reached from Libya via the Gulf to Afghanistan. However, in the international shakeout following the collapse of the USSR, great power interests in the region were far less clear. That tended to raise the profile of the immediate neighbours, and amongst those the Arab states remained particularly concerned. Egypt especially had vital interests concerning the Nile waters flowing from and through IGAD member states; Saudi Arabia and Yemen were also connected by security concerns regarding the Red Sea and the Arabian Sea. Other African states also showed a measure of concern, not least because the Organisation of African Unity (OAU) and the African Union (AU) were headquartered in Ethiopia's capital Addis Ababa, raising continental awareness of the troubled region.

Developments within the Horn did also in time impinge on the wider international community. Famine in the 1980s had contributed to the international encouragement for the founding of IGADD and its later efforts, especially with regard to peacemaking, were internationally encouraged. The US-led UN intervention in Somalia in the early 1990s was largely instigated by reports of growing famine. Beyond what were broadly humanitarian concerns, which continued in one form or another, new interests asserted themselves as well. One of these was international Islamist terrorism, which appeared in the Horn in the early 1990s as a new radical Islamist regime seized power in Sudan in 1989 and subsequently invited Osama bin Laden and al-Qaeda to set up shop there. Recognition took time to emerge but eventually the USA in particular came to recognize the threat, long before 9/11. The issue of Islamist terrorism also returned to the region with developments in stateless Somalia in the post-9/11 period. Talk of 'an arc of crisis' also returned, with possible terrorist links from Afghanistan via Pakistan and Yemen to Somalia, which could then stretch on into the Islamic areas of Africa. Since 9/11 in particular the whole question has even bred 'terrorism studies'.[10]

There was also new international interest in the Horn in the shape of intensified exploitation of its resources. In spite of talk of development, in reality much of the international economic interest has continued to be centred on resources. Minerals were at the forefront, with Asian involvement in the Horn led by China, Malaysia and India all developing oil in Sudan and also exploring elsewhere in the region; a number of other minerals were being developed as well. With the start of the twenty-first century raising fresh concern about food security in the face of climate change and rising population, there was also a renewed interest in the possibility of foreign agricultural investment in a region that seemed overall to have relatively low population (approximately 150 million) for such a vast area.

Somewhat more unexpectedly there was a new geo-strategic concern connected to trade. The poverty and instability of Somalia contributed much to the somewhat unexpected growth of piracy in the seas off its coast. In a short time the range of operations of the pirates extended to hundreds of miles offshore while the number of ships attacked, and in some cases seized for ransom, rose to a level which led to new international action to try to keep the shipping lanes free. This Somali development coincided with the new issue of Islamist activity, giving rise to fears that the two might become interlinked, thus extending the threat of both and mounting a real challenge from the Horn to international security more widely.

Wider international concerns also raise the subject of international organizations which have also produced specialized studies. Reference has already been made to IGADD/IGAD as a regional organization spawned by crisis in the Horn in the 1980s. Its work has been largely connected to subsequent crises; particularly its engagement in conflict resolution. The Horn has also involved both the Arab League and the Organisation of African Unity (OAU) as well as the latter's successor the African Union (AU). Both organizations have been drawn into the various crises at different times on issues ranging from Somalia in the east to Darfur in the west. In addition, the UN has been involved in the region since the end of World War II. All the international organizations raise issues of both their relations to one another and their respective capabilities in impacting on the various crises.

Strategic and security studies as aspects of international relations have in the past focused largely on military matters, but in recent years have broadened to the point where they touch on almost all of the above themes. In the past, state security was largely conceived in terms of other states. Internally states purported to contain nations, each with its own unique sense of identity. But it has become increasingly recognized that in many areas of the world, especially in Africa, such a sense of nationhood is often limited and its absence has become one of the possible sources of insecurity: one has to look inside the state as least as much as outside it for the addressing of security.[11,12] In turn, endeavouring to find solutions internally often raises issues of liberty and security, with some arguing that statebuilding for security has to take precedence over liberty. Since the end of the Cold War this has been increasingly challenged by proponents of 'good governance' who have promoted a faith in liberal democracy in particular as an expression of community: the acceptance of such an outcome is itself the creator of security.

The search for state security globally has led to both international alliances and rivalries. In the Cold War it was largely about the military rivalry of two superpowers. The most obvious manifestation was the Iron Curtain, but beyond Europe there was also military rivalry, particularly in areas judged to be of strategic significance. While the military confrontation of two superpowers ended with the collapse of the USSR, it did not mean that there were no longer security threats in the international system. One already mentioned which emerged as a growing concern was Islamist terrorism. Terrorism is timeless, and there had been incidents associated with Islamists on and off for much of the twentieth century. However, Islamism as an international force increasingly associated with terrorism as a major tactic has been mainly a feature of the past 30 years. This obviously illiberal tactic poses considerable problems for liberal societies confronted by it, largely because of the asymmetric character of the conflict to which it gives rise. Identifying the areas affected and addressing the challenges concerned is wide ranging and demanding and goes well beyond military responses, though they in themselves may be hard enough.

Issues of legality may arise for states with regard to decisions to use force, and to their military agents in the field with regard to the conduct of operations. At times the extent to which the challenge can be met may appear to threaten security. Somali pirates, for instance, appear to have a degree of protection from the laws of the sea, at least as long as their challenge is perceived as motivated by financial rather than political objectives. But while the superpower military rivalry of the past has largely gone, there may instead be a growing superpower economic rivalry. As mentioned, in Africa this has long been linked to international rivalry for access to resources, and appears to be going through a new phase with Asian penetration of the continent. But that also impacts on security in the way that it affects both states and their peoples. Good governance had included ideas of economic governance and these could well be challenged by the comparative newcomers. When they are taken to extremes, such rivalry for resources in a world of rising populations and possibly diminishing resources in some areas at a time of global warming could produce major challenges with regard to economic and political security in many regions.

With the possible exception of piracy the crises of the Horn are not new. Most have deep historical roots, some predating the current state boundaries, others were shaped by the imperial era and some manifested themselves more clearly after the system of independent states had been established in the region. To seek to clarify them this book will sketch the historical background before shifting to review the independence era at national, regional and broader international levels. Particular reference will be made to the challenges the region was to give rise to in respect of any hopes that the end of the Cold War would produce a new liberal political, social and economic order.

CHAPTER 2

The Evolution of the Horn

The term 'The Horn' derives from the region's shape on the map, and geography clearly plays a major part in its history. Current thinking places the Greater Horn as including the areas where the first humans are believed to have evolved over millennia before spreading across the world: the first 'globalization'. That evolution is often associated with the Rift Valley and the open plains areas surrounding the Ethiopian highlands, while the highlands themselves were vital to the emergence of one of the world's most ancient civilizations – that of the Egypt of the pharaohs – the two being connected by the waters of the Nile. While it is only one of the two major tributaries of the Egyptian Nile (with the White Nile flowing from Lake Victoria) it is the Blue Nile which carries by far the greater volume of water, and also delivers the rich highland silt spread by the annual flood which follows the seasonal rains in Ethiopia's highlands.

However, as well as providing a link in the form of the Nile waters, the Ethiopian highlands also served as a fastness. Based on settled arable agriculture, distinctive political and economic developments were to take place beginning with the rise of Axum in the second century AD in modern-day northern Ethiopia and Eritrea. A trading empire developed, with links stretching out not only in Africa, but also across the Red Sea to 'Arabia felix' – now Yemen – as well as wider Arabia.

Axum was to be the first in a series of statebuilding developments. A series of wars followed which saw the spread southwards of an Abyssinian state dominated by the semitic Tigrean and Amhar peoples from the north. Sucessive states rested on two main features. The first was the Coptic church which had its origins in Palestine and then Egypt, and whose influence was to extend into the Abyssinian highlands. While retaining a link with its Egyptian counterpart the church was to develop a distinctive character and to become in effect a state church. Amongst the many legacies of its past are the famous rock-hewn churches of Lalibella, started by the king of that name. The other main support lay in the nobles – the *ras* – who managed their own lands, and could also be called on by the monarch for soldiers. The system has loosely been seen as having some similarities with the feudal age in Europe. The power of the state waxed and waned due not only to external challenges but also the ambitions and aspirations of the nobles. At its height the state could create such accomplishments as the city of Gondar in the seventeenth century, but it also experienced later decline into struggles known as 'the age of princes' before beginning a recovery from the mid-nineteenth century, first under Tewodoros and then Menelik II. Menelik was to expand his empire in the lowlands surrounding the country, relocate his capital to a new city called Addis Ababa and fight off the attempt of Italy to incorporate Abyssinia into its growing empire at the Battle of Adowa in 1896.

To the east of Abyssinia lay the arid plains running down to the coast, and here the Somali people had evolved. The Somalis are a Cushitic-speaking people who have lived mostly as nomadic and semi-nomadic pastoralists. They have acknowledged a common ancestor, Somal, and have a common religion in Islam which spread from Arabia, as well as a common language. However, pastoral life had also contributed to a segmented society with deep divisions of clans, sub-clans and extended families. While Somalis have been described as a 'pastoral democracy' because of the extent of local community management and lack of hierarchical authority, there were also repeated clashes amongst Somalis over scarce grazing and water resources. The Somalis were also traders with a number of Muslim sultanates developing along the coast, with trading links to Arabia and the Indian sub-continent. In the sixteenth century there had been a major confrontation when the Muslim Galla (now generally known as Oromo) swept up into south-east Abyssinia led by Imam Ahmed Gran (the left-handed). Though he was driven back, the area to the south and east of Ethiopia remained largely inhabited by Muslims, and tensions between the Coptic state and its surrounding Muslim communities were to remain.

To the west of Ethiopia lay the vast plains of what was to become Sudan. The major geographical feature was the Nile. The Blue Nile flowed down from Abyssinia to be joined by the White Nile from East Africa at what became Khartoum, from where it flowed north to Egypt. Just north of the river's junction, a distinct Meroitic civilization was to emerge in the third century AD, a development related to the decline of pharaonic Egypt to the north, with which the area had long had connections. Meroe was also involved in long-distance trade and was a rival centre to Axum. While Meroe itself was to decline, it contributed to a continuing experience of state formation along these middle reaches of the Nile. The peoples of the Nubian kingdoms that were to succeed Meroe were Coptic Christians, and served to check the spread of Islam; however, as they weakened by the fourteenth century, Islam was to enter the area mainly from Egypt in the north and across the sea from Arabia.

From the sixteenth century the Funj kingdom emerged and converted to Islam. It was based on Sennar on the Blue Nile to the south of the junction of the two Niles, with its influence extending east and west of the Nile in the rain-watered areas. It stretched as far as Darfur, another distinctive state and one of a series that rose and fell right along the Sahel, the southern fringe of the Sahara. Like the Funj kingdom, Darfur had significant trading activities extending to the

Mediterranean. North of the Funj kingdom and Darfur, and away from the Nile with its settled communities, the deserts and semi-arid areas sustained only low-level populations of mainly nomadic pastoralists. As well as indigenous peoples, the pastoral communities had received a steady flow of Arabs from across the Red Sea, many of whom married into the local communities which often absorbed Islam, and sometimes Arab identity and culture as well. In time northern Sudan was to become frequently characterized as an Arab and Muslim society.

However, south of the Sahel lay a very different world. Behind the *sudd*, a barrier created by the vast swamps of the White Nile, the influences of Islam and the Arabs had not penetrated and instead pastoral societies had evolved in a harsh and demanding terrain. The best known are the Dinka and Nuer peoples, later to make significant appearances in social anthropology as classic acephalous or stateless societies.[1] There were also more settled societies along the river, notably the Shilluk, while further south in the equatorial regions mixed agricultural communities grew up including the kingdom of the Azande. In total, what was to become the southern Sudan was populated by a variety of ethnic communities which maintained distinctive ways of life rather than evolving a common language, culture or any form of collective identity, at least prior to the coming of nineteenth-century imperialism.

The ancient world of the Horn was by no means isolated or cut off from developments in the wider world. The Egyptian links with Africa have been increasingly recognized; the Romans and the Greeks had knowledge as well, with Herodotus writing of Egypt as 'the gift of the Nile'; while the Bible speaks of 'the land beyond the rivers', an allusion to southern Sudan, some have claimed. Later, Ethiopian monarchs liked to claim descent from the fabled union of the Queen of Sheba and King Solomon. European awareness of the Horn also grew, including the intrusion of the Portuguese into the interior of Abyssinia in the sixteenth century.

Yet when the external world penetrated the Horn, what was encountered was very varied. Ancient kingdoms flourished, most notably Abyssinia, while complex stateless societies existed in Somalia and southern Sudan in particular. The ancient Coptic Christian church survived in Abyssinia while largely surrounded by Muslim societies which themselves were of varied character. Trading economies existed, while many people were self-subsistent agriculturalists or pastoralists. What they had in common was that none were accustomed to living within a fixed set of state borders; that was to be a development that owed much to the arrival of nineteenth-century imperialism.

The imperial era

Imperialism's division of the Horn did not begin with European powers, but started nearer home. One of the first European incursions into Africa was that of the French under Napoleon in 1798, though they were soon forced out by Britain's victory at the naval Battle of the Nile three years later. Britain, however, was not then interested in replacing France; rather Egypt returned officially to the Ottoman Sultan. In reality power was seized by one of the Sultan's men, Mohammed Ali, who was an Albanian soldier of fortune. Mohammed Ali consolidated his position as Khedive of Egypt and, inspired by his interest in France, embarked on a programme of economic modernization of Egypt. It proved less than successful, but in the attempt he turned his thoughts to the acquisition of an African empire, with hopes of it extending down to the East African coast. That ambition was never to be fully realized, but the first step of invading the territories to the south of Egypt known as *bilad al-sudan* – the land of the Blacks – began in 1820. At first Egypt's rule extended only to the central areas of what is now northern Sudan, but in time it reached into southern Sudan in search of first ivory and then slaves, as well as to the Darfur sultanate in the west. Egypt was to be driven from Sudan by the revolt of Mohammed Ahmed ibn Abdullah, the Mahdi, which led to the fall of Khartoum – the new capital of the country – in 1885, but Mohammed Ali had effectively created a state which was beginning to correspond to what would become the independent Sudan in 1956.

The other indigenous imperial power was located right at the heart of the Horn in Abyssinia. The recovery of the state, which was begun in the mid-nineteenth century by Tewodros, was continued by Menelik, who also embarked on the acquisition of new lands to the south and east. It was to lay the claim of Ethiopia becoming a multi-national empire, one that sought in the twentieth century not only to retain the lands it had already acquired, but to extend its power as well.

Egypt and Abyssinia had been expanding their territories before the growth of European interest in extending empires into Africa. But in the latter part of the nineteenth century that was to change with Britain, France and Italy all becoming actively engaged in shaping the future borders of the Horn. Its geo-strategic importance was greatly enhanced in 1869 by the completion of the Suez Canal, opening up the Red Sea route to the great trading centres of the east. It intensified Franco–British rivalry for control of Egypt with the latter proving the victor, first by acquiring a majority shareholding in the Canal itself, and then in 1882 taking the country by force, even though it remained nominally a part of the Ottoman empire. The rivalry for Egypt, and the need to protect it once acquired by Britain, has been seen as triggering the scramble for Africa, or at least for the Horn and East Africa.

Italy was the first to establish a colony in the region, in Eritrea in 1869. It was small, and in itself possessed no major source of wealth, but it provided a port on the Red Sea at Massawa, and some agricultural land for settlers inland around the new capital of Asmara with its equable climate. In 1885 France took an even smaller slice of the coast known as French Somaliland and established the port of Djibouti. Britain already had Aden on the eastern shore of the Red Sea, but decided to follow its rivals by adding British Somaliland in 1887; the following year Italy moved again to acquire a long strip of the Somali coast running south from the tip of the Horn with its capital at Mogadishu.

None of these developments had caused significant tension or conflict, but moves in the interior were to prove much more competitive. Italy was keen to move into the interior of Abyssinia, and even thought that it had achieved a protectorate over Menelik by the Treaty of Wuchale in 1888. However, this was not what Menelik believed he had agreed to, and he subsequently built up his armoury with equipment from Russia and France. Relations with Italy deteriorated, and in 1896 an Italian force attempting to enter Abyssinia from Eritrea was roundly defeated by Menelik. It was seen in Europe as an embarrassing defeat, but with their new weapons the Ethiopian forces were a substantial obstacle for the Italian troops. It proved a famous victory and preserved Abyssinia as the one country in the whole of Africa that was to prove capable of resisting European invaders.

Following Britain's success in Egypt, it appeared for some time that France had switched its attentions to the Mahgreb, and West and Equatorial Africa, but it was to become apparent that it had not entirely lost dreams of west–east expansion across Africa. However, Britain had also started to think of moving south from Egypt. The disaster of the fall of Khartoum, following the failure of British troops to rescue General Gordon from there in 1885, had left the Mahdi's latter's successor – the Khalifa Abdullahi – in control of Sudan. By 1896, though, Britain decided – for complicated diplomatic and strategic reasons – to embark upon an advance up the Nile by an Anglo-Egyptian force. This ended in the battle of Omdurman in 1898 and the downfall of the Mahdist state. Word then reached the British commander, General Kitchener, to the effect that a French tricolour had been planted further up the Nile by a small party of Frenchmen. Captain Marchand had led his men from the equatorial coast carrying a metal boat, which they then

assembled on the Nile at Fashoda and proclaimed the annexation of
the area by France. Kitchener hurried south to disabuse him of that
right, but with Marchand's tiny force there was no question of conflict
in southern Sudan and the Fashoda incident, as it became known, was
down to the two governments in Europe to resolve. There was a brief
fit of jingoism on both sides, and some sabre-rattling, but the French
could do little at Fashoda and the matter was hardly worth further
damaging Anglo–Egyptian relations. From then on relations between
the two improved, leading to the Entente Cordiale of 1902, due in part
to the growing recognition by both countries of the rising power of
Germany. It left the Sudan under British control, but instead of being
given colonial status it was to be called the Anglo-Egyptian condominium. It was a rarely used formula internationally, which in practice was to give rise to difficult relations between the co-domini that
were to prove poisonous to Anglo–Egyptian relations for decades
to come.

On the southern flank of the Horn it was to be Germany that emerged
as Britain's rival. Having established itself in Tanganyika with its capital
in Dar es Salaam on the mainland – facing the Sultanate of Zanzibar,
the main commercial centre on the East African coast – Germany was
looking towards the fertile inland Great Lakes region. So too was Britain,
with its eyes on the kingdom of Buganda and its surrounding fertile
areas, and Lake Victoria encompassing the head waters of the White
Nile, with its approach coming through what became the colony of
Kenya. In the end Britain held off Germany to add Uganda to Kenya,
and complete the map of the Greater Horn which was to survive the
imperial era and for many years thereafter. With the exception of
independent Abyssinia it was a map that bore little relationship to
indigenous societies, and in the case of the Somalis divided them five
ways, a division that was to be significant in the years to come.

Other changes were also underway. Following Menelik's death in
1913 there was a contested succession before his daughter, Zauditu,

was finally installed on the throne in 1916 with the backing of a group of noblemen. One of their number, Ras Tefari, from Harar in the east, managed to make himself the leading figure amongst them and on Zauditu's death in 1930 he was proclaimed Emperor Haile Selassie I. Under him there had been cautious steps to make Ethiopia a more modern state. Officially a bi-cameral parliamentary system was established, though in reality power was firmly retained in the monarch's own hands. Economically there was development of the coffee exports mainly from the south and east which were so important for the state's revenues, facilitated by the French-built railway from Addis Ababa to the French port of Djibouti at the southern end of the Red Sea. In social policy a ministry of education was opened in 1930 and a small number of students were even sent abroad, while a few hospitals were also established. At the other end of the social spectrum slavery was officially abolished under Western pressure.

Internationally there were still some events to punctuate the imperial era. World War I passed comparatively quietly, although there was fighting between Britain and Germany in East Africa. However, in the interwar years there was a serious development when Mussolini decided to revive Italy's imperial ambitions, including a brutal invasion of Ethiopia in 1935, in the process of which he sought to avenge the humiliation of Adowa. The Emperor Haile Selassie attracted much sympathy when he appealed in person to the League of Nations in Geneva, but the lack of any active support proved one more nail in the League's coffin when faced by fascists. When World War II finally arrived, one of the Allies' earliest successes was in driving the Italians out of Abyssinia. Italy also lost Eritrea, which was to be administered by Britain for the UN, although in 1950 Italy was allowed to act as UN trustee in its former Somali territory. However, the era of European imperial dominance of the region was soon to wane and be challenged by the various nationalisms that had been growing in different parts of the Horn.

Ethiopia had emerged from the era of the European scramble for Africa not only as an independent African state but as a flowering empire of contiguous territory in its own right. In the process a variety of peoples had been incorporated on a variety of terms. As new lands to the south and east of the new capital were acquired, so many of them were handed over to Emperor Menelik's senior military commanders, some of whom proved eager exploiters of local communities. Even if not originally of Amhar ethnic stock, many new power holders were assimilated into Amhara culture and regarded themselves as part of the ruling group.

In foreign policy Ethiopia continued to play astute policies holding off Britain, France and Italy for decades before Mussolini's invasion and conquest in 1935. Italy's rule became known in Ethiopia not as a period of colonization but as one of occupation, and it was to be a tough and uncompromising experience. However, the occupation was to last only until 1941 when Britain restored Haile Selassie to his throne.

After the war Haile Selassie once more entrenched himself in power. There was again a supposed parliamentary system, but power still lay in the court which revolved around the Emperor who appointed and dismissed the ministers. Economic policies remained similarly conservative, with coffee still the major export and very limited industrialization. The majority of the population remained in poverty, with periods of extreme severity and even famine.

In foreign affairs Haile Selassie continued to judge the changing international scene acutely. Although it was Britain that had restored him to his throne, it was to the USA that he turned most readily. The Emperor was keen to incorporate Eritrea into Ethiopia, especially as acquisition of its ports of Massawa and Assab would end his country's landlocked situation. After World War II, the UN had placed Eritrea under a British mandate and in 1952 its parliament voted for federation with Ethiopia, encouraged by both the USA and Britain. Over the following ten years federation became incorporation under the rule of the Emperor. In return Ethiopia was to become America's closest ally in sub-Saharan Africa at a time when the Cold War was deepening globally.

Somalia

While Ethiopia had a long history of statebuilding that had become more centralized throughout the nineteenth and twentieth centuries, the experience of Somalia could hardly have been more different. On the face of it Somalis have much in common: they claim a common ancestor in the legendary figure of Somal, they have a common language and culture, and are virtually all Muslims. In their harsh and arid environment in the very tip of the Horn they evolved a pastoral system around camels, goats, sheep and cattle; only in the south of the Somali lands was there sufficient water for settled agriculture in the river valleys. On the coast there were some ancient ports, including Mogadishu in the south and Berbera in the north, with trade passing into the interior and up to the highlands of Ethiopia, but the bulk of the population remained pastoralists. Although all Somalis, the pastoralists were segmented into clans and sub-clans. Amongst the pastoralists there were four major clan-families; the Darod, Hawiye, Isaaq and Dir, as well as numerous sub-groups. 'Each level of segmentation defines a person's rights and obligations as well as his/her standing in relation to others.'[2] These relations are flexible and situational in character and thus, 'Pastoral clan organization is an unstable, fragile system, characterized at all levels by shifting allegiances. Power and politics are exercised through temporary coalitions and ephemeral alliances of lineages.'[3] At the same time there were rules, known as *heer*, deriving from a mixture of Islamic and traditional law and administered through *shirs*, or informal assemblies, where men gathered to resolve common problems and disputes. These were open and egalitarian gatherings where all men participated and decisions were made in a very fluid manner. At its best it was 'a pastoral democracy'; at its worst, a place of instability and conflict.[4]

In addition to internal divisions, the imperial carve-up of Africa also served to further separate the Somali peoples. Ethiopia's imperial expansion of the nineteenth century incorporated the Somali-inhabited lands of the Ogaden. As seen, France established a port at Djibouti in 1885, incorporating the lands immediately surrounding it into French Somaliland. Two years later Britain took an adjacent area which became British Somaliland. In the following year, 1888, Italy took a long swathe of land to the south beside the Indian Ocean, while the most southerly Somalis of all found themselves in Britain's colony of Kenya.

The various imperialists had somewhat differing policies. Ethiopia was particularly keen to raid Somali herds in the Ogaden, sometimes with considerable force. Early resistance was centred on Said Mohamed Abdile Hasan, who was from the Ogaden and became a Somali legend in the early nineteenth century. He waged a guerrilla struggle for nearly two decades against not only Ethiopia but also the Italians and the British (who dubbed him the 'mad mullah'). France was concerned mainly with geo-strategic matters and, as well as establishing the port of Djibouti, built a railway to Addis Ababa with a view to expanding its commercial and political influence there. Britain did little to develop Somaliland apart from exporting meat to Aden. In contrast Italy, which had few other colonies, did develop the infrastructure, including education and health services, especially in the south around the capital Mogadishu, and there were even some Italian settlers. It seemed for a while that Britain's expulsion of the Italians in World War II might lead to a shifting of borders and greater unification of the Somali peoples, however, after a certain amount of manoeuvring the imperial borders were restored.

Sudan

Britain saw Sudan largely in relation to Egypt, Suez and the Red Sea rather than as an African colony, as indicated by the fact that it was to remain the responsibility of the Foreign Office, managed through the British Embassy in Cairo. Development of Sudan was a secondary matter, though in time a vast cotton scheme was established in the Gezira, between the White and Blue Niles, which became the backbone of the country's economy. Faced with rising Egyptian nationalism at the end of World War I, and what was seen as its influence on Sudan where there was a revolt in 1924, Britain sought to remove Egypt from the condominium government. Egyptian troops and officials were expelled but that only encouraged Egypt – where Britain had recognized independence in 1922 while retaining considerable power – to continue to press its claim that Egypt's crown should once more be recognized in Sudan.

Within Sudan, Britain sought to encourage native administration in the inter-war years, a policy which gave recognition and administrative powers to the heads of selected tribes. As a further safeguard to this fragmentation in identity, and avoidance of the possible spread of nationalism, this policy was encouraged in the south by effective isolation of the region from 1930. While Islam and Arab culture brought a degree of integration in the north, neither of these features were present in the distinctive African south and were further checked by the promotion of Christianity and the English language instead.

During World War I, the Mahdi's successor, his son, Abdel Rahman al-Mahdi, had been allowed to rekindle his father's followers, the *ansar*, to counter the call of their enemy, the Ottoman Sultan, for an Islamic jihad against the British across the Middle East. However, when Abdel Rahman continued his rise after the war, the British had then encouraged the Khatmiyya sect to become more active as a counterweight. When Sudanese nationalism emerged during World War II it was to take the form of political parties linked to the two sects; the Mahdist movement created the Umma Party, and the followers of the rival Khatmiyya sect led by the Mirghani family supported the National Unionist Party. Since Mahdism had been anti-Egyptian the Umma backed Britain while the rival Unionists turned instead to Egypt and its claim to Sudan. It appeared as something of a deadlock until Nasser's coup in Egypt in 1952 was followed by the retraction of the claim to Sudan. Egypt then persuaded both parties to give notice to Britain to leave, to be followed by self-government before national self-determination. However, defeated Britain used the self-governing period to out-manoeuvre Egypt, leaving the Sudanese politicians to reject Egypt as well and move to full independence in 1956. The biggest losers, however, were the southerners. Less economically and educationally developed than the northerners, especially those in the central areas of the country along the Nile, they found that Britain was increasingly powerless to achieve recognition of their special needs, while the north was keen on maximum speed to end imperialism. Fobbed off with vague promises for the future, the south was effectively dragged to independence in the unitary state of Sudan.

The era of independence

Ethiopia

Although Ethiopia had not come under European control, the imperial era had provided the context in which the country developed from the late nineteenth century. And with independence across Africa taking place from the late 1950s, characteristics of the continent's emerging politics were to be felt there as well. Opposition to Haile Selassie was to grow in various quarters, with pressures for modernization becoming apparent, even from quarters close to the Emperor. In 1960 there was even an abortive coup amongst the Imperial Bodyguard in which it appeared the Crown Prince may have had a hand. Students and industrial workers were others amongst whom critical ideas were circulating. In the countryside there had long been intermittent peasant revolts but they became more frequent, although they were mostly repressed comparatively swiftly. However, in the north matters were becoming more serious. The government's apparent indifference to famine in Tigray in the early 1970s brought criticism from within as well as outside the country. In addition, the takeover of Eritrea was followed by the rise of local resistance that grew from the early 1960s and in time added to national disquiet. Matters came to a head following an army mutiny in 1974 which led to demands for reform from the army and beyond. In time the army opposition coalesced around the Dergue, a committee drawn from various units and ranks. Eventually Haile Selassie was deposed and detained: one year later he was murdered. A new era was about to begin in the country.

Like many starts to a revolutionary period, the Dergue's time in power began with uncertainty and bloodshed. Initially General Aman Andom, a respected figurehead, appeared to be in charge, but he was soon murdered, and from the shadows a little-known major, Mengistu Haile Mariam, was to force himself into power. In turning its back on the former regime, the Dergue instead took a path to the left leading eventually into an explicit Marxist–Leninist agenda. (The central square in Addis Ababa was to be flanked by portraits of Marx, Engels, Lenin and Mengistu.) The new military leadership was supported in this by its revolutionary allies, especially student intellectuals of the Ethiopian People's Revolutionary Party (EPRP) and their rivals in the All Ethiopia Socialist Movement (MEISON). In the end the Red Terror, which continued until 1977, saw the Dergue destroy both groups, with Mengistu emerging ever more clearly as the regime's ruthless leader.

Perhaps because of his military background and the repression of the radical intellectuals, Mengistu moved slowly in his creation of a one-party state. However, in 1984 the Workers' Party of Ethiopia (WPE) was established and spread its tentacles across the country, supported by an array of attached organizations intended to mobilize the people. Predictably Mengistu also invoked Ethiopian nationalism, especially when the country was invaded by Somalia in 1977–78 in support of the latter's irredentist adventure. This political agenda was backed by efforts to strengthen and further centralize the country's administrative structures. Much of the local administration in both town and countryside was carried out through the establishment of *kebelles*, neighbourhood associations, which sought to shape much of the social life.

Economically the Marxist programme proved difficult to implement. Inevitably there was a Ten-Year plan started in 1984, but the task in such a backward country was huge. There was nationalization of the limited industrial development that had taken place, but there was little subsequent growth and urban living conditions grew harsher in general. However, the vast majority of the population remained in the rural areas where the policy was to centre on the reallocation of land through the establishment of Peasant Associations (PAs). In practice these became less productive over time as the state sought to impose ever more direct commands. As a result, some areas saw efforts at more direct control through the establishment of collective villages, in which some 12 million people were living by 1988, although predictably these proved largely unsuccessful as in other Marxist states. The failure of agricultural policies was one factor which contributed to the widespread famine in the north of the country, which was to focus massive and unexpected international attention on Ethiopia in 1984–85.

That attention was to be mainly in the West, on which Ethiopia had largely turned its back following the revolution. Continuing to recognize the geo-strategic significance of the country, the USA had endeavoured to maintain its relationship with the government in spite of the revolution; however, by 1987 that was no longer possible. Instead, Ethiopia turned towards the Soviet Union and was soon one of its major allies in the Third World. The USSR also recognized its strategic position as the Cold War intensified in the early 1980s and the Soviet Navy became more active in southern oceans. Its importance was underlined for Mengistu when (in 1997) the USSR switched support from Somalia to Ethiopia as a result of Somalia's attack, and gave vital aid to Ethiopia, including a vast airlift flying in *inter alia* Cuban troops, enabling it to drive back the invaders.

wrong yes was in 1977

However, it was the internal challenge to Mengistu which was eventually to prove a greater threat than his external enemies. In the north of the country a rolling revolt had started as far back as the early 1960s. Its origins lay in the takeover of Eritrea in 1952, which triggered the emergence of the Eritrean Liberation Front (ELF). The ELF was largely nationalist in orientation but it was to be challenged at the start of the 1970s by a more radical movement, the Eritrean People's Liberation Front (EPLF). At the start of the revolution it seemed that the confusion in the capital was an opportunity for the Eritreans, however, Mengistu's consolidation as well as victory over Somalia in 1978 allowed the Ethiopian army to go on the attack in the north where the EPLF had finally replaced the ELF. The EPLF was forced to retreat until it finally dug in at the town of Nacfa. The EPLF also encouraged other groups in Ethiopia to rebel and in Tigray, immediately across the border from Eritrea, it saw success with the emergence of the Tigrean People's Liberation Front (TPLF). Tigray had been a historic heartland of Ethiopian monarchs, and the southward drift of the state's centre towards what became the new capital at Addis Ababa had encouraged a feeling of Tigrean marginalization. While the EPLF sought secession, the aim of the TPLF was to replace the military regime at the centre, but the two were generally allies in their struggle against a common enemy. Their struggle appeared at something of a deadlock until 1984 when the EPLF broke out of Nacfa and the conflicts became more fluid. However, it was another four years before a decisive step occurred when the EPLF achieved a major victory over the Ethiopian army at Afabet. This proved damaging for the morale of the army which found itself on the retreat. *Afabet!*

While the aim of the EPLF was to consolidate its position in Eritrea, the TPLF encouraged fresh revolts in Wollo and Gondar provinces, eventually bringing various groups together in a new umbrella movement, the Ethiopian People's Democratic Front (EPRDF). Mengistu took increasingly desperate measures both to stiffen the army and bring civilian reforms, but all to no avail and in 1991 he fled the country for refuge in Zimbabwe. The EPRDF led the subsequent occupation of Addis Ababa, with the EPLF fully victorious in Eritrea.

Somalia

After World War II the Somalis showed the beginnings of a nationalist movement, similar to those growing in so many areas still under European rulers. The movement known as the Somali Youth League (SYL) began in 1943 and spread such that it eventually led towards democracy, encouraged by the UN. Following elections in 1959, Britain and Italy encouraged their respective territories to come together in one state that became fully independent in 1960. There were hopes that with a common language, culture and religion Somalia might be well placed to forge a new nation. However, from the outset the new government was keen to remind the international community that there were still many Somalis in the neighbouring territories of Ethiopia, Djibouti and Kenya: only two points on the five-pointed star of the new country's national flag had come together, and irredentist impulses were strong.

The independence elections were won overwhelmingly by the SYL with the notion of 'youth' referring to the aim of creating a more modern society, breaking down the 'traditional' powers of local leaders and clan and sub-clan divisions. The constitution of 1961 was also 'modern' with the influence of the Italian model apparent. There was a unicameral National Assembly elected by proportional representation on a list system. The president was then elected by the assembly, and in turn he had significant powers including appointing the prime minister and, if necessary, dissolving the assembly. Due to its British influences Somaliland in the north largely boycotted the referendum on the constitution, subsequently claiming that it had never agreed to the new set up.

Recognizing the problem, President Adnaan Abdullah Osman and Prime Minister Abdirashid Ali Shermarke put together a regionally balanced government in an effort to see, 'how a vibrant democracy placed within an anarchic society could address itself in a sustained way to a broad agenda of problems'.[5] In the 1964 elections the SYL was once more the winner, but its majority was down and new parties were emerging to challenge it, especially in the north. Osman replaced Shermarke with Abdirizaq Hussein, but after the 1967 elections Shermarke defeated Osman for the presidency and appointed Mohammed Egal as prime minister. It looked like another balanced ticket, but the two men soon showed different approaches to policy and political unity was increasingly threatened. By the 1969 elections fragmentation was very apparent with some 63 parties fielding over 1,000 candidates. Though the SYL managed to win again it was becoming clear that clan and sub-clan identities were emerging as the basis for democratic politics all over the country. At the same time the increasingly bitter rivalries contributed to both the assassination of President Shermarke in 1969 and the effective paralysis of developmental policies. In some quarters at least there was almost a sense of relief when the army's senior officer, Mohammed Siad Barre, seized power in October 1969.

Siad Barre had started his career as a policeman, but with independence had been transferred into the new national army. After seizing power he established a Supreme Revolutionary Council (SRC) of military officers, initially to oversee the work of a new 'technocratic' government. Encouraged by the Soviet Union, with which Somalia's forces had had links since independence, Siad decided to move sharply to the left by adopting 'scientific socialism' in the Somali style, led from 1976 by the Somali Revolutionary Socialist Party (SRSP).

With the rise of 'clannism' after independence it was unsurprising that the practice soon received the socialist treatment. Publicly the main thrust of policy was to ban all references to clan or sub-clan allegiances, though in reality they continued to grow. The leading clans of the 1960s were marginalized and in their place the new regime came to rely increasingly on Siad's own clan, the Majerteen, as well as on the Ogadeeni (from which Siad's mother came) and Dulbahante clans, which was to lead to references simply to the 'MOD'.

At the same time Siad tried to engage the public more in the new directions the state was taking. Somali had not been a written language and there was some tension about the choice of adopting a Latin script rather than Arabic, since it was a Muslim country. Protests from leading Islamic scholars were forcefully repressed, and there was some progress in implementing a new literacy campaign. Siad had also incurred the wrath of the Islamic leaders for his efforts to 'modernize' the position of women in Somali society.

On the economic front the new regime nationalized the major economic institutions such as the banks and started some new state-run enterprises, while leaving the small-business sector in private hands. There were also efforts to encourage the pastoralists to form cooperatives, but it was a very challenging aim, given the structure and culture of Somalia's rural peoples, and met with little success. Instead the pastoralists were hard hit by years of famine in the 1970s, which called for other measures. Food aid programmes, mainly with supplies from the West, went quite well; some pastoralists were encouraged to re-settle in the more fertile farming areas of the south, while others were encouraged to look towards the expansion of fishing in Somalia's long coastal waters. However, the overall picture was still one of poverty, with exports consisting largely of livestock from the north of the country to the Arabian peninsula and bananas from the south to Europe.

The significance of underlying clan identities became more overt with time. The Ethiopian revolution of 1974 had an impact, especially amongst the Ogadeeni Somalis living in the lowlands of eastern Ethiopia. With Ethiopia in apparent disarray and Ogadeenis well represented in the SRC, pressure mounted on Barre in 1977 to fulfil part of Somalia's irredentist agenda by invading and annexing Ethiopia's Somali-occupied territories. The belief was that a successful military campaign would not only reunite the Ogadeenis with Somalia proper, but also encourage a nationalist resurgence raising support for the regime. However, when the invasion's initial success was reversed in 1978 it was unsurprising that clan tensions rose. Shortly after the defeat of the Somali forces there was an attempted coup by a group of Majerteen officers, but it was soon put down. Some surviving Majerteen soldiers crossed into Ethiopia where they set up the Somali Salvation Democratic Front (SSDF) and embarked on guerrilla attacks in their home areas, only to find that these efforts too were forcefully suppressed.

The SSDF was followed by the establishment of the Somali National Movement (SNM) in the north, which won the support of Ethiopia and the then-South Yemen due in part to Barre's turning to the USA to replace his former ally the Soviet Union. The SNM was essentially based on the Isaaq clan, but not exclusively so as other smaller groups remembered the better days when they were all a part of British Somaliland. The successes of the SNM brought increased efforts at repression by the Somali forces, but as so often they proved counterproductive and opposition in the north continued to grow.

Following the war with Ethiopia, Somalia's economic situation also deteriorated as a result of trade restrictions on livestock exports and intermittent drought that affected much of north-east Africa in the 1980s. The government's response was at best inept with rising corruption, inflation and clan favouritism widely observed. With time it became increasingly clear that Barre was relying on the MOD. Even America's support could not prevent the IMF becoming an ever more reluctant backer. The rapid growth of refugees from the Ogaden following the war led to UNHCR funds coming into the country, but this source too was widely seen as exploited by Barre's regime.

In an effort to repress the SNM in the north more effectively, in 1988 Barre surprised many by suddenly signing a pact with his old enemy Mengistu. Under it Ethiopia agreed to stop supporting the SNM, and in return Somalia would cut its assistance to the peoples of the Ogaden, as a result of which Mengistu could deploy more of his troops to the conflicts in the north of his country. While Barre's action was seen by many Somalis as a betrayal, it failed to allow him to crush the SNM despite widespread devastation by his forces in the north.

Barre's failure to contain the north after his pact with Mengistu was followed by the spread of fighting to the more southerly areas of the country, accompanied by rising clan rivalries as the state weakened and Somali society appeared to be fragmenting. The United Somali Congress (USC) was mainly comprised of Hawiye, the major clan in and around Mogadishu, and by 1991 its factions were threatening the capital itself. Barre, by then known just as 'the mayor of Mogadishu', decided to flee. He had started out two decades earlier with talk of ending clannism, but by the time he fled inter- and intra-clan identities had given rise to ever more violent conflicts even as the state itself disintegrated.

Sudan

After independence in 1956 the issue of the south remained unresolved, with talk of constitutional change never seriously pursued. Feelings of alienation grew in the region, and by 1962 led to the growth of a sustained civil war headed by a separatist movement known as Anyanya. Instead of addressing the southern problem, the northern politicians who took over power spent their time in disputes with one another, especially as the balance between the major parties made it necessary to establish successive coalition governments. As party politics fell into fractious disarray, in 1958 the Umma Party encouraged the army to intervene under its commander General Ibrahim Abboud. Although major coups had taken off in the Arab world in Egypt in 1952, this was the first coup in the Horn or indeed in post-independence Africa. However, unlike its Arab counterparts to the north, it was more conservative than radical, and still did little to address the problem of the south in a constructive manner. Instead, when sustained conflict broke out, Abboud's response was to seek to repress it, including the closing of Catholic mission schools and targeting the small number of educated elite, while also imposing Islam and Arabization. His failure, and the expansion of the conflict as the numbers of southern rebels grew, was a major factor in a popular uprising in the north in October 1964. Instead of trying to crush his fellow northerners, in the face of what became known as the October Revolution, Abboud simply handed power back to the civilians and walked quietly away. However, at the Round Table conference the following year hopes of peace in the south failed to materialize, and instead new elections returned power to the old political parties to no greater effect than before Abboud's coup.

It was not long before there was talk of a new coup, and in May 1969 it duly arrived, in the same year as Barre in Somalia and Qaddafi in neighbouring Libya, partly reflecting the disillusionment with liberal democracy in the Third World. This time the coup in Sudan was more typical of the Arab world than Abboud's had been. It came from a group of radicalized middle-rank officers led by Ga'afar al-Nimeiri who called themselves the Free Officers and established a Revolutionary Command Council (RCC), the same nomenclature as Nasser and his colleagues in Egypt in 1952. The May Revolution, as it called itself, was soon embarking on extensive state control of the economy and in 1970 crushed an attempted Mahdist uprising, the first such attempt in the north since independence. However, it soon became clear that there were differing strands of radicalism amongst the new rulers. Nimeiri was essentially for Arab socialism and favoured a proposed union with Egypt and Libya, but others in the RCC supported the approach of the influential trades-union-backed Sudan Communist Party (SCP), with its suspicions of the projected union as well as the threatened increase of Egypt's anti-communist influence. In 1971 the Communists launched their own military coup, but it was narrowly and bloodily stopped by Nimeiri: the SCP was never to regain its former strength.

Having defeated both the conservative civilian parties and the communists, Nimeiri then made a determined and successful effort to negotiate peace in the south, which concluded in the Addis Ababa agreement of 1972. The south was to have a semi-autonomous elected government of its own, while Nimeiri constructed a new one-party state in the north under the Sudan Socialist Union (SSU). Its main aim came to be one of seeking to develop Sudan's agriculture, using the new Gulf funds from the oil price rises of the 1970s together with Western technology, to make Sudan the bread basket of the Arab world. In conjunction with Egypt, a start was also made on the long-mooted Jonglei Canal in the south which would carry water around the *sudd* swamps and improve the supply for agriculture in northern Sudan and Egypt. In addition, oil was discovered in the south and Chevron arrived from the USA to exploit it. However, Nimeiri still had opponents in the north, and successive attempts to overthrow him in the 1970s eventually led to an apparent compromise in 1977 known as National Reconciliation. Nimeiri was joined in reconciliation by Hasan al-Turabi, leader of the growing Muslim Brotherhood, and Sadiq al-Mahdi, leader of the Umma Party, though the latter soon pulled out again.

National Reconciliation brought a return to an emphasis on the politics of the north, but at the price of reducing the significance of the south and the arrangements agreed at Addis Ababa in 1972. In order to take control of the newly discovered oil field, Nimeiri meddled in the south's regional government and changed the north–south border to incorporate the main field into the new and sadly misnamed

'Unity State'. The Jonglei Canal was seen as exploiting the region for the north and Egypt, and could have damaging consequences for the south. At the same time reconciliation with the Muslim Brotherhood was seen as opening a path to the expansion of the influence of Islamism, a development encouraged by events elsewhere in the Muslim world, including the Iranian revolution. It was all to lead to the alienation of the south once more. In 1983 war restarted in the south with the Sudan People's Liberation Army (SPLA) led by John Garang: it swiftly forced the cessation of work on both the Jonglei Canal and the Chevron oil field. Just as war in the south had been a trigger for a popular uprising in 1964, so it was again in 1985 and Nimeiri was swept from power by a second uprising in the cities of the north.

Nimeiri had reshaped Sudanese politics. The north as well as the south had experienced the use of force, first against a major 'traditional' group – the Mahdists – then the communists, before battling with all opposition groups until National Reconciliation in 1977, but that had been made at the price of risking renewed conflict in the south. It left the question of whether it was possible to make a peace between north and south that could hold up. He had also shown overtly the clientelistic and corrupt nature of much of Sudanese politics. It was not new, but it had probably never been as overt before.

As in 1964 there were hopes for a while that a new political order would emerge, although the presence of the military under Siwar al-Dahab still hung heavy over the transitional government. But as 20 years earlier, following the elections of 1986 power was once more shared in a coalition of the old party politicians under Prime Minister Sadiq al-Mahdi, who had briefly held the same post in the 1960s. Thus it was back to the future for the second time, and little more was achieved than under the previous elected civilian coalitions.

However, there had been a development underway for some years, the full scale and significance of which would only become apparent later: the growth of the Muslim Brotherhood. Originally, after World War II, it was an offshoot of the better-known Egyptian movement. The rise of a new leader, Hasan al-Turabi, a lawyer trained in the universities of Khartoum, London and Sorbonne, was to spark a more active role in politics for the Brotherhood, starting with its involvement in the October Revolution of 1964. This offered greater freedom for the Brotherhood to recruit amongst students in particular, and to campaign for an Islamic constitution. However, Nimeiri's coup sent it into opposition where it played a leading part until National Reconciliation in 1977. Turabi then moved into government and, as well as supporting Nimeiri's introduction of *sharia* in 1983, the movement undertook a programme of entryism encouraging its followers into all arms of the state as well as new business enterprises. Following Nimeiri's downfall in 1985 the movement campaigned as the National Islamic Front (NIF). It won only 18 per cent of the vote but proved very active in the period of coalition governments that followed. When it did finally appear in 1989 that there might be serious negotiations with the SPLA to end the war in the south, the NIF staged its own coup using a group of sympathetic officers led by Brigadier Omer al-Beshir, thus opening up a new and very different chapter in Sudan's modern history.

Djibouti

While the end of the Cold War came just at a time when significant changes were taking place for the major states of the Horn, the smallest state, Djibouti, was experiencing nothing of comparable drama, indeed it was often referred to as the calm in the eye of the storm. Djibouti had been created as a French foothold at the bottom of the Red Sea, essentially to maintain a strategic presence. French Somaliland, as it was long known, had two main communities, the largest being the Issas, a Somali clan, and 20 per cent of the population were Afars connected to the wider Afar community in Ethiopia. For much of the colonial period France was said to have advantaged the Afars, but in 1967, in the era of African nationalism, the name was changed to the 'French territory of the Afars and Issas' to appear more even-handed. In addition to these communities, there were other Somalis and some Arabs (mainly from Yemen) engaged in local trade. The hinterland was very arid and unproductive, though the building of the railway to Addis Ababa in the early nineteenth century produced some commercial development. The French base was also a significant part of the local economy.

In 1977 France agreed to formal independence and the state of Djibouti was established, although the French base, and with it French influence, continued. The new president was an Issa, Gouled Aptidon, who cultivated an informal approach to government, while also being cautious and balancing the allocation of posts around the communities. The 65-member National Assembly was similarly balanced, with the whole system linked by a single party, the Rassemblement Populaire pour le Progrès (RPP). There were some tensions, most notably at the time of the Somali–Ethiopian war, when the Issas and the Afars tended to side with different protagonists; nevertheless, stability was maintained well into the 1980s. Economically there was an attempt to create a free port, but it suffered from the number of competitors in the region, although the service sector made some progress. The hinterland, however, remained very impoverished.

International politics: regional and wider

The domestic issues across the Horn were to prove a vital factor in relations with neighbouring states. Indeed, the idea of the problem of 'the Horn' as it first emerged after World War II was centred on Somalia and Ethiopia, and especially the view that the opportunity for the international community to redraw the map to bring Somalis together had been missed. Government encouragement for armed unrest amongst fellow Somalis in northern Kenya and the Ogaden region of eastern Ethiopia became a feature of the 1960s, at least until 1967 when a new Somali prime minister, Mohammed Egal, saw it as counterproductive and embarked on a policy of restraint. Initially Siad Barre also displayed caution, even taking Somalia into the Arab League in the hope of benefiting from the new oil wealth of the 1970s. However, the Ethiopian revolution of 1974 was to impact not only on him, but on Somalis generally. The uncertainty that is part and parcel of revolution, coupled with the growing Somali military capability thanks to Soviet support, appeared to offer an irresistible opportunity, and Barre came under growing domestic pressure to act. The USSR warned against invading Ethiopia, seeking instead the building of friendly socialist relations between the two countries, but that hope was in vain. Somalia's invasion in 1977 led to its abandonment by the USSR which instead gave massive support to Ethiopia, which turned the tide in the conflict.

From 1978 it was Ethiopia that gained the upper hand in relations between the two neighbours. For much of the 1980s Mengistu was ready to encourage Barre's Somali enemies, especially in former Somaliland in the north, thus contributing to the weakening of the regime. The surprising agreement between the two rulers in 1988 to end the tit-for-tat assistance to their respective insurgents was widely perceived as giving Ethiopia greater weight in their relationship. It was an advantage some would say it sought to maintain thereafter, underlining its basic distrust of Somalia following the invasion of 1977: long memories are a feature of Ethiopia's political culture. Barre's downfall in 1991 caused few tears to be shed in Addis Ababa.

On Ethiopia's western flank the challenge had once more started with its neighbour Sudan, and here too it dated from the early 1960s.

However, it was not any irredentist ambitions Sudan held that started the involvement, rather it was the Eritrean movement that had begun in the early 1960s. The ELF believed that Eritrea had been tricked into the supposed federal union with Ethiopia in 1952 and it should be reversed. The ELF was able to draw on concerns among the pan-Arab movement at the time, led by Nasser's Egypt: Ethiopia was threateningly friendly with the USA and Israel, and a separatist movement whose success would make the country a landlocked state would be strategically advantageous from the pan-Arab perspective. In addition to the pressure that Egypt could put on Sudan to facilitate the ELF struggle, there was much sympathy in Unionist Party circles in particular since many followers of the Khatmiyya *sufi* sect were to be found in lowland Eritrea. Conflict in Eritrea soon brought refugees into eastern Sudan, and they in turn were often radicalized so that the Eritrean movement largely became supplied and organized from Sudan. The later decline of the ELF and its replacement by the more radical EPLF did nothing to alter this pattern, which was to continue right through until Mengistu's downfall.

The price for Sudan was Ethiopia's support for the Anyanya fighting in the south. Changes in Sudan led Nimeiri to end this situation at Addis Ababa in 1972, and as well as meaning peace in the south his government put pressure on the Eritreans but with little effect, as Nimeiri's efforts to broker a deal for Ethiopia similar to his own in Sudan came to naught. Instead, conflict in Eritrea continued and by the end of the 1970s had spread into neighbouring Tigray province led by the TPLF. With the USA and the USSR now playing a more active role in both countries it came as no surprise that the collapse of peace in southern Sudan, and the appearance of the SPLA in 1983, was an opportunity swiftly seized on by revolutionary Ethiopia. In 1991, as the EPRDF advanced on Addis Ababa to oust Mengistu, it was accompanied by units of the Sudanese armed forces before which it was necessary for the SPLA to hastily evacuate the capital.

Mutual intervention

These 'un-neighbourly' relations contributed directly to the de-stabilization of the region. The origins of the conflicts were essentially domestic, but their regionalization was very important in arriving at the outcomes for various regimes. It is probably impossible to assign weights with regard to the internal and neighbourly aspects of conflicts, but it is still true to say that events within all three countries would not have played out as they did without the involvement of neighbours.

While so much of the shaping of the state system of the Horn had developed from the intervention of Europe in the region, in the post-war period the influence of the European powers was to decline fairly rapidly. Britain had been the major actor, but with the independence of Sudan in 1956, and its Suez misadventure in neighbouring Egypt in the same year, Britain's influence fell rapidly. Somaliland had also become more marginal to Britain, which was happy enough to see its responsibility ended with Somaliland's incorporation into Somalia in 1960. Meanwhile, any hope that Britain's role in restoring Haile Selassie in Ethiopia would be followed by gratitude in the latter's foreign policy was soon dispelled. Italy, though restored by the UN to administer Somalia, was happy to withdraw. Only France stayed on in Djibouti, but the tiny enclave was of little interest to anybody else.

Europe's retreat was in time filled by newer global actors drawn, as the Europeans had been, by the Horn's strategic significance. First on the scene was the USA which saw Ethiopia's potential, especially with the attachment of Eritrea. America soon opened a communications base at Kagnew near Asmara, capital of Eritrea, as well as arming and training Ethiopia's armed forces and supporting various development projects. In return Ethiopia sent a token force to fight in Korea. The USSR took longer to become involved, and instead the USA hoped to see it isolated by the 'northern tier' states of the Middle East cemented by the Baghdad Pact. However, the USSR escaped the trap by exploiting Nasser's coup in Egypt: with the West refusing his wish for substantial arms, the way was open for the Soviet-approved Czech arms deal of 1955. Once installed in Egypt the USSR embarked on what was to become a game of dominoes with the USA in the region, beginning with involvement in the 1960s in developments in Yemen, including becoming the backer of Marxist South Yemen.

The 1970s proved an important decade for the spread of Cold War engagement, especially with the revolution in Ethiopia in 1974. At first the USA hoped to hold its position, but by 1977 it had been ejected and instead focused on containment by developing relations with Sudan and a little later Somalia. Military and development activities in both countries were undertaken, while the USSR sought to consolidate itself in Ethiopia where Mengistu was enthusiastically embracing Marxism. By the time of the Second Cold War, as the early 1980s became known, the Horn was an integral part of the so-called 'arc of crisis' running through the war torn areas of Afghanistan, the Gulf and the Horn and on up to President Reagan's bogey man, Colonel Qaddafi, in Libya. But the decline and eventual collapse of the USSR at the end of the decade was to have a dramatic impact. Mengistu's failure to defeat his enemies in Ethiopia led to a loss of Soviet confidence in his regime and support rapidly drained away. In Sudan, America had seen Nimeiri brought down in 1985, while the increasing conflict in Somalia brought growing criticism in the USA and eventual abandonment of Barre.

The impact of the Cold War had been substantial. The respective superpowers had backed major figures in the era of 'personal rule' by 'big men' in Africa: Barre, Mengistu and Nimeiri. That backing had assisted these rulers in their natural inclinations towards increased authoritarianism and attempts to crush opposition movements, by force. The propensity to use force in turn meant large supplies of arms, especially from the USSR to Ethiopia, and arms often leaked from central governments to the opposition movements, contributing to the escalation of conflicts. At the same time, the spill-over of what had started as domestic conflicts into neighbouring states contributed to the worsening of regional relations, diminishing the chances of achieving domestic stability. In spite of their arms supplies the super-powers could never fully control their unruly clients: in particular, Barre in Somalia attacked Ethiopia in spite of Soviet warnings, while Nimeiri ended southern Sudan's few years of peace and embarked on Islamism to the horror of the USA. Both developments were to have long-term consequences for both the states involved and the region.

The region itself stood on the borders of two wider regions which also affected developments. The Middle East had long historic connections with the Horn, and following the decline of Britain and France there after World War II developments soon had an impact on the Horn. Radical nationalist and pan-Arab movements began to rise to power in the 1950s and soon polarized the Middle East in ways that spilled out to surrounding areas. At the centre of the new ideological energy was Egypt. Britain frustrated Nasser's ambitions in Sudan, but by the early 1960s Egypt was encouraging the formation of the ELF in Eritrea, although Syria was later to take over the leading role, to be followed in the 1970s by Saudi Arabia. Egypt's attention returned to Sudan with Nimeiri's coup of 1969, though the proposed union of the two plus Libya soon collapsed. However, as both Egypt and Sudan moved towards the USA in the 1970s, so Sadat and Nimeiri planned a new union between the two countries. Amongst various proposed projects the most ambitious by far was their joint construction of the Jonglei Canal in southern Sudan, which was to fall victim to the SPLA when civil war restarted. In 1985 Nimeiri's downfall was effectively to end this further round of Egyptian ambitions in Sudan.

The failure of the unity project of 1969 also made Libya an implacable enemy of Nimeiri and from then on Qaddafi took every opportunity he could find to bring him down, including facilitating a major armed attack by the Mahdists in 1976, and supporting the SPLA in the early 1980s. Libya even joined Ethiopia and Yemen, all Soviet armed, in the Aden Pact of 1981 but it proved of little significance. In response Egypt and Sudan, encouraged by the USA, were to embark on years of trying to undermine Qaddafi's regime partly via the struggles in which all three were involved in Chad. After Nimeiri was eventually succeeded in 1986 by Prime Minister Sadiq al-Mahdi, Sudan–Libyan relations improved but it proved a relatively short-lived interlude before the coup of 1989.

The other Middle East actor to play a major role in the politics of the Horn was Israel. Having developed its 'peripheral doctrine' of seeking to align with nearby non-Arab states in the late 1950s it was soon developing ties with Ethiopia (as well as Turkey and Iran). Ethiopia was historically fearful of Muslim encirclement, and concerned about Egypt's claim on the Nile waters. Israel opposed the danger of the Red Sea becoming an Arab lake and thus a danger to her shipping. While Israel trained Ethiopia's forces along with the Americans, it also opened a naval base on Ethiopia's Dahlek islands. Meanwhile, in southern Sudan Israel began to support the Anyanya from 1967 as part of its efforts to continue to weaken the Arab states following its victory in the 1967 war.

The Horn's East African neighbours had more modest foreign policies than the ideologists of the Middle East, but could not avoid involvement in such an unstable and violent region. For Kenya, Somalia was to be the main headache, especially in the early 1960s, with armed incursions on its northern borders. However, they were fairly easily contained, and a change of heart by Somalia in 1967 eased the situation. Uganda, however, became more involved in southern Sudan with refugees arriving, and by the mid 1960s the Anyanya were operating through Kampala, while from 1967 Israel gave support generally through the same route. Before seizing power in 1970, Idi Amin, who had a background in the southern Sudanese Nubi community in East Africa, personally spent time fighting alongside the Anyanya. The cessation of the conflict in 1972 eased relations between the two countries, and when war restarted in 1983 it was Ethiopia that was mainly involved. However, Uganda's president from 1986, Youeri Museveni, was a close friend of SPLA leader John Garang and sympathetic to his movement in the last years of the Cold War and beyond.

The years of rivalry and conflict across the Horn, largely centred on Ethiopia, had appeared to be entering a new chapter at the start of the 1990s. While it was no coincidence that the moment came at the end of the Cold War, with Mengistu in Ethiopia and Barre in Somalia seeing their superpower support fade rapidly, the victorious revolutionaries in Eritrea, Ethiopia and northern Somalia were largely the product of indigenous political developments assisted by the regional politics of the Horn. The USA in particular supported the evolving scene hoping that it would prove a peaceful transition that would be followed by developments across the poverty stricken and war torn region. This, in turn, would reflect its hopes for a New World Order in which democratization, and liberal economic policies contributing to globalization, would replace the era of the Cold War.

CHAPTER 3

Ethiopia

Two traditions have been writ large in Ethiopian politics since at least the nineteenth century. One has been the efforts of successive regimes to dominate the central highlands of the country, first under decades of monarchical rule and then for a shorter but still substantial period under a military regime. The second has been the spread of the power of the highlands to incorporate neighbouring lowland areas in a generally subordinate relationship. The downfall of Mengistu Haile Mariam's military regime in 1991 was accompanied by plans that appeared to offer a different future.

On the face of it Mengistu's downfall was the work of a popular revolutionary movement; perhaps a series of such movements as resistance had spread. Revolt in Eritrea in the north, the most recent of the centre's acquisitions and always the one most capable of resistance, had led to eventual victory for the Eritrean People's Liberation Front (EPLF), and it had also helped to inspire revolt in neighbouring Tigray, historically more central to the shifting tides of highland Abyssinia's politics. As the Tigrean movement, the Tigrean People's Liberation Front (TPLF), made rapid progress towards taking power in Addis Ababa it encouraged similar groups in other regions, giving the appearance of an ethnic melange coming to power. The arrangement between the EPLF and the TPLF, which led to Eritrea's referendum on secession and its agreed independence in 1993, seemed not just a solution to the struggle in the north, but the logical possibility of the whole project that had put the TPLF in power in Addis Ababa. Ostensibly, the Ethiopian People's Revolutionary Democratic Front (EPRDF) was as an umbrella organization over regional and ethnic People's Democratic Organisations (PDOs), but the relations between the handle and the spokes of the umbrella were initially far from clear.

The answer appeared to lie in the unofficial formulation by which Ethiopia's government was to become best known: 'ethnic federalism'. Perhaps influenced by its historic route to power, building on ethnic and regional organizations rather than attempting a coup or a wider 'national' revolt, as well as its own Marxist–Leninist–Maoist–Albanian thinking during the long years of struggle, the TPLF hit the ground running with regard to ethnic federalism. Its ideology concerning federalism was largely informed by, and had clear overtones of, Stalin's approach. There were supposedly clearly formed 'nationalities' with distinctive languages and cultures, and the approach should have been to recognize and incorporate these rather than seeking to combat and perhaps replace them with a single new externally imposed identity. The new rulers saw themselves as capable of identifying and defining the territories of such national groupings, with a view to incorporating them in a new federal system constructed primarily from the centre in 1991. Within weeks of taking power, the EPRDF called a national conference where various groups, some hurriedly established, came together to construct the Transitional Government of Ethiopia (TGE) which served for two and a half years. A Council of Ministers was set up which included representatives of seven ethnic groups or nationalities, as well as a Council of Representatives. Ethnic federalism, the one principle to which the TPLF appeared irrevocably committed, was now to be brought to life through the drawing of a map of the regions which were to be incorporated into the new constitution. To its defenders it was historically necessary in view of the record of centralism under first the Emperor and then the Dergue, both of which had acted in ways that had promoted ethnic conflict. To its critics ethnic federalism was in effect a way in which Tigray, a poor area with some 10 per cent of the population, could potentially dominate through a system of divide and rule.

Apart from the federal capital itself and a second chartered city, Dire Dawa, there were nine geographical federal states designated by the elite of the TPLF and its regional allies in the EPRDF, and certainly without any direct reference to the 'nations, nationalities and peoples' involved. According to the criteria, this was decided on the basis of culture, customs, language, identity and identifiable contiguous territory. Six of the nine had a recognized dominant ethnic group which gave its name to the new state. In the north Tigray was most obvious as the homeland of the TPLF, even though its population was comparatively small. The old ruling peoples, the Amhara, lived north of the capital and were to have their own larger state with Tigray on its northern border. Taken together Amhara and Tigray were made up of comparatively homogeneous ethnic and cultural societies known for their history of involvement in Ethiopia's state formation as well as the prominence of the orthodox Coptic Christian church. The TPLF's most numerous allies in the war to overthrow Mengistu were the Oromo who, according to the official census of 2005, comprised about one third of the total population of 73.9 million and lived in a large swathe of territory to the east, west and south of Addis Ababa. This became the state of Oromia. The Oromo are made up of several sub-groups and historically their political and cultural subordination by the state has included suppression of their language. To the east of Tigray and Amhara lay Afar state, whose dominant ethnic group, the Afars, were also to be found in Eritrea and Djibouti, although the largest number were in Ethiopia. In the south-east was the Harari city-state around the historic trading centre, while further east still was Somali, the largely Somali-inhabited arid lowland area that had been subject to two irredentist attacks by neighbouring Somalia, first in the 1960s and then in the 1970s. The Afar and Somali clans of the east comprised the largest number of pastoralists in the country. The three most clearly multi-ethnic states were in the west bordering Sudan: Benishangul-Gamuz, Gambella, and the large Southern Nations, Nationalities and People's Regional State (SNNPRS). These three states were the most heterogeneous in the country with numerous ethnic groups, some of which spanned the border with Sudan. In all 64 ethnic groups are officially recognized in the country.

According to the 1994 'Constitution of the Federal Democratic Republic of Ethiopia' the federal states have extensive powers including their own legislative, executive and judicial powers. However, land and natural resources are under the control of the federal government; in a very poor country, states' finances come largely from the same federal government which also manages much of the country's economic development and social policies. The federal government itself appears to be bi-cameral but in an unusual manner. The House of Peoples' Representatives is the main legislative body, made up of 548 members elected by a first-past-the-post system on a single member constituency basis for a five-year term. Meanwhile, the states themselves are represented in the House of Federation. However, this house is intended to function largely as a constitutional court on issues relating to the states, although initially at least it contributed little. The best-known reference in the constitution is that which states that, 'every Nation, Nationality and People in Ethiopia has an unconditional right to self-determination, including the right to secession'. In a continent noted for its fear of recognizing secession, and with Ethiopia hosting the headquarters of the Organisation of African Unity (OAU) and its successor the African Union (AU) in Addis Ababa, this clause in the constitution has been seen as unexpected. However, it has to be remembered that the TPLF was founded on, and fought for, regional recognition, and that from the outset it recognized the right of Eritrea to *was there an alternative?*

secede. When regional recognition was granted following Mengistu's defeat it made sense for it to be included to emphasize the federal priority of the new constitution – albeit one heavily influenced by Marxist–Leninist canon – in the knowledge that the Soviet Union's constitution had included similar provision for the Soviet republics.

According to the constitution the federal states had substantial powers. In view of the commitment to 'nations, nationalities and peoples' it was no surprise that states could promote their own cultures, languages and histories, even though in theory there was a possibility this might encourage secessionist sentiments. They were supposed to be self-governing with the ability to establish their own political institutions giving the appearance of each being unitary in character. However, they also had to set up their own districts, known as *weredas*, and local administrations, *kabelles*. In addition, they had the right to levy some taxes of their own (though such were the levels of poverty that in practice over 80 per cent of funds would come from the federal government) as well as developing their own plans for economic growth. In view of the decisions on boundaries having been made by the federal government at the outset, and the designations of six states as having dominant groups with the remaining three states being multi-ethnic, there were criticisms that the system could entrench and perhaps even create forms of ethnic dominance within states. To answer this the constitution referred to the right of minority ethnic groups to seek to establish their own states, though in reality this amounted to no more than one or two setting up their own *weredas*.

While the virtual inevitability of the EPRDF and its allies setting up a system of ethnic federalism has been widely recognized, many have pointed out the extent to which the centre has still predominated in Ethiopia. Some of the explanations seem as inevitable as the system itself. Politically, the federal system had been set up from the centre at a time when it appeared possible that there could be at least partial collapse of the state itself: in the situation after Mengistu's flight there was little prospect of putative states coming together to establish a US-style federal system. Many of the central civil service survived the collapse of the Dergue and were in a position to continue in central government or be seconded to the new states which were themselves very short of the human resources for the tasks of state management. Financially, the centre was dominant and continued to make the key decisions with regard to matters of finance, economic development, natural resources and – for the rural majority – property rights, which would remain under some form of communal control rather than free-hold private property. In 2001 as if to emphasize this central dominance, departments were amalgamated to create a new structure of Ministries including Capacity Building, Infrastructure Development, Rural Development and Federal Affairs.

With regard to the management of the centre, much has revolved around the character and performance of the EPRDF, and especially its core from the old TPLF led by Meles Zenawi, the prime minister from the early 1990s. A former student leader turned liberation fighter, he was known more for his political than his military capabilities; he was also known for being very intelligent and well read. Many have pointed out the TPLF's Leninist and Maoist past in the mountains of Tigray, as well as the similarities of its terminology – at least with regard to the question of nationalities – with that of Stalinist theory. The TPLF has had a traditional Leninist structure with a central committee and an executive committee (formerly called the Politburo) and is secretive in character. In this it may be reflecting not only the customary nature of such organizations but also an aspect of highland Ethiopian culture which has frequently been remarked on in relation to successive regimes. In this regard the public emergence of a leadership crisis in 2001 was most unusual, but so were the circumstances, with the unexpected war with Eritrea that had first broken out in 1998, followed by a second round of fighting in 2000. By 2001 the TPLF leadership was appraising its performance after a decade in power, including the conduct of the war. While the leaders had been united in agreeing to Eritrea's independence, some of Meles' challengers argued that a tougher political stance should have been taken before the conflict, and that in the second round of fighting in particular Ethiopia should have taken a more aggressive strategy leaving Eritrea substantially weaker. However, the critics were eventually overcome and expelled from the party. And while the TPLF had kept its firm hold on Tigray itself, the split had an impact on some parts of the state since at least some of those who were expelled had their own popular following as heroes of the liberation struggle. However, in regard to central government, the leadership of Meles Zenawi, if anything, became more entrenched in the years that followed, while he personally became ever more reclusive within the country, although not in his growing international role. He had suggested that he might stand down after the 2010 elections, and had also spoken of the need for a new generation of leaders to be developed, but in practice there was little sign of his growing personal control being reversed. The split of 2001 was, however, a reminder that behind the secretive facade of the government, differences of a personal, ideological and strategic character could still be festering.

The TPLF had also been the creator of the EPRDF which, as mentioned, operated as an umbrella organization. An early ally in 1989 was the Amhara National Democratic Movement (ANDM), an important constituency in view of the power the Amhara previously exercised and their continuing presence in many of the organs of the central state. In the following year the Oromo People's Democratic Organisation (OPDO) also joined: while the Oromo were widespread in area, they constituted a major part of the population and had given rise to another long-running liberation force, the Oromo Liberation Front (OLF). The somewhat fragmented character of the OPDO led to growing and vociferous opposition to the EPRDF, especially amongst those who went into exile. The EPRDF also encouraged the formation elsewhere of

People's Democratic Organisations (PDOs), including a number in the south where in 1994 they came together to form the Southern Ethiopian People's Democratic Front (SEPDF). At the time of the TPLF leadership struggle these other parties in the EPRDF played a part, but it was a subordinate role and the overall leadership remained dominated by Meles Zenawi and his fellow Tigrayans. Away from the central areas of the country, on its eastern and western flanks in particular, the EPRDF has encouraged the construction of affiliated parties with which it maintains working relations.

A number of studies have been undertaken that indicate the reach of the EPRDF into even the most outlying areas of the country. Having created the new federal structure around designated ethnic identities, it was necessary for the system to see representatives of those communities in the various 'national' governments while simultaneously ensuring that they were brought into the country's overall political direction and development plans. To achieve this, the EPRDF needed to exert its control over the newly established organs at the levels of state governments – *weredas* and *kabelles* – by ensuring the presence of members of the local parties who were safely under the discipline of the Front. In addition, there were EPRDF 'advisers' who were often involved in training programmes for state officials that generally expressed the ideological party line: they also undertook promotional activities amongst the local communities. The EPRDF was also helped in its efforts by the extent to which the new state governments remained heavily reliant on central government for financial support; if necessary the security forces would apply more repressive measures.

The system was at its clearest in the highland states such as Tigray and Amhar. As the place of origin of the TPLF, Tigray has understandably come in for considerable scrutiny with regard to development, and local research has shown some of its strengths and limitations. On the plus side, officials down at local levels have shown a real endeavour to promote rural development programmes such as the

Food Security Programme of 2003. At the same time the development programmes have generally emanated from above rather than drawing on local initiatives and decision making, often involving communal efforts but led by the officials of the vanguard party with various 'development' targets to be met. The TPLF deployed a number of techniques to mobilize the peasants. One was to invoke the historic legacy of the party and the peasants working together to defeat the Dergue, with the struggle extended to fight 'the enemy' of poverty as well. Cooperative peasants were offered access to various improvement measures for their land, and the chance to gain privileged access to public works programmes such as the Productive Safety National Programme (PSNP). In addition, participation in programmes was encouraged by various associations such as those for farmers, women and youth. Participating farmers were encouraged to join the TPLF, and in some areas as many as a quarter of heads of households joined, sometimes participating in self-criticism sessions known as *gemgam*.

Oromia, the state in which Addis Ababa is located, caused more problems. The Oromo are the largest 'nationality' in Ethiopia, scattered over a large central area. They were linked to the EPRDF through the Oromo People's Democratic Organisation (OPDO), but the region had also spawned the Oromo Liberation Front (OLF) during the Mengistu years. After his downfall the OLF had worked briefly with the EPRDF, but it soon broke with many of its leaders going into opposition – where they complained increasingly of harassment – or into exile. They also endeavoured to launch a guerrilla warfare campaign, though with little success. However, although that was generally contained, doubts remained about Oromo sentiment towards the new system. These doubts were supplemented by the fact that most Oromo are Muslims – some 30–40 per cent of Ethiopia's population overall – and that religious issues had been rising due in part to the spill-over effect of increased signs of militant Islam in neighbouring Somalia. In turn the government has shown increasing concern about the teachings of Arab-funded preachers in the country's mosques. Yet the prospect of any collective action by the Oromo is tempered by the fact that, although numerous, they consist of a number of clans, and historically there has not been a distinctive Oromo political identity of the kind that has contributed to the shaping of Tigray and Amhar states.

In spite of the particular problems of Oromia, it appeared that the highland states were the greatest beneficiaries of the new system, while the outlying lowlands were fairing less well. In the Southern Regional State there are 45 recognized ethnic groups, all of which, although comparatively small, appeared to feel that in the new political dispensation it was necessary for them to express their ethnic identities in order to gain the recognition which could bring access to resources distributed from the centre via the state. Some of them had begun to develop their own political parties, but these were brought together by the EPRDF to create Wegagoda People's Democratic Organisation. However, this soon became associated with the use of the Welayta language, which helped to generate growing opposition amongst ethnic groups who felt themselves excluded from power. To contain such sentiment it proved necessary to re-organize the districts, but it also transpired that, in 2002 in particular, brutal force was used when scores of unarmed civilians were shot as they protested about this local issue.

In neighbouring Gambella state to the west, an area only incorporated into Ethiopia in 1902, there were two major dimensions. First, the penetration of the Ethiopian state during the twentieth century had brought highlanders to the lowland area as traders, officials and even as farmers during the famines of the 1980s. Secondly, the coming of ethnic federalism brought opportunities for highlanders to take positions in the new state, since they were more in tune with developments emanating from the centre than the historically more isolated lowlanders. The situation encouraged the latter to assert their ethnic identities afresh as they sought access to state resources. However, this in turn opened up competition between the lowland ethnic groups, and there were violent clashes – particularly between the largest 'indigenous' groups, the Anywaa and the Nuer – as they struggled for positions and resources in the new state. Instead of incorporating ethnic groups, the new system appeared to be exacerbating ethnic identities and seeing their mobilization into conflict.

However, the most testing of the states has been the Somali region of the Ogaden, also known as Region 5. Here, local issues have focused on the relations between the majority Ogadeeni Somali clan and peoples of other Somali clans who have been generally favoured by the EPRDF, as well as the impact of Chinese exploration for oil. But it is also a region much affected by international developments based on neighbouring Somalia. Ever since Somalia's independence in 1960, relations with Ethiopia have rarely been less than difficult, and, at their worst, a major irredentist war was launched by the then-Somali government of Siad Barre on Ethiopia in 1977. Although effectively stateless since Barre's downfall in 1991, southern Somalia continued to be seen as a threat by Ethiopia, and the rise of the Islamic Courts Union in 2005 was to lead to Ethiopia's attack in the following year. The situation also gave rise to intense concern for the stability of the Ogaden from the late 1990s which intensified in 2007 with the growth in attacks by the Ogaden National Liberation Front (ONLF). Ethiopia saw this not only as a local uprising but one encouraged by its northern enemy, Eritrea, which it accused of being active in both Somalia and Ogaden. The subsequent crackdown included a trade blockade of the Ogaden in 2007 which greatly affected the livestock trade at the centre of the local economy – much of which was destined for the lucrative markets of the Arabian peninsula – and contributed to growing humanitarian problems. At the same time, Ethiopian security forces stood accused of substantial repression and unconcern for human rights, about which growing information filtered out in spite of obstacles to relief efforts.

The festering situation in Region 5 amounts to the strongest indictment of Ethiopia's claims to be building viable federal states, but it is not the only one. More broadly it appears that it has been a top-down programme from the centre, driven by and through the power of the ruling EPRDF, more than a genuine effort to engage with the local communities in all their variety. As a model for federalism it appears to draw on Stalin's ideas of discrete, established 'nationalities' – rather than the complexity and fluidity of identity in many parts of the country – accompanied by a Leninist approach to political party building that limits bottom up initiatives. Neither at the local level nor in the centre does it appear to seek to embrace multi-partyism in relation to the exercise of power. As a result, some have questioned whether or not it amounts to federalism at all, and wonder if, in addition to eastern European ideological inspiration, it owes something to the divide and rule of European imperialism, especially since large swathes of the present country were incorporated in a not-unrelated piece of empire building by Emperor Menelik in the late nineteenth century. Indeed, it may be that, instead of building on 'primordial' ethnic identities as claimed, Ethiopia is building new 'situational' identities which may remain under central manipulation but which could provide the bases for fresh challenges in the future, perhaps citing the constitutional provision of their right to secede. That said, there has been a degree of pragmatic success. While there have been some conflict areas they have remained localized and the country as a whole has enjoyed greater peace than for many decades. The theory of ethnic federalism may have its obvious limitations, but with pragmatism from the centre it has proved more manageable as something of a compromise between the neglect of Haile Selassie and the all-out repression attempted by Mengistu.

In addition to establishing its ethnic federalism, the EPRDF also committed itself to democracy, a move that made it even more legitimate in the eyes of the USA and other Western powers, who saw Ethiopia as a new opportunity in the light of the downfall of Africa's last, and arguably most significant, outpost of Marxism–Leninism. But it has been argued that the new rulers' conception of democracy owed more to similar revolutionary thinking than to liberal–democratic theory. The revolution in Tigray had involved collective, class-based mobilization of the peasantry. In a country still as poor as Ethiopia that involved the leadership in assisting the bulk of the community in participating, at least formally, in the formation of a consensus on collective development: as the EPRDF put it in 1995, 'For our democracy to be guaranteed and to strike roots it should be based upon the all inclusive participation of the people'.[1] This did not sound like an invitation to the kind of pluralistic democracy that Western donors in particular widely sought to foster in Africa in the 1990s, although hope might be drawn from at least some of the terms used. However, for the donors in particular, the proof of the pudding would be in the eating.

Free and fair elections were an important feature of the 1995 constitution, but from the outset there were tensions between the character of the EPRDF and the expectations of political freedoms ultimately played out on an electoral level playing field amongst both Ethiopian opposition parties and the Western international donor community. On paper, opposition parties could operate freely, and, in fact, at different times there have been a range of such parties, some seeking to conduct country-wide campaigns and others more locally and regionally focused. However, it became clear in the early years of the new regime that freedom to campaign and contest elections fairly related closely to the threat to its power perceived by the EPRDF. International monitors and observers suggested that, where there was no significant opposition party to the EPRDF elections at national and local level, in 2001 and 2002 they were conducted with general observance of the proprieties. These areas included much of the key central states of Tigray, Amhara and Oromia. However, in areas as varied as the major urban centres of Amhara and the rural southern SNNPRS a very different picture was seen. Tactics used to disrupt opposition parties included intimidation and disqualification of candidates, harassment and even killings of opposition party supporters, as well as various pressures on voters at the polls themselves. A US State Department report of 2001 drew on the National Electoral Board itself to write, 'There were also credible reports of ballot stuffing, vote count fraud, voter intimidation or bribery, dismissals from work, withholding of salaries, detentions, abductions and killings'.[2] How far these occurrences were encouraged by the EPRDF centrally, and how far they reflected the fears and ambitions of local leaderships, is not clear but it is possible to suggest that the original dichotomy of revolutionary and liberal approaches to democracy had a part to play.

The concerns expressed in early studies of democracy in Ethiopia appeared to be fully borne out in the 2005 national elections which are regularly described as the first truly competitive elections since the EPRDF took power. The early years of the decade had proved testing. Early hopes of rapid development were proving to be hampered by very real economic difficulties and consequent frustrations, especially among the large numbers of young men drawn to the growing urban centres, notably Addis Ababa itself. In many of the outlying areas there was also a sense that they were not experiencing the opportunities of the more central areas. However, it appeared that these growing tensions were not fully appreciated by the EPRDF, especially if its behaviour before and after the elections is compared. As the elections approached it appeared to be less obstructive to opposition parties that were growing rapidly, especially the Coalition for Unity and Democracy (CUD), which drew support from urban areas in particular, and the United Ethiopian Democratic Front (UEDF) with support in the south and west. The main line taken by these parties was the need for greater equality and unity; important themes in their core areas of support. In the period before the elections it appeared that things were going smoothly, and with high voter registration it seemed that a real contest was possible. Quite what the millions of peasants made of the election is hard to tell, though one researcher thought that calculation was central from his interviews, 'With which candidate do I stand the least risk of reducing my chances of survival?'[3] Perhaps the EPRDF was over-confident of the outcome, as Prime Minister Meles Zenawi did not personally campaign at all and announced shortly after the elections – and before much of the counting had taken place – that his party had won an overwhelming victory.

The official results showed that it was indeed victorious with 371 seats in the 547 contests, but the opposition parties' seats went up from 12 to 179, in addition to which there were numerous calls of foul play, though demands for recounts and reruns were summarily dismissed. In contrast to the comparatively restrained way the EPRDF had behaved in the run up, the shock of the result led to a rapid confrontation between it and the opposition parties. Demonstrations were officially banned for a month after the elections, but they occurred nevertheless and in the resulting protests some 200 people were killed and 18,000 protestors, mainly young men in the urban areas, were detained. The situation threw the opposition parties into disarray with the CUD deciding to boycott the assembly in which it had officially won 104 seats. This caused a good deal of dissension within the party; a number of leaders choosing self-exile abroad proved to be a major factor in its fragmentation thereafter. Western observers who had had high hopes that the elections would usher in a more open and multi-party era voiced varying degrees of criticism, but on the whole went along with the outcome of the whole electoral process.

In addition to the crackdown, immediately following the election itself, the EPRDF set out to recover from what it had regarded as a very testing period. This included bringing in a variety of new elements of control as part of what Meles Zinawi called an 'Ethiopian Renaissance'. In 2008 there was a clampdown on the media, which had substantially grown in scale and scope since 1991, further extending government domination of the sector. There were now to be significant restrictions on reporting as well as on publishing and broadcasting, and the new law was followed up by harassment and arrests of journalists. In the following year a new anti-terrorism law was introduced that was justified in terms of growing threats to national security. A third law introduced restrictions on NGOs aimed in part at the role of international NGO activities in the country, and referring specifically to political life. It was widely seen as an attempt to crack down on a civil society once apparently described by Meles as an 'opposition in disguise' and also referred to as 'the foot soldiers of neo-liberalism' who were insufficiently accountable to the people of Ethiopia, with the government stressing that the provision of services was its responsibility rather than that of foreign-backed independent local NGOs.[4] For the latter to work in their preferred fields of development they had to give up their customary rights-based approach aimed at empowering the population, and switch to the language of service delivery working alongside government. At the same time the government did see the need to work with the international community, including NGOs, on some humanitarian issues, notably food aid – especially in drought-prone areas of the south and south-east where in bad times some 2–3 million people were affected – though it did so repeatedly on its own terms. (In 2008 Ethiopia had the largest World Food Programme (WFP) operations in the world, overtaking that in Sudan.) With the international NGOs held at arm's length there was also less possibility of a challenge from local NGOs which in practice often required state patronage. For its part the government saw them largely as relevant only in local affairs such as dispute management.

This effort at closing down political space after the scares of 2005 was accompanied by the rapid expansion of the numbers belonging to the EPRDF. From a membership of 760,000 it grew to around four million by 2008 in time to extend the party's influence substantially in the local and regional elections that had been postponed from 2006. Indeed, to have an opportunity of employment in the public sector, or to access almost any form of state-provided resources, it was desirable

to be a party member. The number of local councillors was sign
cantly increased and, with the rise in EPRDF membership coupled
with the decline in the opposition parties, councils were largely filled
by the ruling party which proclaimed a further success for 'participatory democracy'. Indeed, it appeared that most adults in the population were, if not actual members of the party, close to someone who
was. At the same time the main opposition parties were becoming
weakened and fragmented. Ethiopia was in the process of becoming
a dominant party system, a move that Meles Zenawi sought to justify
with references to the country's political culture, which he depicted as
not having 'internalized' the building of a competitive democratic
system. At least one critic suggested the reverse, seeing an attempt to
establish a hegemonic 'oppressive, control-minded political culture' by
a leader who knew his Gramsci, and depicted an autocratic ruler behind
a democratic facade. As if to indicate that he was not simply a dictator,
at the same time as extending government control, the prime minister
announced, as mentioned, that he would serve only one more term
and that it would then be time for a new generation of EPRDF leaders
to emerge. By the end of the decade some opposition leaders were
released from detention, but this was widely seen as a sign of the
government's regaining of confidence after the experiences of 2005
rather than indicating a reversal of the trend towards greater control.
Opposition was now largely regional, especially amongst disaffected
Oromo and Somalis in the east, to which the government response
was a combination of sticks and carrots.

The success of the EPRDF's strategy was borne out in the 2010
national elections. Although there were opposition parties, they were
in a much less challenging position than in the previous national elections and were overwhelmingly crushed by the EPRDF which, with its
regional allies, won 545 of the 547 seats. Meles Zenawi duly assumed
the premiership once again and his cabinet was largely a continuation
of personnel, leading some to question the extent to which there might

ship in the foreseeable future. However, the sudden
of Meles Zenawi in August 2012 once more raised
the future direction of a country long led by a close
ve group.

Develop.. its since 2005 have led some to write the epitaph of liberal democracy in Ethiopia. No government has ever come to power through the ballot box; there has been a lack of national cohesion, especially in the lowland areas conquered in the nineteenth century; historically there has been a hierarchical rather than egalitarian culture, in the core highland areas in particular; and violence and revolution have characterized the taking of power – hardly circumstances in which those who are successful will be willing to surrender power at the ballot box. Instead the developmental state is given priority, which in practice is used to justify the severe restriction of opposition, expansion of the EPRDF in close cooperation with the state and, when judged necessary, tough coercive measures. As one leading Ethiopian scholar put it:

> One must understand that the Constitution is only meant for foreign consumption, and not for internal implementation ... Some policies might have changed from the former regimes of Haile Selassie and the Dergue, but one thing always remains intact in Ethiopia: politics is run from the centre with a top-down control. This is also the case today.[5]

A further dimension of government control lay in its approach to the economy. The large majority of Ethiopia's 85 million people live in the rural areas where there is poverty and swathes of areas still prone to drought and food shortages. About half of the population has been heavily dependent on subsistence economy, with around four million in need of food aid. The state continued to own all land while recognizing forms of local access. It also sought to promote agro-industries as an approach to economic development and had the support of the World Bank in its efforts, which included the controversial building of new dams, partly to increase the electricity supply – ideally to the point where power could be exported. It was, however, notable that the companies engaged in the process were closely linked to the EPRDF, and Ethiopia was far from being an open-market economy. According to the World Bank nearly half of the business sector of the economy was controlled by EPRDF-affiliated companies operating in fields such as telecoms, transport, cement, construction and pharmaceuticals, with many companies receiving large foreign aid contracts as well as easy financial terms from the banks. One conglomerate closely linked to the party has been the Endowment Fund for the Rehabiliation of Tigray (EFFORT), while another has been the group of companies led by the wealthy Ethiopian–Saudi businessman, Mohammed al-Amoudi, who is close to the government and associated particularly with investment in agricultural schemes.

This growth of politically linked conglomerates has not been simply a matter of business opportunism, but a sign of the continuing lack of faith by Meles Zenawi in leaving the economy in the hands of the free market. He forged an intellectual and later personal relationship with economist Joseph Stiglitz in his resistance to the nostrums of the IMF. The prime minister's own advanced studies had focused on economic development and he argued that historically, rising economies had employed a degree of protectionism; simply opening the country up to multinationals to operate in a free market would have damaging effects for Ethiopia's own development in the long run. Major areas for investment included infrastructure and telecoms as well as agriculture. Controversially, the latter included a programme of leasing land to foreign investors who saw agricultural development in Africa as important for their long-term food security, and not simply for profit in world markets that were generally rising after years in the doldrums. The countries from which the new investors came included China and

South Korea in the east (as well as Saudi Arabia and other Gulf interests); countries that in theory or practice were seen as examples of being 'developmental states' of different kinds, and on which Meles was very well read. There was concern that expansion of this sector could lead to the government claiming lands from the peasants who would have little access to any redress, especially as there were repeated doubts about the independence of the judiciary. (The senior positions in the judiciary were political appointments and often regarded as cowed by government.)

Strategically, economic growth was based around the Plan for Accelerated and Sustained Development (PASDEP 2007-11) which aimed at agriculturally led industrialization, and it was seen as successful with rates of growth of up to 10 per cent annually in the years after 2000. However, this was driven in part by good rains, foreign investment and generous donors who made Ethiopia one of the three largest recipients of international aid. Within the country the freedom and dynamism of Ethiopia's own business sector was more in doubt. In particular, critics maintained that the patronage of the ruling party was often a prerequisite for business development, and that members of the government and civil service were increasingly directly involved. This criticism was accompanied by allegations of growing corruption. Thus, although the economy was growing overall, comparatively few benefits were trickling down to the largely rural population which, in many areas, was still mired in poverty. There was action at this level, but it was largely the rolling out of programmes designed centrally with which local peasants had to conform in their own interest, not least since land was ultimately controlled by the state. In addition, in 2009, 1.6 million hectares of land were marked out for foreign investors in agricultural schemes, a figure which, if successful, could be extended to 2.7 million. Provision of education and health services of a basic character was taking place, but income levels for most remained low and overall Ethiopia remained listed as one of the ten least-developed countries in the world. At the bottom of the social hierarchy was the position of women, against whom there was continuing social and economic discrimination. The global financial crisis of 2008 proved testing, but the IMF was helpful with support to the balance of payments, although ominously price levels remained significantly higher in 2010 than they had five years earlier.

In the international community Ethiopia was frequently seen as a considerable success. There was less conflict after 1991 than in the preceding decades of civil war; ethnic federalism appeared a suitably devolved approach in such a large and diverse country; long-term democracy was not entirely ruled out; and economic growth rates appeared encouraging. However, after 2000 in particular there were a growing number of concerns. The reduction of 'national' conflict could not hide the fact that there were conflicts, particularly in the peripheral areas. Resistance in Oromia and Region 5 was not as threatening as the pre-1990 wars in the north and Eritrea, but nonetheless flared up intermittently. There were also localized conflicts, often of an ethnic character, in parts of the periphery, especially in the south and west. These areas of instability raised questions concerning the ethnic federal model: was there sufficient autonomy in relations between the regions and the centre?: and were the regions really reflective of Ethiopia's ethnic 'map', which might itself be a somewhat inflexible approach to local identities that could fail to accommodate inevitable social changes? Expectations that democracy would follow a multi-party direction seemed increasingly to give way to forms of a more 'revolutionary' model, accompanied by growing control by the TPLF-led EPRDF. Yet the 2005 elections showed that there was a spirit of opposition, especially in the urban areas of the central regions – including the capital itself – where the social pressures of frustrated urban populations could prove explosive. Meanwhile, development in the countryside remains uneven, with poverty and unrest in outlying areas in the east and south in particular.

Ethiopia is experiencing its third wave of 'modern' statebuilding. Its first was that of Menelik in the late nineteenth century. Inspired by the era of imperialism he both acquired new territory for the state he was building and fought off a European rival in the shape of Italy, which was left with only the crumbs of neighbouring Eritrea and Somalia. His legacy was to survive well into the twentieth century as Haile Selassie took up Menelik's imperial mantle, developing the model with its limitations in a changing, less imperial, Africa. His military successor, Mengistu, embarked on an Afro–Marxist experiment, with Soviet support in a strategically significant area in Cold War rivalries. As a model it had severe limitations in terms of the people, but what brought it down was revolutionary mobilization, first in Eritrea and then Tigray, with the latter largely resulting from the traumas of the early years of the revolution itself, as radical Tigrayan students quit their studies for the northern highlands and the gun. The latters' eventual success brought the downfall of Mengistu's Marxist experiment. This was to be succeeded by Meles Zenawi's vision of the 'developmental state' in Africa as the way forward, as it had been in parts of Asia, against the tide of neo-liberal political and economic orthodoxies so widely pushed in Africa in the wake of the Cold War. What has been notable about Ethiopia is not just that it has seen development attempted along these different lines, but the seriousness with which it has been taken. Elsewhere in Africa, lip service and sometimes more has been applied to ideology, but rarely with the sustained determination of Ethiopia. Whether the third way will succeed is for the future: for the present the most notable feature has been the top-down single-mindedness with which it has been pursued, just as Haile Selassie and Mengistu Haile Mariam pursued their chosen paths.

CHAPTER 4

Somalia

Amidst the change of rulers in the Horn at the end of the Cold War, it was Siad Barre who left the legacy of the greatest chaos. As he headed south from his capital pursued by his enemies, those same enemies were even then turning on each other. The main group that had forced Barre out of Mogadishu was the United Somali Congress (USC), a movement mainly based on the Hawiye clan, which was one of the largest in the country and dominant in and around the capital. With Barre's flight, one of its main political leaders, wealthy businessman Ali Mahdi Mohammed, was proclaimed interim president. However, he was swiftly challenged by one of the key military figures in the USC, Mohammed Farah Aideed, a former prisoner of Barre's, whose faction felt that its leader was not being given the recognition due to him for his role in ousting Barre. Aideed's followers were the strongest of the various militias, but his group was soon challenged by others, including the Somali National Front (SNF), led by Mohamed Said Hershi 'Morgan', and the Somali Patriotic Movement (SPM). In all there were some ten significant militias contesting central and southern Somalia, including Mogadishu itself, the leaders of which were often described in the media as 'warlords'.

While individual militias were often identified by clan and sub-clan labels, these labels were more reflective of the collective identities of the young men involved than of the backing of 'traditional' clan leaderships and structures. 'Clannish' identities had been more politically utilized by Barre as his years in power had rolled on, and it was hardly surprising that with his downfall they were a potent factor within the opposition that had overthrown him and now contested the space he had left. Nor was it surprising that the rivalries were predominantly conducted through violence rather than political accommodation and compromise, in spite of an attempt by the government of Djibouti to convene a conference in July 1991, shortly after Barre had fled. Barre himself had resorted to increasing use of force throughout the 1980s, and with his fall the country was awash with weapons – augmented by supplies from Ethiopia when Mengistu fell – with which the factions could now conduct their competition. The individual militias were quite small, about 2,000–3,000 in number each, but that in itself reflected the frequent splintering that occurred, and raised rather than restricted the overall level of violence in a situation in which there was no control either by the state (now non-existent) or 'traditional' clan elders. There were, though, large numbers of footloose young men, many of them just teenagers, for whom any form of livelihood seemed tied to the gun.

With no state over which to fight in order to gain resources, militias had to look to other targets for their incomes. Looting became widespread. In the farms of the fertile south around the river valleys there were increasing attacks that were soon to contribute to famine conditions in the country. In towns and cities as well, looting contributed to a growing picture of insecurity. There was also business to be done, especially the supplying of the burgeoning market for the mild narcotic qat, which provided opportunities in 'protection' of all kinds. As the violence mounted it contributed to new refugees pouring out of the country to Kenya and Ethiopia, as well as farther afield to Yemen and even the former colonial power, Italy.

It was this lawless environment, as much as natural famine, that contributed to the necessity of food aid. The uncontroversial response of the international community was to seek to meet the humanitarian need, but this in turn became a new source of wealth. By 1992 food aid was increasingly being hijacked by armed groups, both for their own consumption and to sell it on to an increasingly desperate population, a situation which was of immediate concern to the aid agencies and the UN itself. The overall delivery of food aid was by now the responsibility of the United Nations Operation in Somalia (UNOSOM), and early in 1992 UN Under-Secretary James Jonah arrived to seek to address the problem. He made temporary progress with relations between Aideed and Ali Mahdi, and went on to propose a UN force to keep the factions apart, although this was more than the UN was then prepared to accept. However, within months, and as the situation continued to deteriorate, the UN thought again. Five hundred UN troops were deployed, but found themselves pinned down at the airport by the rampaging militias and unable to intervene effectively in a situation that the aid agencies and the media were increasingly calling one of famine. With memories of the impact of images of famine elsewhere in the Horn less than 10 years earlier, the question of an effective response rose on the international agenda.

The UN was also influenced by the approach of its still fairly new Secretary-General, Boutros Boutros-Ghali, the former deputy foreign minister of Egypt. Boutros-Ghali saw the end of the Cold War as creating a new opportunity for the UN to take a lead and, if necessary, to be ready to make greater use of force in a situation such as that unfolding in Somalia. In his previous incarnation Boutros-Ghali had been responsible for Africa and thought he knew what was needed, in the course of which he dismissed his own representative in Somalia, Mohamed Sahnoun, an Algerian diplomat. Sahnoun had proposed decentralizing the delivery of aid by dividing the country into five regions to avoid the concentration on Mogadishu. He also proposed working through the cooperation of local leaders rather than relying on force. However, Boutros-Ghali sought a major military commitment to UNOSOM demonstrating the power of the UN that he wished to project, and turned to the USA. Sahnoun in turn went public with his criticism of Boutros-Ghali's approach, whereupon the latter reciprocated in kind.

Following the end of the Cold War, President Bush was seeking to shape what was being labelled 'The New World Order'. As a first step, in 1991, the USA had led a successful rejection of Iraq's forces from Kuwait following the illegal occupation of the previous year. Such American leadership of determined international action to address crises of whatever kind appeared to accord with the ambitions of Boutros-Ghali, although it was not guaranteed that Bush would decide to send American troops to Somalia. There were those in his administration who saw Somalia as essentially a food problem, and that the apparent famine situation should be addressed by focusing on expanding deliveries. Others, however, saw security as the top priority, and it was this view that predominated, although even then it was not clear that this would involve the deployment of American ground forces. Cynics thought that the rising media attention, at a time when the presidential election was approaching, encouraged Bush to go to full US leadership of all aspects of a new UN military intervention. He was backed in this by the military chiefs, especially Colin Powell, the normally cautious chair of the Joint Chiefs of Staff, who thought it would be eminently 'doable' as well as necessary. The only warning that reached the public domain came from the US ambassador to Kenya, a former journalist Smith Hempstone, who wrote, 'If you liked Beirut you'll love Mogadishu ... do not think Somalia is amenable to the quick fix so beloved of Americans'.[1]

Bill Clinton's defeat of Bush for the presidency in November 1992 did not stop the momentum for intervention. Clinton had been critical of Bush's initial response to the Somalia crisis in his electoral campaign, but once elected gave his support for Bush's commitment to UN resolution 794 in early December 1992. Under this, US forces were to take the lead in the Unified Task Force (UNITAF), which would be a Chapter VII operation allowing for the use of force to make peace amongst the factions and not just to keep the peace to allow food to be distributed. It was intended to be a short-term operation, and Clinton was even told it could well be over by the time of his inauguration. Tactically it was decided that the operation should concentrate on Mogadishu and confront the main warlords there, rather than more dispersed operations in different areas. UNITAF was swiftly built up to 37,000 men, 28,000 of whom were American forces.

Initially there was a measure of success, with food aid more easily distributed and the death rate appearing to fall (although some were later to claim that local food was also more available as well). However, the major issue to emerge was the political question of what, if anything, to do about the militias, who had largely created the situation in the first place. The thinking in the American camp was that there was no need for a systematic focus on disarmament, although occasionally action was taken. However, Boutros-Ghali was once more keen to see a strong stance taken with the warlords as part of steps to bring about the reconstruction of the Somali state. Inevitably the Somali faction leaders were actively calculating how to respond to the situation. At first there was apparent compliance with UNITAF's arrival, and, in addition to participating in US-led talks, Ali Mahdi surrendered some weaponry. However, the rivalry between the leading figures remained intense, with Mohammed Aideed in particular reluctant to give up arms.

The factions were watching UNITAF carefully, and by March 1993, with the food situation apparently improving, the USA felt the time was ripe to begin to wind down the operation, although Boutros-Ghali continued to say that more time was needed to address the underlying problems of state collapse. Indeed, he appeared to have had a measure of success when, at the end of March, UN resolution 814 established a successor operation, UNOSOM II, which had a clearer commitment to disarmament. However, with Boutros-Ghali physically forced to curtail his one and only visit to Somalia, the UN appointed as its Special Representative a US military figure, Admiral Jonathon Howe. Largely of his own volition, and with little input from Washington or New York, Howe decided to embark on a military crackdown, apparently encouraged by the tougher terms of resolution 814. He targeted Aideed and his SNA faction in particular, attacking its base in south Mogadishu. In response Aideed smuggled arms back into the city (they had been hidden outside when UNITAF arrived) and whipped up opposition through his radio station.

It is indicative of the problem of intelligence that there is still uncertainty about the extent of outside help to Aideed, if any. At the time there were virtually no reports of that kind, but subsequently a number of claims appeared. Sudan was then home to a new-ish Islamist regime that had welcomed various groups associated with terrorism, including Osama bin Laden and al-Qaeda. Early in 1993, some disparate Islamist groups from Somalia also visited Khartoum, and there was subsequent training of fighters who ended up assisting Aideed. It was the first time that Somalia had been alleged to be linked to the wider phenomenon of international terror groups, but it was far from being the last.

Fighting between the forces – led by an American commander on one side and the most militarily experienced Somali faction leader on the other – intensified as 1983 wore on, and reached a peak on 3 October in a battle that left 18 Americans dead as well as numerous Somalis, both fighters and non-combatants, in one of the largest ever engagements on behalf of a UN peacemaking operation. The outrage of the American public was predictable, and Clinton responded by announcing that there would be a surge followed by withdrawal by the end of March 1994, a formula that was to be repeated in comparable circumstances in other parts of the world in the years to come. His announcement was followed by the effective replacement of Admiral Howe with an experienced diplomat, Bob Oakley, who returned to talking to the factions, including Aideed, who turned out to have quite elaborate plans for a system of proportional government to stabilize clan politics and reconstruct Somalia. However, no progress was made on this front as US troops departed, to be followed in 1994 by the remainder of the UN forces, leaving the Somali factions to continue their destructive rivalry.

The first effort at armed intervention in the name of humanitarianism in a situation of conflict, led by the liberal West on behalf of the UN, had ended ignominiously. Supporters of the operation claimed that Somali lives had been saved by the enhanced food distribution, but whatever the truth on that score there had been notable shortcomings in the whole operation at conceptual and operational levels. Conceptually there had been public differences within the high command of the UN over how the operation should be conducted. Ambassador Sahnoun had wanted dispersed engagement with local leaders, but Secretary-General Boutros-Ghali favoured a version of what became known as 'shock and awe' to boost the capability and future role of the organization. Within the USA there had also been a comparable difference of approach, with Admiral Howe appearing to be of the Boutros-Ghali school of thought, before Clinton was brought down to earth by the outcome, and an agreed withdrawal was negotiated by an experienced diplomat and local faction leaders. It had been an experience of 'shock and horror', and, as Clinton was later to admit, contributed *inter alia* to the lack of an effective response to the Rwanda genocide of 1994. In addition, there was a lack of clarity between the UN and the USA over the purpose of the operation. For President Bush the US involvement had been for humanitarian relief only; but for Boutros-Ghali it was the start of an operation of nation-building, a theme that was also to have resonance in subsequent years. The USA was left no closer to resolving that issue in the longer term, although Boutros-Ghali was to move to a less confrontational approach. However, partly due to Somalia, he was losing the confidence of the world's only remaining superpower, and his reputation never fully recovered.

The broad picture of much of Somalia after the UN departure was similar to that before the intervention. Factional struggle continued to embrace the capital and much of the surrounding area. Mohammed Farah Aideed died in 1996 but his faction was inherited by his son Hassan; ironically he had been educated in the USA and unwittingly been deployed as a translator by the US forces in the UN operation. Ali Mahdi continued to pursue his claim backed by his clan faction. Another contender to emerge was businessman Osman Otto who had broken with Aideed's SNA, which he had previously financed, to pursue his own ambitions. As the three main factions divided Mogadishu, they and others contested the more fertile areas down to the border with Kenya. To the immediate north the situation was quieter. Here clan and sub-clan leaders, backed by local Muslim figures, established a less intensely competitive environment showing what could be done, while not going as far as trying to construct a regional state in that area of the country.

There were also economic activities that continued to sustain local populations. Ironically the UN even contributed to this in the aftermath of its withdrawal as a result of all the material – and indeed debris – that it left behind. One long-time student of the country was to write of 'The scrap merchants of Mogadishu', especially in urban areas.[2] The acquisition of property was also worthwhile, especially for rent to the international NGOs that still continued to operate in various parts of the country. In agriculture the fertile far south continued to grow and export bananas, in spite of intermittent fighting over land. In the more arid central areas pastoralism continued, as did trade in livestock to neighbouring countries. On the back of these activities new developments were also emerging, including a thriving telecoms sector and banking, much of it linked to the substantial expatriate communities and to the growing centres for these activities in the Gulf, especially Dubai.

While the southern part of the country remained without a capable government, in the north there was a remarkable contrast as in the wake of Barre's collapse two small states appeared to be evolving: Somaliland and Puntland, with the former attracting particular interest. The origins of the emergence of Somaliland lie partly in the Somali National Movement (SNM), which had fought such a determined struggle with Barre from its founding in 1981 and had withstood the horrors of his regime's brutal attacks. Like the movements in Eritrea, Tigray and southern Sudan, the SNM had proved itself a successful liberation movement against an autocratic and violent regime. At the same time, Somaliland had inherited societal structures which had survived through the colonial era and into the independence period. Indeed, the British practice of using clan and sub-clan elders for the purposes of local administration had brought them into working relationships with the state, in contrast to the Italians to the south who had been hostile to clans as a drag on 'modernity'. Though the years after independence had seen attempts by the Somali state to suppress clan powers – especially under Barre – they had survived, and in the north had largely been allies of the SNM, especially in the face of the devastation wrought by Barre's forces.

The combination of the SNM and clan elders proved to be pillars around which Somaliland first survived, and then built anew. But it was a hard task and, in 1991, as Barre fled from Mogadishu leaving conflict and chaos in his wake, there were fears that the same could happen in Somaliland. The SNM appeared to lack the capacity to develop a stable security environment, while there were reports of clan and sub-clan rivalries. On the SNM side it appeared increasingly that its leader, Abdel Rahman Ahmed Ali 'Tour', who was declared president of the self-proclaimed Republic of Somaliland, was less successful as a politician than as a fighter, and in 1993 he was replaced by the veteran northern politician and former prime minister, Mohamed Ibrahim Egal, who proved much more enduring. The SNM had a core from the Isaaq clan family and although there were some internal tensions these were contained, while non-Isaaq groups were accommodated rather than repressed. At the same time, local elders and other leaders were brought together in large and lengthy traditional gatherings known as *guurti*, which were to become an established feature of the new system and helped to resolve both local issues and relations with the centre in what was, in effect, a functioning and distinct feature of the evolving state that appeared to be unique in the Horn.

However, the building of the new political system still proved challenging. Political rivalries and undisciplined militia factions contributed to civil war from 1994 to 1996, but it ended in reconciliation rather than conquest, and subsequently the situation largely stabilized. Institutionally the system evolved into an executive presidency accountable to a bicameral parliament, with an elected lower house and a higher chamber of elders, called appropriately the *Guurti,* all of which was confirmed by a constitutional referendum in 2001. With the death of President Egal in 2002, the growing strength of the system was shown in the orderly succession of his deputy Daahir Rayah Kahin, who went on to win the 2003 presidential election. In addition, there was an emerging multi-party competition by the time of the 2005 legislative elections, although there were fears of signs of authoritarianism on the part of the new president constraining the opposition parties' activities. As a result, there was concern when the elections due in 2009 were stalled amidst fears that Rayah Kahin was trying to entrench himself in power by changing the constitution to allow himself a third term. Instead, however, in the delayed elections held in 2010, Kahin was defeated by Ahmed Mohammed Silanyo, who had himself lost the 2003 elections, with the system adjusting successfully to the peaceful transfer of power. In addition to the central government institutions, the six districts into which Somaliland was divided represented the continuation of the decentralized approach to statebuilding which has characterized the country throughout.

All was not totally rosy in the garden: that would have been too much to expect. There were tensions in some districts, especially in the east where the emergence of Puntland in 1998 led to a border dispute. More generally there was some concern in the districts with the growth of a bureaucratic state based in the capital Hargeisa, which appeared challenging to the traditions of local societies. There was also alarm when there were acts of terrorism perpetrated by Islamists, which seemed out of line with the character of Somali Islam. It was notable, however, that in addition to outside Islamists there was a growth in the number of *madrasas* (religious schools) in the country, while unemployment among the youthful population was high and appeared to contribute to radicalization. This growth in *madrasas* reflected the long-standing Islamic faith of all Somalis, and the influence of religious leaders in the country as a whole, where traditionally there had been a quiet and essentially spiritual approach to religion rather than a militant expression. Indeed, the growth of cohesive movements in civil society as a whole, including women's groups and popular oral poetry gatherings, were important in consolidating the peace after 1996.

Economically Somaliland was making slow progress. The raising and export of livestock remained at the core of the economy especially for the rural areas. At the same time the capital Hargeisa was becoming something of a regional business centre, not least because of the comparatively stable environment and developing infrastructure that it offered entrepreneurs. There was also a growth in mineral exploration, with hopes entertained for oil and natural gas in particular. However, for many of the fast-growing population, nearly 3.5 million by 2008 and mainly young, remittances from the diaspora of around two million remained a vital part of their income.

The great disappointment for Somaliland though was the failure of the international community to recognize its call for independence in spite of a number of grounds for its claim. There had never been a pre-colonial Somali state of the kind that Ethiopia had been able to present to the world. Nor had Somaliland been part of a wider colonial territory, as the post-Barre Somaliland was the territory that Britain

Somaliland

had carved out nearly 100 years before. In 1960 Somaliland had been granted its independence by Britain, and three days later had agreed to cast its lot with former Italian Somalia on what was subsequently claimed to have been a false prospectus. Instead of the proposed fair and democratic state, political and economic power had shifted south to Mogadishu where in time it had been taken over by a military regime that proved to be cruel and rapacious, especially with regard to Somaliland in the 1980s. Unlike the rest of Somalia, Somaliland had reconstituted itself as a functioning multi-party democracy after Barre's downfall. If self-determination deserved anything more than lip service in international relations, then Somaliland's government believed that its call for recognition should be recognized. Moreover, following the fall of the dictator Mengistu in Ethiopia, the international community had recognized the full independence of Eritrea. In addition, a number of international institutions and agencies dealt with the Somaliland government. The UN itself had agencies working with the new government, the European Union has helped in development and a number of respected international NGOs had also joined in.

legitimate call for recogn.

Strong though the Somaliland case has been, which has won it admiration and support from individuals and some sympathy from governments, including the USA and Britain, there has still been resistance in the international community. In particular, existing African states have felt the potential threat of secessionist movements across the continent would be boosted were Somaliland to be successful. The acceptance of Africa's colonially drawn borders had been written into the charter of the Organisation of the African Union (OAU) in 1963, and was continued by its successor the African Union (AU). An exception was made for Eritrea because of the agreement for a referendum on separation by the new post-Mengistu regime in Ethiopia, while in 1994 a second possible exception had been advanced by a regional body, the Inter-Governmental Authority for Drought and Development (IGADD), for southern Sudan. At the time of Eritrea's independence the two former guerrilla movements, the EPLF and the TPLF, which had mostly cooperated in their respective drives for power, believed that the division would be workable. For Somaliland there was no comparable partner in Mogadishu with which to seek agreement on separation. When there were efforts in 2000 to create a Transitional National Government (TNG) there, its intention was to be a federation for Somalia as a whole. In recognition of OAU/AU intransigence on separation, and support for the concept of the TNG, President Egal came to the conclusion that it might be necessary to accept 'special status' for Somaliland, for a while at least, rather than continuing with the seemingly impossible quest of international recognition of his country's claim of independence. His successor, Kahin, was, however, to revive the independence claim, though with no greater success.

While the potential emergence of Somaliland was clearly on the radar from 1991, it took longer for the area immediately to the east and south – the very tip of the Horn – to emerge as an entity calling itself Puntland. The name this time was not an imperial echo so much as the adoption of the ancient name of the land of Punt. Like Somaliland it had a clan core, in Puntland's case it was the Majerteen, a branch of the Darod clan family, though as with other clans there were to be sub-clan tensions and rivalries throughout. Puntland first established itself as a putative authority led by a military figure, Abdullahi Yusuf, in 1998, and for the first three years was comparatively peaceful. It was then plunged into a short but bitter conflict as clan elders came together to oppose the alleged growing authoritarianism of Yusuf, especially in the area around its main port of Bossasso. From 2005 Puntland had a new leader, Mohamed Muse Hersi 'Adde', who was later replaced by Abdirahman Mohamed Farole. However, by 2009 the stability of the government was proving increasingly threatened, including challenges from the spread of Islamist groups and growing tensions within the dominant Darod clan grouping arising from allegations that the ruling Majerteen sub-clan was becoming over mighty.

Puntland was to evolve a different political agenda to Somaliland. It always defined itself not as seeking to become an independent state, but as an autonomous part of a reconstructed federal Somalia. Indeed, after the movement for the TNG emerged in 2000, Abdullahi Yusuf sought to put himself forward as the putative president of Somalia. Puntland's emergence was thus something of a challenge to Somaliland which always resisted the aims of the TNG, and also disputed Somaliland's claim to the border areas of Sool and Sanag where a number of clashes occurred.

Puntland was also to prove contentious with regard to its economic development. In addition to the traditions of livestock rearing and exporting, it became known for its fishing in the rich offshore waters. The major issue, however, was to be the growth of piracy after 2000. Puntland has claimed some of the ports associated with piracy as being in its territory, and has indicated its readiness to help address the problem if supported by the international community. However, there have been doubts about Puntland's capability and determination to tackle piracy seriously.

Meanwhile, in central and southern Somalia, especially the latter, there had been little in the way of indigenous authority growing beyond a degree of localized development. It was not for lack of effort by outsiders, as there were repeated attempts throughout the 1990s that ended in failed talks. In 2000 Djibouti, which had always been suspicious of a potential rival in an independent Somaliland, promoted a new effort with UN support which became known as the Arta process, named after the venue of the initial talks. It resulted in the emergence of the TNG led by Abdiqasim, who endeavoured to launch this latest initiative into Mogadishu itself but soon encountered rejection at the hands of both local warlords and Ethiopia, which always sought a part in developments in its traditionally troublesome neighbour. It seemed like just another failure until 9/11, after which the US-led net to capture Islamist terrorists was widely thrown to include Somalia: perhaps the failed state was or could become another haven for such holy warriors? But though Somalia might be a threat, the USA still felt some bruising from its previous engagement, and so restricted itself primarily to anti-terrorism and letting the European Union (EU) take the initiative politically.

New talks on Somalia were to take place in Kenya under the auspices of IGAD which became known as the Mbgathi process. It was intended that the conference would be more inclusive than its predecessors and include representatives of the faction leaders, the clans and leaders from what is always optimistically known as 'civil society'. The EU-funded conference was expected to have about 300 representatives, but in the event around 1,000 arrived with very mixed credentials. In an effort to create some kind of organization a Leaders' Committee was set up and in the event it was the clan strongmen who stood out.

Mbgathi process [handwritten marginal note]

When it came to actual negotiations on the shape of the future state, the trend was towards eventual federalism. There had been talk since the early 1990s of 'building blocks' for the future, although it was noticeable that Somaliland omitted itself by refusing to participate in the conference, a fact that some equated with disintegration should federalism be established. But a unitary state had been given a bad reputation by the Barre years, and there seemed just as much danger of attempted clan domination should it be established again. This was to be the most important issue addressed by the committees into which the conference had officially broken up, although other key questions such as land and economic development were also being discussed. Talks on these various fronts dragged on seemingly endlessly with attendees coming and going and appearing more interested in the perks of participation than the substance of the discussions. Indeed, amid international frustration, it seemed at one time that the talks might just fade away until, after nearly two years, President Museveni of Uganda stepped in as Chair of IGAD to push for a conclusion in October 2004. Eventual agreement in Kenya on the formation of the

TFG (margin annotation)

new Transitional Federal Government (TFG) did not, however, mean that its return to Somalia would be straightforward. The TFG's President Yusuf, the former Puntland leader, realized the danger of trying to move directly into Mogadishu and instead settled for nearby Baidoa hoping to negotiate a return to the capital from there.

However, while the talks were taking place for the formation of the TFG, there had been further gaining of power by Somalia's Muslim leaders. The role of Muslim leaders had been strengthening since 1997, partly due to the ability of popular local *sharia* courts to create some kind of order in and around the capital with indigenous legitimacy. In accordance with the traditions of Somali Islam their doctrines were comparatively moderate, and the leaders willing to cooperate with each other to extend a network of influence known as the Islamic Courts Union (ICU). They numbered about 30 at their height, under the chairmanship of Sheikh Sharif Sheikh Ahmed. In addition to the Muslim leaders themselves, some businessmen also saw opportunities in a more peaceful environment and were prepared to give their support. Local clan and sub-clan leaders increasingly recognized their authority while other backers were opponents of the attempt to establish the TFG. At the height of the success of the movement in 2006 there was a noted reduction in the level of violence in and around Mogadishu, and there was even a clampdown on what had hitherto been the growing activities of pirates, with the number of attacks on international shipping reduced sharply.

Islamic Courts Union (margin annotation)

While the ICU movement was developing greater authority in the south than any previous attempt at law and order since Barre's downfall, it was also running into opposition. The TFG, with its vital international recognition, was one strand, especially when the possibility of talks between it and the ICU came to nothing in 2006. In addition, the rise of the courts was being viewed negatively in some international quarters. There were also older 'warlord' militias that felt under threat and in danger of losing their power as the ICU was growing, and they had the backing of the USA which feared Islamist potential in the new movement. However, the 'warlord's' disruptive efforts had only encouraged support for the ICU, whose fighters successfully resisted. Nevertheless, once more firmly in place, the ICU encountered further international opposition, especially when it emerged that amongst the movement's leaders was Sheikh Hassan Dahir Aweys, who had been associated with the more modern Islamist movement al-Ittihad, originally an offshoot of the Egyptian Muslim Brotherhood.

Such credentials were anathema to Ethiopia, which had itself felt threatened by al-Ittihad and Islamist terrorism since the late 1990s, and also to the USA, following its failure in the covert use of local 'warlords' to assassinate leaders of the courts. Fearing the rise of a strengthened Islamist government, and in the name of supporting the internationally recognized TFG, in late 2006, Ethiopian forces, with the support of American air power, attacked Mogadishu and forced the courts out amid considerable carnage, creating many thousands of refugees. Following the comparative peace for most of 2006, 2007 was to be a year of intensified conflict, much of it directed against the Ethiopian troops who were now seen by many as an occupying foreign force. In an attempt to bolster the TFG, the AU appealed for other African countries to commit troops to its peace-keeping mission – the African Mission in Somalia (AMISOM) – but few were willing and the overall number of troops was initially small. In time, however, Burundi and Uganda led the response to the call as it built towards the 8,000 troops deemed necessary; a figure later raised to 12,000.

Out of the wreckage of the ICU there emerged a new movement, Harakat al-Shabaab al-Mujahideen (Mujahideen Youth Movement), formerly the armed wing of the ICU. This soon became a rapidly growing Islamist militia, spreading its influence widely in the centre and south. Its growth was accelerated as a result of the Ethiopian invasion, making use of the continuing effect of a foreign presence to act as a uniting experience for Somalis, in this case leading to what was in effect a new insurgency against the invaders from across the country's western border. It was not so much that al-Shabaab was widely popular for its own teaching, as that its core members were ideologically committed, had a common Somali cause against the Ethiopian invaders – the traditional enemy – and were organized and capable of being ruthless in imposing their tough interpretation of *sharia*. But while there was a committed core it was by no means clear that it was a wide and stable movement rather than one of militias of questionable unity and stability, with which young men brought up in circumstances of actual or potential violence became involved. In addition, al-Shabaab was in turn to be challenged by Hisbul Islamiyya (the Party of Islam) led by Sheikh Aweys, who had fled to Eritrea and later returned with the latter's backing. There were attempts to try to woo Aweys towards the TFG and a common front against al-Shabaab, which might have the additional advantage of loosening his ties with Eritrea, but he once more proved an elusive figure to pin down.

With the situation worsening, Djibouti sought once more to be the peacemaker, with the support of the UN, and by the middle of 2008 had brought agreement between the TFG and some of the former ICU figures, with the court's former leader, Sheikh Sharif, being made the next president of the TFG. Having been driven out by the Ethiopians and Americans only a few months before, the Sheikh was now being proclaimed as the new leader of what his former attackers hoped would be a more inclusive and reconciliatory government. At first it seemed that the new TFG might have a greater chance of success. The Sheikh himself had had comparative success with the ICU before he was forcibly ejected, the last of the hated Ethiopian troops had finally withdrawn early in 2009, and there were promises of renewed international support. Indeed, there was a lull in the level of conflict in the capital as the TFG sought to establish itself in the early months of 2009, but it proved tenuous as the reformed government was no nearer to becoming an accepted authority. Instead there were accusations of weakness, division and corruption, which grew rather than diminished.

Meanwhile, the struggle between the Islamist groups in the south as a whole continued. The major grouping was al-Shabaab which remained rather opaque. It appeared to be a conglomeration of groups rather than having an overall command, and indeed there were reports of disagreements amongst the various leaders. The groups have used typical tactics of modern guerrillas including roadside bombs and suicide attacks. During the Ethiopian presence from late 2006 to early 2009 they had a degree of popular support of a nationalistic character but, after 2009, repression as much as support appeared to be their basis of power. While often claiming to act in the name of Islam, the interpretation and practices appeared more like those of the Taliban in Afghanistan than of the more moderate *sufi* traditions of Islam in Somalia. In addition, they financed themselves through various forms of extortion in the name of 'taxes', including road blocks and levies at airstrips and ports. Ideologically the leaders have linked themselves increasingly with international groups such as al-Qaeda, which has encouraged foreign Islamists to join them, though for many the appeal was still more of a local nationalism.

While al-Shabaab controlled much of the south-central area, an Ethiopian-backed group known as Ahlu Sunna Wal Jama'a (Followers of the Prophetic Way and Consensus), reflecting a more traditional *sufi* style of Islam, checked its advance northwards into Puntland and Somaliland. In addition, in 2006, the ICU's success in defeating the 'warlord' militias had allowed the area immediately south of Puntland to set itself up as Galmudug, with a similar ambition of being recognized as a part of a future federal Somalia. However, in the southern part of the country there was little sign of progress towards peace. Instead in the West there were growing fears of the growth of Islamism and with it international terrorism; a fear which al-Shabbab at least appeared to justify with its links to al-Qaeda and a new influx of foreign

Al shabab labelled a terrorist org in US in 2008

2009 drought in Somalis

fighters. It was sufficient for the USA to put al-Shabaab on the list of terrorist organizations in 2008, and to target and kill those it knew and traced. After the death of Osama bin Laden in Pakistan in 2011, al-Shabbab even went so far as to announce that it would avenge his death, though nearer home it suffered a setback when a wanted terrorist leader, Faisal Abdullah Mohammed, was killed shortly after bin Laden. For its part, al-Shabaab had already claimed responsibility for the bombings of bars in Kampala during the 2010 soccer World Cup, in revenge for Uganda's leading role in AMISOM, al-Shabaab's main enemy force in Mogadishu. In 2011 it also sent suicide bombers into Mogadishu partly in response to the US use of drones against its leadership.

Al-Shabaab was also an important factor in the drought in the south-central area of the country where the humanitarian crisis which developed from at least 2009 was the worst in the world, causing up to 3.5 million Somalis to be in need of food aid. (It affected neighbouring countries as well and was said to be the worst drought in the region for 60 years.) International relief agencies struggled not only in the face of a conflict on the ground, but also with the attitudes of the parties to the conflicts. The TFG and Ethiopia were suspicious of food aid reaching al-Shabaab, which was virtually inevitable since it controlled many of the areas affected. Instead the TFG sought to control the dispersal of humanitarian aid while still controlling only the capital and lacking the ability to deliver aid more widely itself. It was backed in this position by the UN and the international community, which indicated its determination to see the TFG succeed. Al-Shabaab itself banned the relief supplies, fearing that the actual delivery of aid by international NGOs could assist foreign operations against it. Food aid appeared to have become a possible instrument of state rebuilding – however far-fetched that looked in the light of the tiny area under the TFG's control – as well as a victim of al-Shabaab's determination to resist, at virtually any cost to the communities in areas where it operated.

The links between al-Shabaab and al-Qaeda also made the USA concerned at the effects of aid on what it regarded as its international counter-terrorism operations and, with growing political pressures and security threats from all sides on aid deliveries, some agencies withdrew or suspended their programmes. That suspension contributed to the growth in refugee numbers, and, by 2011 there were hundreds of thousands in the largest Kenyan refugee camp, with newcomers arriving at the rate of several thousand per month. Eastern Ethiopia and Puntland to the north also received many seeking food aid. This situation gave rise to renewed questions about the US policy on stopping its food aid reaching areas controlled by al-Shabaab groups. The blocking of food aid from the USA, the largest source in the world, had taken place under the Patriot Act, passed shortly after 9/11 and intended to weaken Islamist movements. However, it had been suspended to allow food to Hezbollah-dominated areas of south Lebanon, and some felt that the severity of the crisis in Somalia warranted a similar response; nonetheless, in some Republican and military circles in particular it was resisted for fear that al-Shabaab would also be beneficiaries. There were some efforts to try to use local agents to deliver food aid, but conditions remained both difficult and fluid, with great uncertainty about the strength, organization and attitudes of al-Shabaab itself. In May 2011 there were hopes of greater access when al-Shabaab announced that it was pulling out of Mogadishu, but it also said that the move was purely strategic and the uncertainty and difficulties persisted. As if to indicate that the pull-back was not a defeat but signalled a change of tactics, in late 2011 al-Shabaab turned to terrorist bombing in the city, akin to its bombings in Kampala in 2010.

With the TFG's mandate expiring in August 2012, there were fresh international efforts to implement a 'Roadmap' agreed in 2011, including a new constitution. However, the international community continued to back a process which demanded the exclusion of al-Shabaab, which remained a significant force in the south-central areas.

Somalia's state collapse, which is generally regarded as the most complete in the world, and which has lasted for 20 years, has resulted in a great deal of analysis and interpretation. For some the levels of its clan rivalry and violence are primordial. Clans and sub-clans have always competed for resources, resulting in conflict. The difference in the context of the Somali state is one of scale. Traditionally relations amongst the pastoralists were very local, concerned extended families and sub-clans and could be contained since conflicts were generally small scale and did not involve sophisticated weaponry. Moreover, peace could be made, for a while at least, through the politics of stateless- ness in which accepted leaders and elders of the parties judged on the basis of mutually accepted 'laws', and punishments were agreed and implemented. After independence the colonially created state was still an alien structure, and in such a poor country its resources provided an inevitable target for enhanced rivalry and therefore conflict, even to the point of destroying the state itself: politics had been reduced to the ultimate zero-sum game conducted with a readily available array of weaponry. The democracy of the early years of independence had only served to encourage multi-party clannism, and under Barre the pretence of banning it served instead to exacerbate the inevitable as he raised the level of rivalry from the local to a full-blown level of clan competition for national resources. This approach has been well summed up by Said Samatar when he wrote, 'Somali state politics is nothing but traditional clan politics writ large, with the difference that the society is today armed with modern, mass-destructive weapons – with Stalin organs and assault rifles. Hence the massive level of the violence.'[3]

It was also suggested that the creation of the state had changed the economy as well as the politics. Traditional reciprocal relations had largely been associated with a subsistence-based pastoral economy, while the colonial and post-colonial economy was partly one of commodity production. But that in turn was largely related to the international market economy in which Somalia could never become more than a small fringe actor. Thus marginal capitalist development had damaged traditional systems of conflict management while being unable to produce a more developed economy: in neo-Marxist terminology Somalia was becoming a classic small-scale case of structural 'under-development'. This situation was made worse by the unevenness of the process in which Italian colonial policy had advantaged peoples from the south of the country over those from the north. The growing but necessarily constrained competition amongst Somalis was at the same time taking place within the political context of Barre's 'developmental state' which, with its socialist agenda of government intervention, served to intensify the competition. And as the limitations of that competition became more apparent, it degenerated into the well-known, if officially banned, rivalry of clans which, once established, was to continue after his downfall.

An understandable extension of this argument was that, in the process, independence had created a state-based class that increasingly operated as the corrupt superstructure of a partially commoditized economy. As opposition grew, notably after the invasion of Ethiopia by Barre in 1977, initially it was inevitably local but was met by repression by the 'clannist' state, which in turn provoked ever more widespread clan resistance. The eventual success of the insurgent clans ended in the demise of the state, but without the creation of any transcending political identity in the process, and hence no effective replacement; a situation that was to persist thereafter. Some thought that only international intervention could reverse this situation, but repeated efforts served only to bring generally fragmented opposition to the various efforts of the outsiders.

Others, however, saw things differently. The existence of clans did not make conflict inevitable. In the north, Somaliland had created a government and a significant degree of security. Although there was a dominant clan there, it had worked to incorporate others with success, showing that state and multi-clan societies could have a future. The lesson to be drawn, it was argued, was to address Somalia in terms of more localized units, an idea suggested by some as early as the first UN engagement following Barre's downfall. Somaliland, and to a lesser extent Puntland, had shown what could be done, and the need was to proceed in this way. To some extent this approach caught on theoretically with the TNG and then the TFG, but Somaliland continued to resist the idea of such federal incorporation, holding out instead for its own international recognition (its representatives at the independence of South Sudan in 2011 wore tee-shirts saying 'Somaliland is Next'). In addition, some critics pointed out that developments in Somaliland and Puntland had reflected indigenous choices and processes, not the imposition of a decentralized or federal formula supported by the international community and promoted through the imposed TFG.

Furthermore, talk of political reconstruction has always raised the question of the people to be involved and the process. In particular, whether to regard 'warlords' as participants in the process was a problem the UN had faced in the early 1990s. Also, how could local leaders be accommodated? And what about the legitimacy of some of those claiming to speak in the name of Islam? The search for 'civil society' has often been raised, but of what did it really consist, and were people such as those claiming to represent local NGOs really credible? Were there leaders and personalities to be found who could transcend the obvious divisions amongst the Somali peoples? In addition, what should the process be? Would the process depend on the international community, or could indigenous 'stakeholders' manage it? Such were the kinds of questions raised by the Mbgathi peace process in Kenya – the 15th attempt at peacemaking since Barre's downfall – which produced a TFG that appeared little more successful than the TNG had been before it.

In any case talk of reconstruction on whatever political basis was faced with economic and security problems that appeared to constitute an interconnected disaster. Economic impoverishment had contributed to violence, especially the combination of large numbers of unemployed young men and the easy availability of weapons. The resulting insecurity further undermined the economy, driving millions into internal displacement, cross-border refuge, and reliance on international food aid that was increasingly difficult to deliver. There had been some attempts to reduce arms by embargoes and, during the brief success of the ICU in 2006, the collection of arms by local leaders, but in the conditions that have prevailed for most of the years of independence in Somalia it is all too obvious why people obtain and then keep their guns. That has led some to suggest that Somalia, at least south of Puntland, should simply be left alone. Let food and other forms of aid go in but, instead of attempting any form of statebuilding, simply work with local communities and see what forms of bottom-up development take place. Others, however, have seen this as a council of despair, and argue that, although more peaceful relations at local levels may develop, the abandonment of support for any form of state-building would be to leave Somalis without any hope of the kinds of development in services and infrastructure of which it is hard to conceive without a more large-scale authority.

Piracy

The search for answers to the problems of Somalia had become more intense as the problem of piracy grew, with doubts about it being addressed without an onshore strategy. But while the rising threat of Islamism in the country had become increasingly linked to international politics, piracy off the Somali coast was a home-grown phenomenon.

Piracy is as old as recorded history and exists in a number of areas of the world, with recent hotspots including the Straits of Malacca and the West African coast, especially off Nigeria. However, the growth of piracy off the Somali coast has made it the area of greatest activity in the world with the opportunities provided by 20 per cent of world shipping passing through the Red Sea, the Arabian Sea and the Indian Ocean. In addition, the piracy has taken on a new form: whereas most modern piracy has focused on ships at anchor or moored, the Somali pirates have had to target ships sailing on the high seas.

The emergence of piracy as an international concern has its roots in a number of the strands already discussed. It is not an entirely new phenomenon, indeed a notable period of piracy in the waters of the Horn had been in the late eighteenth and early nineteenth centuries, when vessels from the southerly end of the Gulf of Arabia attacked ships of European origin trading with India and points further east. It led in the end to a truce with Britain that gave rise to the Trucial states, later to become the United Arab Emirates (UAE). The more recent escalation dates from the collapse of Barre's regime in 1991, and has grown in volume since 2005 in particular. The attacks have also had a much greater range, extending over several hundred miles and reaching as far as the Seychelles. It adds up to a situation in which the seas off Somalia have become the most dangerous in the world for piracy.

The pirates frequently identify themselves as former fishermen, deprived of their living by foreign fishing fleets. In the 1970s Barre had encouraged the growth of the industry as part of economic diversification, but by the late 1980s, it was in decay, with electricity failures and intermittent fighting interrupting the treatment and freezing of catches. In addition, since the 1990s more foreign fleets have appeared off the Somali coast, seriously depleting the catches of local fishermen. Certainly the north-east coast of Somalia, off the area of Puntland in particular, is believed to be one of the richest fishing grounds around Africa and it is not disputed that large operations by fleets from a number of countries have taken place. In a report by Britain's Department for International Development it was said that there was large-scale and illegal foreign fishing, especially for tuna and shrimps.

Indeed, pirates initially boarded the foreign fishing ships to take the catch, but later realized that holding ships to ransom was more lucrative, and then that they could branch out into all forms of international shipping and not just confine themselves to fishing boats. (It has been noted that with foreign trawlers deterred by piracy, local catches have increased, including those off the northern coast of Kenya.) This also involved extending their operations from the main fishing areas off the east coast of Somalia into the much busier international shipping lanes of the Gulf of Aden.

The pirates also claim that some foreign operators have taken advantage of the lack of any effective authorities controlling the coastline to dump containers and even unwanted ships filled with toxic materials and nuclear waste, thereby creating a problem of pollution of the inshore waters. The 2004 tsunami created huge waves on the Somali coast that threw up some of the dumped waste. The UN Environment Program has confirmed that such evidence exists, although the difficulty of obtaining it has made it impossible to quantify the extent. The pirates thus like to present themselves as international victims rather than international criminals, and they do have a case. As 'victims' they can also appear as Robin Hood characters: while they themselves show outward signs of increasing wealth in their home areas, they also claim that there is a trickle-down where many in the local communities benefit from their activities and suffer no significant consequences from the international community.

As indicated, during the period of the ICU in 2006, the number of incidents fell, but following the Ethiopian and American overthrow of 2006–07 it rose dramatically. In 2008 there were 111 pirate incidents which led to 42 ships being seized, and that rate continued to rise into 2009. The result has been the growth of piracy from small beginnings into quite sophisticated operations which appear to involve Somali businessmen, 'warlords' and militia members. There also appears to have been a degree of specialization, particularly with regard to the increasingly sophisticated equipment available to the pirates. There are also international links, with weapons coming from Yemen to add to the many acquired from areas of conflict, especially the ready availability of arms in Mogadishu. In Puntland it was said that some of the Darod clans have also been involved, using ports including Eyl, Bossasso and Caluula, leading to the government there claiming to have taken action to close operations down. It claims instead that Haraderia to the south of Puntland has become the main port, with Hawiye clans involved.

Since 2007 the pirates have become more organized with 'mother ships', often themselves hijacked vessels, helping the smaller boats known as 'skiffs' to attack several hundred miles out into the Indian Ocean, reaching as far as the Seychelles, as well as moving northwards into the southern Red Sea. Their organizations now appear to have quite elaborate hierarchical structures, with the proportional sharing of ransom money forming a significant part of local economic activity, involving a number of clans and sub-clans. It has been estimated that there were probably about seven syndicates operating in 2010 involving some 2,000 pirates. They took at least 49 ships and over 1,000 sailors in 2010, with 35 ships and 700 sailors still being held by the end of the year. In all, it was estimated that the pirates 'earned' $238 million in 2010. Once on shore in their sometimes well-equipped bases, the ransoms are carefully divided up between the financiers, the pirates themselves and those guarding the ships while the money is awaited. Average payouts are believed to be between $10,000 and $20,000, a serious sum in areas as poor as Somalia, turning some pirates into local celebrities.

In addition to more complex organizational structures, the improved weaponry, including RPGs and heavy machine guns, has led to questions about international links, especially among the extensive network of the Somali diaspora. Somali businessmen in Dubai are thought to be involved, as well as others in neighbouring Djibouti, Ethiopia and Kenya. It has even been suggested that informants in London may be

sending valuable shipping information on cargoes, ro
ules. However, it has proved difficult to track possible (
tions, largely because all the activities, and especially
ransoms, are conducted in cash – normally US$100 bills – with ransoms
believed by 2011 to range generally from $500,000 up to $3 million,
with $1 million being the usual kind of figure. In 2008 the pirates even
seized a huge Saudi Arabian tanker, the Sirius Star, with $100 million
worth of crude oil, which was ransomed for $3 million, after which
there was a spontaneous party on the beach in Hoby. In February 2011
pirates seized their third supertanker. Oil tankers seem to have become
increasingly popular as targets largely because they have commanded
the highest ransoms: in 2010 $9.5 million was paid for the release of
the South Korean Samho Dream. In November 2010 it was reported
that no less than $12.3 million was paid for the release of two ships.
Estimates for the total costs incurred in all aspects of piracy have risen
as high as $5 billion per year.

The first international response to the growth of Somali piracy was
to begin putting measures in place to limit the threat within a number
of constraints. The shipping industry already had a monitoring body,
the International Maritime Bureau (IBM) Piracy Reporting Center based
in Kuala Lumpur in Malaysia, which came up with a number of pieces
of advice. These included a recommendation to stay at least 600 nautical
miles off the Somali coast, even though it might increase distances and
subsequent costs in time and fuel. Also, cruise ships took to removing
the western Indian Ocean from their itineraries. However, for merchant
ships coming from or going towards the Suez Canal more detailed
measures were suggested, including registering with The Maritime
Security Center Horn of Africa (MSCHOA) which offered its own
advice on deterring and avoiding hijacking.

With the possible solution of local state action against piracy in the
region ruled out, either by the lack of a functioning state (Somalia) or
a lack of capacity, in the end the most reliable action came down to

.e involvement of larger naval powers. EU countries have played a leading role in assisting ships passing through the Gulf of Aden, including the establishment by the EU Naval Force (EUNAVFOR) of the ATALANTA mission. It was started in 2008 with the aims of protecting the UN World Food Programme deliveries to Somalia, protecting merchant shipping around the Horn and deterring piracy. One of ATALANTA's tactics has been to encourage merchant shipping to make use of a naval corridor to the south of the Yemeni coast with naval vessels in attendance rather than actual convoy formation. Other measures recommended to the ships have included switching off Automatic Identifying Systems (AIS), speeding up for this section of the voyage and moving in zigzag patterns. Ships following this advice have significantly reduced their chances of being attacked, but with so many ships from so many countries passing through the area many do not follow the recommendations and attacks persist. Some shipping companies changed routes, going around South Africa rather than heading for the Suez Canal thereby reducing insurance costs, but the safety of this procedure was called into question when the pirates greatly expanded their areas of operation.

For their part, the naval ships involved in these operations have been very ready to demonstrate their continuing significance to their respective governments, and also saw it as a good form of active training for the sailors involved. Indeed, for most countries involved, confronting Somali pirates was their major international naval operation. NATO has also been involved with its Operation Ocean Shield, while the USA has led a coalition based in the Gulf known as Combined Task Force 150, later 151. A number of Asian countries also sent naval units, including China, India and Japan, since they had a major involvement in the shipping targeted. In all, 14 navies have been involved, with approximately 20–30 warships off the Somali coast at any one time, and in late 2010 the area they patrolled was extended beyond the Seychelles. The international operations have given something of a boost to the tiny economy of Djibouti, which several countries use as a facility for their ships. In spite of these efforts, the continuing rise in attacks has led to criticism that there are simply not enough foreign warships for the vast area of the seas that needs to be patrolled, although it is recognized that the costs for the navies involved are already high and may prove unsustainable for a significant length of time. International concern was also expressed at the UN, where the Security Council adopted a series of resolutions in 2008. With the support of the TFG, supposedly speaking for Somalia, member states were authorized to take whatever measures were necessary to put down piracy and armed robbery at sea.

With the comparative success of the international policing of the Aden corridor, it has been the Somali basin that has remained the most vulnerable area, and the level of attacks has not diminished in the long term. (On an annual basis factors such as the monsoon affects the level.) One newer response has been for naval vessels to patrol close to the coast off the known ports used by the pirates, to try to deter them or chase them back into port. Naval operations have also included seeking out suspected mother ships for the pirate gangs and boarding and searching them. In some cases arrests have been made by international naval forces, and extradition agreements with neighbouring states have been activated, with pirates handed over to Kenya in particular. However, there are limitations in seeking to arrest and imprison pirates since the neighbouring states such as Kenya and even Seychelles have little capacity for imprisoning the kinds of numbers that could be involved to the standards that the international community would require. A number have been tried in Somaliland, which is regarded as a more reliable ally than Puntland, and in 2011 there were about 50 imprisoned in Hargeisa. In addition, when pirates have been captured, the arresting ships are generally reluctant to take them to their home courts for trial, not least because of problems of evidence, which is often circumstantial since weapons are generally hurriedly jettisoned, and instead they have frequently simply released the pirates, probably to strike again later. One exception came in April 2010 when five Somalis were detained by a US warship, the USS *Nicholson*, on which they had fired in the mistaken impression that it was a civilian vessel. They were taken to the USA for trial and subsequent imprisonment.[4] By the start of 2011, with the number of ships being taken continuing to rise, and their range of activity extending right down to the Mozambique Channel to the south and across to the Straits of Hormuz at the entrance to the Gulf, the outlet for much of the world's oil supply, the UN representative handling piracy matters proposed the international establishment of special courts in northern Somalia and Tanzania.

The growth of piracy has also encouraged private security companies to offer their services. These have often taken the form of advice and training in avoidance techniques such as a variety of measures to make it harder for ships to be boarded. However, merchant navies have not generally carried armed guards, and there is a reluctance to do so, though that practice has increasingly been questioned as the scale of the piracy has risen. For the shipping companies themselves the chances of a particular ship being seized remain comparatively small, while the additional expense of armed guards on all ships, even if available, could be prohibitive. Nevertheless, with insurance costs and payouts rising, bodies like Lloyds of London have been contemplating organizing further measures, such as greater use of convoy techniques, as China and Russia have been doing, in an endeavour to counter the growing scale of the attacks.

If the pirates are successful in boarding a ship there is advice for crew members to avoid getting into firefights. In part this is because pirates are likely to be more experienced in the use of arms, and in part because the international legal position with regard to such a fight on the high seas could be complicated. Instead, it is better to try to take measures that improve vigilance, make the boarding of ships more difficult, and in some cases build secure areas on board to which the crews can retreat. A wish to avoid firefights has also generally operated on the side of the pirates whose aim is not to inflict casualties on the crew but to take ship and crew intact and then to negotiate a ransom (although it has been noted that after 2008 there was a rise in the number of incidents of pirates firing on ships, perhaps because defensive techniques were improving). There was a notable exception to this non-violent response to attack in April 2009 when the American crew of the *Maersk Alabama*, carrying food to Somalia, was attacked and fought back successfully, but it was not a response which was taken up more generally. When a ship has been taken the pirates usually turn off the AIS and head for the Somali coast, and once there they open negotiations with the ship owners. Experienced negotiators are available who will talk directly to the pirates on the ship and generally agree a ransom which is dropped onto the ship. Typically it has taken about two months from the seizing of a ship to the completion of the process and the release of the ship and its crew.

The cost is eventually covered by the hull underwriters in the insurance industry, which is legally prepared to cover the payment of ransom to pirates who, for these purposes, are regarded as private criminals. However, if the pirates were regarded as operating for ideological reasons, notably in Somalia's case as part of an Islamist agenda, then it would be regarded as terrorism and it would be illegal for payment to be made. The pirates thus have a strong interest in avoiding being linked to the Islamist factions increasingly active on the mainland, as has al-Shabaab, which would not benefit financially, and there has been no conclusive evidence of any change in this situation, although allegations of links have increased. It was noticeable in the *Maersk Alabama* incident that US Secretary of State Hillary Clinton declared that the pirates were criminals and not terrorists.

The realization of the growing strength of the pirates led to discussion of the prospects of them being tackled in their bases on land, but also recognition that in the longer term this would require the reconstruction of a state in Somalia. At the same time many of the pirates appeared to be operating from the territory over which the government of Puntland claims authority, and Puntland has been making considerable efforts to appear credible to the international community as a partner in suppressing terrorism, including arresting some pirates in 2009. However, there has been scepticism, since it is unclear how far the writ of Puntland's authority really runs. In addition, not all the pirates are currently operating from the territory it claims and those that are may well be able to move south to other ungoverned ports if necessary. There has also been suspicion of connections between some of the leaders in Puntland and the pirates, whose activities also embrace a range of onshore dealings such as arms trading, kidnapping (including people trafficking) and smuggling.

By 2011 it was clear that piracy was continuing to grow and, with the help of more mother ships, was expanding the area of operations up to 1,000 nautical miles off the Somali coast. Attacks on oil tankers exiting the Gulf were recorded, as well as more attempts to seize bulk carriers and container ships, since larger ships could command larger ransoms. There were also signs that piracy was becoming more violent, with a number of deaths of crew members taking place, while some owners were encouraging more armed defence of their ships. One country that did decide to take a tougher approach was India, not only because of the growing threat to its trade, but also because many crew members have been of Indian nationality. As a result, its navy took a tougher attitude, seizing a number of pirates and detaining them for trial in its own courts, rather than letting them go to attempt to strike again. While the large majority of ships passing through the area have not been directly affected, it is clear that the overall problem is continuing and that the seas around Somalia remain the most dangerous in the world for merchant shipping and its crews. In 2011 there were also indications that pirate groups were diversifying into the kidnapping of tourists for ransom in the Kenyan coastal resorts.

Kenya, with porous borders and a significant and distinctive Somali population, has also been linked financially and commercially with the piracy industry.

Somalia has emerged as a failed state of both onshore and offshore dimensions which are interlinked. Onshore, the failure of the state has led to hybrid wars involving violent criminality, conflicts over local power, battles for control of the capital and potentially central government, as well as international intervention from Ethiopia (with US assistance) and AMISOM forces. Offshore, state collapse has facilitated the emergence of piracy on a scale and complexity larger than elsewhere in the world. Figures indicate that it has not been contained by international naval efforts, and it has often been argued that its combating requires onshore action which appears to be beyond the aims and abilities of the international community. This vicious circle is in turn connected to another in the form of a complex humanitarian emergency. Somalia has hundreds of thousands of people displaced internally as well as growing numbers of refugees heading for neighbouring countries, especially Kenya. On the humanitarian front, by 2011 the emphasis was put on drought as a condition affecting Ethiopia as well as Kenya and Somalia. While that may be the case, the political situation in Somalia is clearly a vital factor. It all brings back images of the early 1990s, as state failure and 'warlordism' preventing humanitarian relief was the reason for the US-led UN intervention which achieved little, but was the first chapter in an unresolved disaster that has now lasted for some two decades. Today humanitarian relief has to contend not only with the onshore obstacles to action, but the offshore as well, as piracy has affected delivery of food aid.

Superficially former Somalia looks like a country of two stories. The usual picture of state collapse and violent anarchy in the centre and south is tempered by evidence that reconstruction is possible, as demonstrated by Somaliland and to a lesser extent Puntland. Yet the ICU period of emerging peace, before the Ethiopian invasion of 2006, suggested that it was not impossible for the south to evolve its own more orderly arrangements, while to the north both Puntland and Somaliland have had their own problems. Certainly it is widely thought that without the establishment of some form of stronger authority in the relevant areas on land, almost certainly on a de-centralized basis if it is to succeed, there is little prospect of fully addressing the problem of piracy off Somalia's shores.

CHAPTER 5

Sudan

The coup in Sudan in 1989 was the start of the first attempt to construct an Islamist state in the Arab and *sunni* Muslim world, and the new regime saw itself from the outset as having international as well as domestic significance. It was an ideological agenda, but one very different from the earlier Leftists and their efforts right across the region, described in its heyday as 'garrison socialism'.[1] The *eminence grise* of the project, which had started long before 1989, was Hasan al-Turabi. Born in 1932 in northern Sudan, he was the son of a *qadi*, an Islamic judge, who had ensured that from the outset Turabi studied *sharia* – Islamic law – at the same time as he followed a Western education. His reputation as a contributor to debates about Islam was well established before the coup he masterminded, and had already spread across the Muslim world.

The driving force of Turabi's approach was his view of the place of Islam in the modern world. His views are not to be found in any one work, but in a range of writings and lectures, many of which are quite generalized in their messages. Sometimes described as a fundamentalist, Turabi was certainly not one who sought to turn back the clock to the Arabia of the seventh century, but rather one who endeavoured to understand the contemporary role of Islam. This involved him in a good deal of interpretation starting with the concept of *ibtila*', life's challenges to Muslims, especially those posed by the rise of the West. He argued that in order to meet the challenges, Muslims need to seek *tajdid* – renewal – which requires the stripping away of many of the accretions to the true message of Islam which the religion had acquired down the centuries. In Sudan's case this means the influences of the various *sufi turuq* – mystical Islamic orders – and of Mahdism and their replacement by the establishment of a modern Islamic state. The method was to be by the adoption of *ijtihad*, the revelation of Islam based on first principles, from which true *sharia* could then be constructed to form the foundation of an Islamic state.

Turabi often presented himself as a reformist and was interpreted as being quite liberal for his apparent support of representative democracy, or *shura* as he prefers. However, this was not classic liberal democracy since it required that *shura* operate within an Islamic constitution, which Turabi believed to be the wish of all true Muslims. He also appeared liberal with regard to women and the arts, although once more within an established Islamic society. Indeed, he appeared to think that such an Islamic society should be the prerequisite for the making of an Islamic state. Once established, the beacon Islamic state would spread the message to create a renewed *umma*, a wider community of the world's Muslims.

However, while talking of an Islamic society, since National Reconciliation in 1977, Turabi's plan had involved entryism into many areas of the state, including the armed forces, in preparation for the moment when the National Islamic Front (NIF) would take power. As one insider was to put it not long after the 1989 coup, the leaders were preparing 'to make a bid to control the state and impose their norms on society and hoped to succeed where their opponents had failed by defining a new Sudanese community based on Islam'.[2] The new regime called itself the National Salvation Revolution.

In effect it was a form of vanguardism, starting with a purging of the army itself. Some 40 per cent of the officer corps were summarily dismissed (about 2,000 in all), and when coup threats were detected those involved were summarily executed. Alongside that, a number of new security networks were established which were to prove effective in preventing possible popular uprisings of the kind that had brought down previous military regimes in 1964 and 1985. 'Ghost houses', as they were known, became places of arbitrary detention, torture, mutilation and death as recorded by various human rights organizations and the UN. It was easily the most repressive period in northern Sudan since independence in 1956, and far outdid anything carried out under the two previous military regimes. In addition, the regime established its own militia, the Popular Defence Force (PDF), numbering about 150,000, and PDF training was made compulsory for students and some civil servants. It was seen as a move both to augment the army and at the same time to act as a counterweight to it if necessary.

While *sharia* had been introduced in 1983, those existing laws were revised and a new code introduced in 1991. At the same time Sudan was formally given a federal political system consisting of 26 states, though in effect with government control of all top appointments. In addition, Popular Committees were established along Libyan lines to operate in parallel with the local administration, with roles including distributing rationed goods and acting as local spies. The Revolutionary Command Council (RCC) that had officially taken power in 1989 was dissolved in 1993 when Omer al-Beshir was formally declared president, although most of its members went into the new cabinet which was overwhelmingly NIF in composition. However, it was widely believed that formal structures were a form of smoke and mirrors, and that power was really exercised behind the scenes by a group of the NIF leadership. Widespread purges were also reported in the judiciary, the civil service and education with many others choosing to leave the country for self-imposed exile.

A ministry was established that was specifically responsible for trying to create the new Islamic society, and many pre-1989 civil society organizations came under attack. To the NIF many of these groups – which had been quite vibrant, associated with the uprisings of 1964 and 1986 and known as the 'modern forces', – were leftists and secularists. They included professional organizations such as the doctors and the once powerful trade unions' movement. In their place new Islamic groups, many dating from the 1980s, sought to take over, such as the Islamic *Jihad Dawa*, the Society for Enjoining Good and Speaking Against Evil and the Holy Quran Society. Alongside this was a programme of Arabization and Islamization, which was enforced across the education system at all levels. The role of women was also Islamized, which impacted on the professions, dress codes and family life, with free movement restricted and travel requiring the permission of a male relative or guardian. The economy was liberalized, which meant in practice that the influence of the Islamic banks grew as did that of the small business sector that the NIF had been encouraging since the 1980s. Privatization of state enterprises was actively pursued, generally to the advantage of the regime and its allies. However, liberalization was to be hampered for much of the 1990s by the country's indebtedness and by US and UN sanctions imposing international credit restrictions.

In 1996 the regime felt sufficiently confident to move to no-party elections in which Beshir comfortably defeated 41 other candidates for his post. Similar elections were also held for a National Assembly, where it was subsequently claimed that some of those elected had been members of the banned parties that had held power on and off before 1989. Among those elected was Turabi, who was then chosen as Speaker of the Assembly.

Throughout all this time the government was continuing the war in the south, and in the early 1990s depicted it as a *jihad*, with its own slain troops publicly celebrated as martyrs. However, in spite of the most intense fighting of the war, it still proved incapable of outright victory. Nor did it turn towards negotiating peace with the southern

SPLA. There were international efforts to get such talks going in the early years of the new regime, including the involvement of former US president Jimmy Carter and another effort involving the State Department, before attempts by Nigeria and then the regional Inter-Governmental Authority for Drought and Development (IGADD), but all to no avail.

There had long been doubts about the seriousness of the government, and indeed in 1997 it decided to pursue another initiative of its own. With prospects of victory receding, and deepening international hostility, the government sought to capitalize on an earlier split in the SPLA. In 1991 a variety of factors had led to a breakaway group known as the Nasir faction being formed, and in the following years Riek Machar had emerged as its leading figure. In 1996 he was involved in what became known as the Khartoum peace agreement, and was rewarded by being made vice-president; in reality a largely nominal position as far as he was concerned. Riek Machar was from the Nuer in Upper Nile and, with the protection of his militia, and government troops forcing out local populations where necessary, oil development was restarted in the areas around Bentiu, from which Chevron had retreated under attack from the SPLA in 1983. From 1996 it was Chinese, Malaysian and Indian companies which dominated, since major Western companies were deterred by the sanctions then in place against Sudan. In 1999 Sudan became an oil exporter for the first time. With output rising over the following years towards 500,000 barrels per day, it became sub-Saharan Africa's third largest exporter behind Nigeria and Angola. Spurred on by oil, Sudan's hitherto floundering economy grew rapidly over the following decade, averaging 9 per cent growth per year. The core of the state stood, as it had long done, at the centre of an area of growth that was concentrated on the riverine region of northern Sudan. The main areas of growth, in addition to oil and other minerals, were services, import substitution industries (including a burgeoning arms sector), construction and agriculture, all of which had the support of Asian and Middle Eastern investors. The state itself was largely responsible for managing relations with foreign investors, while the armed forces diversified into commercial and industrial activities and local civilian business, generally amounting overall to 'crony capitalism'. There were even dreams of creating some kind of regional Dubai where the White and Blue Niles meet in Khartoum. Business in Sudan also became a byword for corruption.

Meanwhile, by 1999 Turabi believed that the path to the fulfilment of his Islamic state had evolved to the point at which the new parliament, in which he was now elected leader, should in effect take over the powers of President al-Beshir and his military and security henchmen. The National Congress Party (NCP) had by now effectively been formed as the government supporters in a dominant party system in which some other smaller groups formed a nominal opposition. With support from the NCP and the parliament it dominated, Turabi proposed major constitutional changes that would in effect move power from the president to the legislature and its leader. Faced with this challenge, and supported by the security cabal at the heart of his now more personalized regime, Beshir resisted Turabi's challenge, dissolving the parliament and imprisoning Turabi. Later, upon his release, he formed a new party, the Popular Congress Party (PCP), in opposition to Beshir's NCP. However, the NCP was still dominant in the central areas of northern Sudan, where its new-found oil wealth allowed it to extend its patronage network while easing somewhat on the levels of repression of the earlier years in power. Turabi may have been sidelined, but the state he had inspired still remained garbed in Islamist ideology, though rather more lightly, not least because it was still its only claim to legitimacy albeit mainly in its own eyes.

Clearly Sudan was changing as the new millennium began. After nearly half a century of instability and poverty, the development of oil meant some prospect of the latter being eased, and with 75 per cent of oil reserves in the war-torn south there might also be new thinking about Africa's longest civil wars. Though there was much to be done if peace was to be made, the conflict in the south was 'ripe for resolution', a phrase SPLA leader John Garang was himself to use after signing the final peace document in 2005 (and which was borrowed from two academics: Francis Deng, himself a prominent Sudanese, and William Zartman).

Both the main protagonists, the NCP government and the SPLA army fighting in the south, broadly accepted that there was military deadlock. Politically there was also something of a deadlock following the failure of the NCP to construct its own peace arrangement in 1996 without involving the SPLA. Subsequently, Sudanese politics had largely descended into a stalemate between two armed camps. In the circumstances the regime recognized that having begun its period in power in 1989 by preventing a peace with the SPLA, an agreement with it could strengthen the position of the NCP if properly exploited thereafter. As for the SPLA, it had also had internal problems, as well as being harassed by the NCP-backed Southern Sudan Defence Force (SSDF), and it too could make political gains from an agreement, not only in the south, but possibly also in marginalized areas of the north. Its then-leader, John Garang, had always sought to embrace other marginalized and exploited peoples of Darfur and eastern Sudan, in what he saw as a national programme to redress the political and economic domination of the 'Arabs' of the riverine north of the country. Garang's vision went under the – by then well known – banner of the 'New Sudan'.

It was also increasingly clear that conflict was 'hurting' both parties, especially with regard to Sudan's newly developing oil resources. The NCP was pushing ahead with oil production, including the forced displacement of many local communities that were effectively exercises in ethnic cleansing. Yet there were restrictions on the oil development, especially of likely fields deeper in the south, and access to them would contribute to economic growth that could strengthen the regime. At the same time the SPLA was gaining no benefit at all when both it and its constituents were increasingly aware of the possibilities of wealth that lay beneath their feet. In contrast, peace could unlock not only oil, but Sudan's other resources, notably water and land, of which the south had both in plenty, thus releasing considerable development potential.

Regionally, a number of Sudan's neighbours, especially the leading members of IGAD – Ethiopia, Kenya and Uganda – supported the process. As well as the issues raised for neighbours by civil wars, Sudan's oil fields held possible benefits for certain of its neighbours. Central to the Comprehensive Peace Agreement (CPA), and especially the Machakos Protocol that kicked off the agreement in 2002, was the Declaration of Principles (DoP) put forward by IGAD after the unsuccessful peace talks of 1994. The DoP had included the proposal that if the Islamist government would not accept a secular Sudan, then the south would have the right to a referendum on secession. The SPLA had accepted the idea with alacrity, and the NCP had included something on similar lines to induce Machar to sign the Khartoum peace agreement of 1996. In view of the past cross-border dimension of conflict IGAD's support for peace was a necessary, but insufficient, condition.

A further vital factor was the attitude of the international community, especially the USA. The Clinton administration had hoped to see the NCP fall in the late 1990s, as its support of international terrorism was fully recognized, and in the light of attacks on the US embassies in Nairobi and Dar es Salaam in 1998 and the attack on the USS *Cole* off the coast of Yemen. When the NCP survived, US thoughts turned towards peace, but it was really under George W. Bush that involvement mounted. At first it came mainly from evangelical Christians who had long been involved in the south and were very influential in the Bush circle. They were supported by a number of human rights groups long-concerned at the suffering in Sudan. But there was also impetus following 9/11. Sudan had sheltered Osama bin Laden and al-Qaeda in 1991–96 and feared possible US action after 9/11. The NCP worked swiftly to make its intelligence available to the USA for the 'war on terror', and the USA developed its involvement in the peace process, giving its support to IGAD and its leading member states, especially Kenya where successive rounds of negotiations took place. During the process the USA worked with Britain and Norway, both long concerned with the conflict, in the Troika that supported and sought to facilitate the protracted negotiations leading to the CPA. Equally important was the fact that there were no major dissenting voices in the international community. From 1999 there had been the possibility of a Libyan–Egyptian initiative for a broader peace process with no mention of possible secession for the south. However, diplomacy with regard to both countries, especially through US–Egyptian channels, checked the initiative and brought virtual unanimity of support for peace.

The CPA itself was the culmination of a series of agreements on specific matters and was thus long and complex. It incorporated a transitional period leading to liberal democracy with national elections scheduled by July 2009 and a referendum in the south on separation in 2011. In the interim period there would be a collective presidency consisting of the head of the NCP as president, the head of the SPLA as first vice-president and another NCP vice-president. There would be a Government of National Unity (GNU) with an NCP majority and a Government of Southern Sudan (GoSS) with a Sudan People's Liberation Movement (SPLM) majority. Similar majorities would also be established in the Interim National Legislature, and the new legislature of South Sudan. Six specialist commissions were also to be established, together with special arrangements for three disputed border areas, Abyei, South Kordofan and Southern Blue Nile.

Yet at the same time that the CPA was being welcomed, doubts were being raised in a number of quarters. One concern was that it was an imposed peace. Critics argued that from the Machakos Protocol at the start of the process in 2002, right through to the signing of the CPA three years later, too much of the input was coming from the international community and not enough from the NCP and the SPLM themselves, ranging from the content of the agreement and protocols to the pressure exerted on the parties to sign. As such it was suggested that there would be at the least a lack of a sense of ownership by the parties, which could lead to an unwillingness to implement the CPA in full, and at worst that there might be, at least amongst some involved, a sense of resentment at the process and outcome that could give rise to active resistance to it. The issue of ownership was exacerbated by the untimely death of John Garang in a helicopter crash shortly after his appointment as national first vice-president and president of the GoSS, since Garang had been central to delivering SPLA/M support for the CPA. Following the appointment of his successor and former deputy, Salva Kiir, and the reduction in influence in the NCP of Mohammed Osman Taha, who had been Garang's main counterpart in the negotiations, relations between the two parties deteriorated. The deterioration ranged from mutual allegations of failure to implement the CPA to a virtual standoff in Abyei, an oil-producing area at the centre of the country where the NCP refused to accept the findings of the experts' review as required by the CPA.

A second concern centred on the exclusiveness of the agreement. Throughout it had been negotiated by only two parties, the NCP and the SPLA/M, both of which had numerous critics and probably represented only a minority of the population in northern and southern Sudan respectively. Essentially this was because they commanded the two major armed forces and recognized each other in a way they did not extend to others, while the international community saw other claimants to participation as comparatively weak and/or likely to complicate the negotiating process. Multi-party negotiations of the kind that took place in South Africa with the end of apartheid had been ruled out with the sidelining of the Libyan–Egyptian initiative. This was a blow for the Umma Party and the Democratic Unionist Party (DUP) in particular, which had been the two dominant parties in Sudan's three previous periods of democratic government. In an effort to keep the outside parties informed of developments visiting delegations were invited to the peace negotiations, but only as observers. While the scale of support for the excluded parties was not known, they had long histories as major actors in the country's politics and were thus likely to be concerned with where the exclusive process would leave them. The formal dominance of the NCP and SPLM in the interim period before elections was particularly worrying, since it could provide them both with opportunities to use their access to state resources for eventual electoral support.

There were also concerns about the terms of some of the protocols. One example concerned wealth sharing that seemed to centre on oil in particular. This was unsurprising since Sudan's rapid emergence as an oil producer was already having a significant impact on the national economy and could obviously go a good deal further quite rapidly. Yet its impact had only a limited affect upon the vast bulk of the country's population, particularly in the countryside and especially in marginalized areas of the south, east and west. The concentration on oil was perceived as meeting the concerns and interests of elites, especially in and around the NCP and the SPLM, rather than the majority of the population. Water and land were both highly contentious (and related) issues that were not fully or directly addressed and there were fears that, when combined with the exclusiveness of the process, the pressing economic needs of the majority would be neglected and/or they would be further exploited and marginalized by the apparent concentration on oil. Was Sudan simply going to be added to the countries of Africa in which oil was effectively a 'resource curse' rather than an asset for the benefit of the many?

Another line of criticism lay in the long timespan for developments envisaged by the CPA, with national elections three to four years away and the referendum on separation for the south not due until 2011. This would mean a long period of time for the NCP and SPLM to shape events, which could include consolidation of their respective positions within the processes, or even derail the CPA with the intention of subverting the possibility of a wider share of power nationally and possibly regionally.

While the CPA was being criticized for not being comprehensive with regard to the negotiators, it was very wide ranging in the subjects it tackled. One set of issues related to national government which, according to the agreement, was to function in such a way that unity would be attractive for the south at the time of the referendum. At the same time a new government would be established in Juba and the outlines of that were included in the agreement. Finally, there was a set of provisions designed to deal with issues between the two new governments.

At the core of the interim national constitutional arrangements was the GNU, and central to this was the institution of a new collective Presidency, to comprise the president, the president of the GoSS as first vice-president, and a second vice-president. It was expected that the two vice-presidents would be the leading figures from both sides in the CPA negotiations; John Garang for the SPLM and Mohammed Osman Taha for the NCP. Both were known as ideologues: Garang for his vision of the New Sudan fully incorporating into one country the marginalized areas of the south, east and west, and Taha for his role in seeking to Islamize from above in the early 1990s. But in the negotiations both had also shown pragmatism, and were thought to have reached a degree of respect. However, within days of becoming first vice-president, Garang was killed and succeeded by Salva Kiir. Kiir had been a soldier rather than a politician, and his views on his predecessor's vision of the New Sudan were obscure, while his relations with the northern participants in the negotiations were not as close as Garang's had been. It soon became clear that his new position as head of GoSS was his first commitment and he was to spend comparatively little time participating in the GNU in Khartoum. Critics also suggested that NCP leaders had little enthusiasm for fulfilling the hopes of the collective presidency emerging as an effective institution. Instead there were moments when mutual antagonism rather than effective cooperation characterized the GNU. Indeed, in October 2007 the SPLM briefly walked out from the GNU in a disagreement over the census, another requirement of the CPA. However, it was noticeable that an actual walkout was exceptional: for the most part, although the differences between the SPLM and the NCP were aired publicly and often fiercely, both parties also knew that they still needed each other.

The CPA also required a minority share of ministerial positions for the SPLM, the most senior of which was initially that of foreign minister. However, SPLM appointees frequently found that they had little power and that NCP junior ministers in their departments seemed to have more control, and were part of a wider informal NCP network. Nor were SPLM ministers helped by the civil service: under the CPA there were supposed to be a minority of positions in departments filled by southern officials, but in reality little was achieved, and the long-entrenched overwhelmingly northern and NCP-approved officials continued to run the departments.

In theory the executive was accountable to the new interim National Assembly. Under the terms of the CPA the NCP nominated 52 per cent of the seats with 28 per cent chosen by the SPLM and the remainder to be chosen by other parties. However, in practice the Assembly was little more than a talking shop with scant ability to hold the GNU to account, although some independently minded members did take their opportunities to speak out. They were encouraged to do this by constraints on political criticism outside the Assembly. Although there was a proliferation of newspapers, there were arbitrary checks on publications. Copy was checked as it came off the presses and might appear either with blanks or not at all, leading to a degree of self-censorship, not least because of revenue implications, while journalists were harassed and worse. Radio and television were state-managed, and while outside broadcasters were widely available their coverage of Sudanese affairs was limited. This situation of unpredictable partial censorship was helped by the perpetuation of the power of the security services carefully built up since 1989, which remained at the heart of the regime. Under the CPA they were supposed to be transformed into information-gathering bodies operating under the rule of law, but in practice they largely continued their former activities, if less repressively than in their most severe years in the early 1990s.

At the centre of the progress towards the restoration of a multi-party liberal democratic system, as outlined in the CPA, were the steps towards elections that were due by July 2009, four years after the signing. This required a number of developments, prominent amongst which was the conducting of a national census. For many, Sudan's first census in 1954 was seen as the most acceptable ever held, since when there had clearly been a rapid growth in population. But it was not total numbers that mattered so much as distribution in order that constituencies could be updated, especially after all the deaths and population displacement between north and south caused by decades of wars. The census did turn out to be as difficult as predicted, and was completed over a year after the planned date of July 2007. Equally predictably it was subject to criticism, especially with regard to the figures recorded for the south. Then there was the need to draw up an electoral law, which proved contentious and was similarly delayed, to be followed by the establishment of the National Electoral Commission.

As a result of all of the above, the elections themselves did not take place until April 2010, and when they did they appeared to be enormously complex. There was to be an election for the national president as well as the National Assembly, involving first-past-the-post constituencies, a block of seats to be decided by proportional representation based on party lists and another block for women. All 26 federal states were to have elections for governors and assemblies. In addition to all of these, South Sudan was to have elections for the president of GoSS and for its own assembly. This was to be the culmination of the opening up of political space across the whole country, and another step in the long march to liberal democracy in Africa since the end of the Cold War. Unsurprisingly a considerable amount of international support went into the whole process. However, as seen, the context that had been created between 2005 and 2010 was already somewhat ambiguous, while in practice much would come down to the positions adopted by the political parties.

Many in Sudan had long prided themselves on Sudan's ability to restore liberal democracy as it had done after the popular uprisings of 1964 and 1985 had overthrown military regimes. Each time the restoration had brought back coalition governments dominated by the so-called 'traditional' parties, the Umma and the DUP. Both had deep roots in northern Sudanese political life going back to the nineteenth century. Both had also felt cut out of the CPA process, especially as in the previous competitive elections in 1986 they had once more been the two largest parties.

The Umma Party was led by the former prime minister, Sadiq al-Mahdi, and in spite of factionalism he remained its leading figure and presidential candidate, for a while at least. In the run up to the elections he campaigned actively in spite of a reported lack of funds. However, the party was thought to have lost support in two of its traditional areas: Darfur, where the outbreak of widespread conflict from 2003 undermined both Umma's support and the prospects for holding elections in a number of constituencies, and Blue Nile on the border with the south where the SPLA had made inroads in the war.

The DUP was under the patronage of Mohammed Osman Mirghani, the head of the Khatmiyya *sufi* order, although he was above the fray of campaigning, while beneath him the party was thoroughly split into factions with no clear leader. Nevertheless, the

DUP had a strong traditional base in the riverine north and eastern regions of the country, and in 2005 Mirghani had put himself at the head of a revived coalition of 1990s opposition parties – including the SPLM but not the Umma Party – known as the National Democratic Alliance (NDA). However, the central areas of the country were also those where the NCP had been building its support; indeed, President al-Beshir and some other leading figures were from Khatmiyya families.

The NCP itself was a comparative newcomer since it had been formed only in 1998, but behind it the movement had a much longer history. Moreover, as the hitherto effectively unaccountable party of government, it was in a very advantageous position to exploit its patronage position. It had access to resources and was reputed to have a $500 million war chest for the elections, which it could spend in the central and most densely populated areas that it was targeting. It was also the dominant voice in the national media. In addition, senior positions in the states were held by people who were at least acceptable to the NCP and thus at that level the party also had many opportunities to win votes. With the economy growing the NCP also liked to present itself as the party of progress in contrast to its leading challengers, as well as playing an anti-American card made more popular by events in Afghanistan and Iraq.

While the NCP looked to be in a strong position from the outset it also had to concern itself with the Popular Congress Party (PCP), established by Turabi after the split with his protégés in 1999. Its aim was to be the party of Islamist ideology, depicting the NCP as having deviated onto the path of materialism and corruption. Over the years Turabi had built a personal following, and it was hoped that this could be the basis of a significant challenge to the NCP across northern Sudan. There were also a number of smaller parties, including the Sudan Communist Party which had been a force until the 1970s, but none were expected to play a major part.

The key party, however, was the SPLM. The northern parties were comparatively known quantities, but the SPLM as a party was not. The localism, lack of development and poverty of the south had combined to make it a region in which political parties had never really flourished, nor had the SPLA done much to change this perception during the war. But the south appeared now to be emerging to compete on the national stage, and with the region itself, believed to be about a third of the population, sown up. But it was still unclear how successful the SPLM would be as a political party and how far it would prove itself nationally rather than just regionally.

The vision of the SPLM as leader of the New Sudan derived from John Garang. It depicted the south along with the west and east as having been marginalized victims of the political, economic, social, racial and religious domination of the riverine north. It was a message that found a response not only in the south, but particularly in Darfur in the west, as shown when critics in that region produced the *Black Book* in 2000 detailing their grievances. Although some dismissed Garang's adoption of New Sudan in the 1980s as pandering to the neo-Marxism expected of him by his then Ethiopian and Soviet backers, it was a persuasive case and one taken up in a number of quarters in the north, including some amongst the millions of poor southerners displaced there in the decades of conflict. It was to these constituencies that the SPLM's Northern Sector was expected to appeal, and one of the leading northerners in the SPLM, Yasir Arman, was nominated as the national presidential candidate and began to campaign actively.

With the reasonable assumption that the SPLM would dominate in the elections in the south, and a measure of support on which it could draw in the north, it seemed for a while that it might forge alliances with the northern opposition parties. Even when it was clear that those parties would run independently it was suggested that taken together they might prevent Beshir obtaining the required 51 per cent of the vote in the first round of the elections; in that event there would have to be a run off, and there could then be cooperation of all the opposition parties around an agreed candidate. There was therefore surprise when, within weeks of the election, the SPLM announced that it was withdrawing its candidate from the presidential election and would also only compete for the National Assembly in a few constituencies near the border. The SPLM's decision was followed by similar announcements from the other major parties.

The withdrawal prompted much speculation, some of which related the decision to the negotiations that were ongoing over the referendum. Some argued that the SPLM nomination of Yasir Arman rather than its leader Salva Kiir indicated that it was really separatist at heart: it was suggested the nomination was only intended to bring pressure on the NCP during the negotiations. Others pointed out that the NCP had not expected the SPLM to nominate a candidate for the presidency, and that it had not put up anybody against Salva Kiir in the south. The suggestion was that, with Arman standing, the NCP would be more difficult in the referendum talks and might seek to destabilize the GoSS. Yet others argued that should Arman end up victorious at first or second ballots it would put Kiir and the GoSS in a difficult position, since Kiir was expected to be the elected president of GoSS as well as being head of the SPLM nationally, while divisions in the SPLM between 'New Sudan' and separatist elements within the party could be very damaging. Whatever the reasoning, it was clear that without the SPLM campaigning for the national presidency there was little chance of a Beshir victory being prevented. In addition, with the withdrawal of Arman the northern opposition parties also pulled out complaining that there was not a level playing field. Beshir duly won on the first round with 58 per cent of the vote. Various reports indicated criticisms of the conduct of the elections, but the reality was that once the SPLM had withdrawn from the race the election itself lost much of its political significance. It was also notable that even though he had withdrawn Yasir Arman still received 20 per cent of the vote.

Sudan was not to move towards a more open political system than it had hitherto. True, Beshir announced that he would broaden his government to include some figures from the defeated parties, but this was essentially an exercise in widening his base through extending patronage rather than an indication of the significance of the political opposition he faced, while senior figures in those parties proved reluctant to be embraced in this way. When a new government was finally announced at the end of 2011 the NCP had only attracted new figures from the DUP. The expectation grew that the controls on opposition voices would tighten once more rather than continue the partial easing of the previous few years.

For the GoSS, the decision to pull out of the race concentrated interest even more on the internal developments of the region. The establishment of the GoSS after two decades of war represented an enormous challenge at all levels. Across this large area, approximately the size of France, there was little by way of any tradition of state formation. The Turco–Egyptian period in the nineteenth century had penetrated the south almost only by way of exploitation; British rule had established only the most sketchy of administration and little sense of regional identity for the many ethnically based communities there, a sentiment enhanced by 'native administration' and regional isolation from the early 1930s. War had followed almost immediately after independence in 1956 and, although there had been a decade of peace from 1972, progress had been limited with growing ethnic tensions before conflicts broke out again in 1983; these were to have devastating effects on such services and infrastructure as did exist. In the conflicts it became apparent that, in spite of claims of social development in SPLA-held territories, there was little that had been achieved on which the GoSS could build.

Even establishing the GoSS itself was challenging, especially with the death of its dominating leader, John Garang, so soon after the signing of the CPA. Salva Kiir was a military man little-known outside SPLA/M circles but he was able to emerge as the unchallenged head of the new government. He had a rather small pool of military and political figures around him from which to recruit, and collectively there was scant experience of government. Although the international community was ready with expert advisors on governance, few of them had experience of South Sudan. In addition to the GoSS, it was also necessary to establish functioning authorities in the states and at local government level in areas severely disrupted by the conflicts.

At the same time as building a new government at several levels, the SPLM was also supposedly recreating itself as a political party. It was a major task for an organization that had always been centred on a guerrilla army, which was in turn largely identified with the south's largest ethnic group, the Dinka. It was also difficult for the SPLM to forge a distinct new ideology. The 'New Sudan' concept had been inherited from Garang, but both sentiment within SPLM and attitudes amongst the wider southern population suggested that separation was more attractive. The CPA had of course included the clause that both sides would seek to make unity attractive, but it was actions that would count, particularly the decision not to run Kiir against Beshir for the national presidency followed by the withdrawal of Arman from the race. But was the SPLM just responding to developing sentiment, or was it providing leadership? In the event it was not to be seriously challenged in the south by any other party. Other parties did emerge, but once again it proved very difficult terrain in which to develop parties of any scale or depth, and they ended up as not much more than personalized factions with little by way of a clear ideological appeal. The NCP did have branches in the south and resources around which to build. But for many it was identified with the 'Arab' north and, in any case, once the SPLM had withdrawn Arman the NCP largely backed off. Thus the SPLM's dominance of the new state ensured that it had an overwhelming victory in the 2010 elections.

The one field in which the new government did have experience was in problems of security which included many south–south clashes;

some inherited from the decades of war and some exacerbated by the problems of peace. One of Kiir's early successes was to bring an agreement with Paulino Madeep, head of the Southern Sudan Defence Force (SSDF), a large militia that had been allied with the national government against the SPLA and which was widely feared might still be used to destabilize the new rulers in the GoSS. However, there were clashes in several parts of the region (as indeed there had been in the 'peaceful' period of the 1970s) and by 2009 the UN figures of 2,500 killed and 350,000 displaced suggested that casualties at that time were higher in the south than in Darfur. Some clashes related to local SPLA forces, now the army of the GoSS (while retaining its 'rebel' name). They could be overbearing, and many of the police were hurriedly recruited from there with little or no regard for qualifications such as basic literacy. Cattle raiding was another cause of clashes, as too were land disputes, partly due to years of south-south conflict and partly because of returning refugees and IDPs. Additionally, despite some attempts to collect the vast number of weapons circulating in the region, many remained in private hands. The GoSS also laid blame on the NCP for deliberately raising conflicts, which have in turn been linked to rising ethnic tensions. While Kiir was generally seen as trying to take a conciliatory approach to conflict resolution it was noticeable that by far the largest part of the budget, at least 30 per cent, went on the army. The CPA included the establishment of a 10,000-man UN force – the UN Mission in Sudan (UNMIS) – but its mandate was to monitor the peace agreement rather than to be involved in peacemaking, and its number was limited for such a vast area.

In spite of the spending on the army, the share of the oil revenues due to GoSS meant that there was money for development, which was bolstered by promises of international support. The figures do indicate expansion of education and other services, but from such a low base and with such limited human resources it is inevitable that many felt that there had been little by way of a peace dividend, especially at a time when hopes of a secure peace were being repeatedly challenged. It was also noticeable that the World Food Programme (WFP) was importing sufficient supplies for half the population of the south.

While there were several areas of contention between the parties following the signing of the CPA, a number stood out. Power sharing was a running problem mentioned before, to be replaced by brinkmanship and bargaining between the two parties. Another important political issue was the national census which had been necessary for the elections. This had considerable implications since the allocations made in the CPA had accepted the general assumption that approximately one third of the population lived in the south. There was a long delay in holding and then compiling the census, and when it finally appeared it gave figures suggesting that the proportion of the population in the south was significantly less than claimed. However, amid complaints over the conduct of the census, it was agreed that it would not be strictly interpreted and so the elections eventually went ahead.

Another major political issue was the question of the Transitional Areas, as they were known in the CPA, on the north–south border: Abyei, Southern Blue Nile and South Kordofan, all of which had mixed populations and many of whom had supported the SPLA in the wars. Abyei, a significant oil-producing area, was promised its own referendum on being part of north or south at the same time as the southern referendum scheduled for January 2011. Abyei's own borders were to be set by a group of international experts, but its decisions were not accepted by the NCP, and it was only after the matter was referred to the Permanent Court of Arbitration at The Hague that an outcome more acceptable to both sides was made. In the meantime there had been violent clashes in 2008, during the course of which much of the town of Abyei had been destroyed and 50,000 people displaced: Abyei remained a centre for disagreement and conflict. Southern Blue Nile and South Kordofan were to have their futures decided by somewhat ambiguous processes of popular consultation, but like Abyei experienced growing tension and violence which grew worse as the south's referendum approached. While the future of these three areas was still uncertain, a joint boundary commission was seeking to agree the whole of the north–south border which also turned out to be a slow and disputatious process.

The violent clashes at Abyei also reflected the confrontational positions increasingly adopted by the two armies. The CPA included the formation of a Joint Integrated Unit (JIU) from units of both armies, with international help. However, in practice it proved hard to integrate and make an effective force that could work alongside the 10,000-man UNMIS force in peacekeeping activities. The limited development of the JIU contributed to the atmosphere of two increasingly separate military–political camps in Sudan rather than ever closer cooperation that would help 'to make unity attractive'.

There was also the question of oil revenues. The agreement called for a 50–50 split of the revenues from oil that had been produced in South Sudan, which meant in practice around 75 per cent of total production. In addition to being the main driver of national economic growth as it accelerated over the decade from 1999, oil contributed over half of the national government revenues and almost all of the revenues of the GoSS. The problem was not that the agreement itself was in dispute so much as there was a certain opaqueness regarding the actual revenues received, with the Ministry of Oil and Energy firmly in the grip of the NCP – at least until after the election of 2010 – and complaints about delays in transferring money due to the GoSS.

As the implementation of the CPA progressed towards the referendum, the terms of the referendum law became a further growing area of contention. Amongst many issues one obvious one was the involvement of the many southerners who, for various reasons, including forced displacement, had moved north during the decades of conflict: there were also a smaller number of northern counterparts in the south. Both issues of citizenship and practical issues associated with relocation for those who had moved meant that much was unresolved as the referendum approached.

Some critics argued that there were areas of the CPA that the two sides, particularly the NCP, were reluctant to see implemented. One of the most obvious examples was the NCP's rejection of the findings of the commission of experts into the border area of Abyei. The rejection was a breach of the CPA and indicated the NCP's determination to retain at least a significant portion of the oil-producing area. It also retained troops there in defiance of the CPA, and as such it was a dangerous flash point that led to renewed clashes between the two parties to the CPA. While Abyei did not reopen a wider conflict between the two governments it contributed to the increasing tension in the run up to the 2011 referendum. Additionally, conflict intensified in 2011 in the two other disputed border areas leading some to refer to them as 'the new south'. Both areas included former SPLA forces now committed to what had become SPLM-North (SPLM-N), a particular *bête noire* of the ruling NCP which sought to repress it.

The international involvement in support of the implementation of the CPA was also distracted by the unfolding developments in Darfur. International leaders sought initially to keep the two areas separate in engagement with Sudan, but came under growing pressure from their own constituencies to give their attention to Darfur where the scale of the violence that flared in late 2002 and early 2003 was not widely foreseen. The economic problems of the region were well known and had caught wide international attention with the famine 20 years earlier. These problems had not gone away, and political discontent had been rising, as indicated in the appearance of *The Black Book: Imbalance of Power and Wealth in Sudan* in 2000 which was believed to reflect the views of young radicalized Darfurians in particular. Nevertheless, the scale of the conflict was a cause for surprise. There was also surprise at the ferocity of the NCP's response, much of it through the agency of local armed militias known as *janjaweed*.

Amidst a growing international outcry some 300,000 were estimated to have died, with about two million displaced in camps in Darfur or in refugee camps in Chad.

The peace process between the NCP and the SPLA had inevitably had an impact on the rebel groups in Darfur. The SPLA's call for a 'New Sudan' had embraced all marginalized areas in the country, and there had been links between the SPLA and Darfur rebels as far back as the early 1990s, yet the latter were not direct beneficiaries of the CPA process and feared the consequences of exclusion (including some former NCP Darfurians who had split along with Turabi in 1999). Their conclusion appeared to be that the NCP was significantly weakened by the extensive concessions it had been forced to make to the SPLA, and that the way to advance their cause was to follow the SPLA's example and take up arms.

After initial concern that the situation in Darfur could damage the process towards the CPA which was then underway, and perhaps a lack of initial awareness of the scale of the violence in the region, the international community was slow to respond and it was not until 2005 that efforts to achieve another negotiated peace, this time the Darfur Peace Agreement (DPA), began in earnest. The question then was whether the Darfur situation was 'ripe for resolution' as that in the south had been.

While the DPA document of 2006 was long, detailed and impressive, the circumstances were far from propitious.[3] For a start negotiations did not have long roots in the relations between the parties, unlike the CPA which had built on a history from the DoP of 1994. In the course of that process the NCP and SPLA had become accustomed to many of the issues and also increasingly experienced as negotiators who, however reluctantly, took each other seriously. In contrast it has been said that the DPA talks in Abuja were not proper negotiations between the parties. Rather they behaved in a manner that suggested substantial mutual suspicion, bordering on contempt; instead of those feelings being dissipated over the weeks and months of talks they remained firmly in place. Nor did the sides regard each other as equal parties, with the NCP in particular not fully accepting the status of the Darfur rebels, an imbalance that reinforced distrust and intransigence amongst all parties. Instead of working towards common ground they generally did little more than reiterate established demands and exchange insults. Indeed, instead of talking directly with each other they more often sought to negotiate with the mediators in the apparent expectation that the latter would then argue their case with the other side. For their part the mediators were said to have drafted texts and then presented them to the parties on a take-it-or-leave-it basis.

The latter point was not helped by the splits in the rebels themselves. Initially seen as comprising two main factions, the Sudan Liberation Army (SLA) and the Justice and Equality Movement (JEM), the situation at Abuja became more complex. In addition to some disagreement between these two factions, the SLA itself was to split again, apparently along personal and then ethnic lines.[4] Thus, instead of having two comparatively united and cohesive parties negotiating directly, as had been the case with the NCP and the SPLA, the Darfur talks consisted largely of indirect talks in which one side, the Darfur rebels, was prone to factionalism. Their own divisions and consequent vulnerability were to make a number of them retreat into intransigence, while the Sudan government felt little need to respond to the kinds of demands for concessions being made to them.

Eventually the international community turned to strong-arm tactics. Senior figures in government in the USA and UK – Robert Zoellick, US Deputy Secretary of State, and Hillary Benn, Minister at the Department for International Development (DFID) in the UK – were brought in to add weight, but also to set a final deadline after earlier deadlines had passed unsuccessfully. However, this was to have the opposite effect on the rebels, as, faced with new pressure and fearful of the consequences of signing the DPA text presented to them, it was signed by only one faction of the SLA, that of Mini Minawi, while the other faction of the SLA led by Abdel Wahid, as well as the JEM, refused to sign.

The disagreements in Abuja were also reflected in the continuing violence in Darfur itself. The existence of comparative political and military stalemate had been part of the context for the CPA: both were missing in Darfur. Apart from the political differences mentioned there was the fact that violence was continuing on the ground, which at least some believed was more important than the peace talks in Abuja. Following the rejection of the DPA by two of the factions, both they and the NCP intensified the conflict in the following months with neither side appearing to gain the upper hand. Instead the scale of the conflict and disintegration grew, and within a year there were some 20 groups fighting in Darfur in a situation that resembled 'warlordism' as much as regional rebellion. In time the level of conflict in Darfur diminished, but was far from over, and an air strike at the end of 2011 killed the JEM's leader, Khalil Ibrahim. By that time the government was trying to sideline the armed rebel groups by signing a peace agreement in Doha with a new group, the Liberation and Justice Movement, though it was in fact comparatively weakly supported in the region.

Meanwhile, the position of the international community was much more sharply divided at the regional and broader international levels. At the regional level Chad was a major problem. The links between the politics of Chad and Sudan, especially involving Darfur, have been long and complex. Nevertheless, it is clear that the government of Idris Deby was under intense pressure, including an attempted armed attack from the east in 2008 which came close to success; Deby himself blamed the NCP as well as his internal enemies for this situation. Deby in turn supported the continued use of force by some of the Darfur factions, and shortly after the attack on Ndjamena he backed JEM's attack on Khartoum, which reached the outskirts of the neighbouring city of Omdurman before being halted. However, following the downfall of Qaddafi in Libya there was agreement between the two governments.

The CPA was broadly supported by the international community which applauded the work of both the parties and the Troika. It was not that there were actual opponents of the DPA in the wider international community so much as disagreements about what to do in the event of its failure, the continuing fighting and especially civilian suffering in Darfur. Led by the USA, there were increasing calls for UN action including the possibility of significant new sanctions against Sudan. However, the NCP had developed other allies and they took a different view. China had become Sudan's biggest trade partner and Russia also became a significant source of arms for the government, and both made it clear in the UN Security Council that they were opposed to the imposition of new sanctions. Thus the international unity that was a significant part of achieving the CPA was missing from the search for peace in Darfur.[5]

The conflict in Darfur also gave rise to an international first when, at the height of public concern, the UN Security Council referred Sudan to the newly established International Criminal Court (ICC). In 2009 the ICC issued an arrest warrant against President al-Beshir for crimes against humanity and war crimes committed in Darfur. It was the first time that a serving head of state had been indicted by the ICC. In 2010 a charge of genocide was added for alleged further attacks on ethnic groups associated with the rebels: the Fur, Masalit and Zaghawa. Beshir's government of course rejected the charges and tried to use them to arouse national criticism against Western persecution.

The potential separation of the south in 2011 under the terms of the CPA led to renewed discussion that further dissolution of the country might take place. The most obvious question was that of Darfur, which seemed poised between government efforts at enforcing a new peace and rebels making common cause against it, and might seek to overthrow the government if not seek separation for Darfur.

However, the position of Darfur was significantly different to that in the south in the run up to the CPA. The level of conflict by 2011 was not as great as it had been following the outbreak of fighting in 2003, and the government's continued use of force indicated that it felt that the rebels could be contained if not further reduced. That aim has been helped by the downfall of Qaddafi, who had been a constant meddler in Darfur, and in 2011 by the agreement with Chad not to support their respective rebel movements. At the same time after repeated unsuccessful negotiations with the main rebel groups – the SLA and the JEM – the government developed a working relationship with a more compliant group, the Liberation and Justice Movement (LJM). Making peace with the south on terms that included possible secession was one thing, doing the same thing in the north in Darfur would be a very different matter. In addition, the potential outcome for the south had had growing international acceptance at regional and wider levels since the 1990s, but that is unlikely to be repeated for Darfur. A peaceful Darfur remained a long way off, but secession appeared unlikely to be the solution without major change in Sudan and the international community.

In the east the NCP had a measure of success in 2006 with the signing of an agreement – the Eastern Sudan Peace Agreement (ESPA) – which bore some resemblance to the terms of both the CPA and the DPA, and with the cooperation of Eritrea which hosted the talks in Asmara. The agreement had at best a limited impact on the underlying fragility of the region, but the east showed little sign of seeking separation; because of its strategic position as Sudan's only direct outlet to the sea it is seen as essential to the state's survival that it does not do so.

With the increasingly likely separation of the south, Sudan was left after the CPA as a weak state in the hard grip of the NCP, at least in central areas of the country. Part of strengthening the state depends on weakening that grip and sharing power more broadly at both national

and state government levels. Having accepted the referendum on secession in the CPA in the name of retaining *sharia* in the north, and then
having done little or nothing to 'make unity attractive', the NCP had
little option other than to attempt to claim legitimacy through its 'protection' of the 'Islamic state'. There were efforts to make deals with other
political parties, but most had been weakened by the NCP's past political exploitation of the new oil economy and had little appetite to be
seen to shore up the government at a time when it was clearly under
growing political and economic strains which were increasing in severity
as a result of the financial implications of potential separation. With
conflict continuing in Darfur and the 'new south', as well as fragility
in the east, in the centre the main threat came from the expectation
of a period of severe austerity following the likely south's secession and
the resulting drop in income from oil revenues. The government's media
made no attempt to hide this, even projecting it as the price to be paid
for north Sudan's assured Islamic future. However, doubters pointed
to the long politicization of Islam in Sudan and the rivalries it had
engendered.

As for the south, the decision of the SPLM to pull out of the 2010
presidential elections effectively ended any prospect that the referendum on the secession would be more than a formality. Neither side
wanted to be seen as publicly choosing separation, but few in either
the NCP or the SPLM doubted that this would be the outcome. Before
the end of the year the GoSS finally called for a vote for separation
which proved overwhelming, with 98 per cent support in the 2011
referendum followed by full independence in July of that year. Often
described as oil-rich, it remained an extremely poor country. Decades
of conflict had left it with few services, an 85 per cent illiteracy rate,
widespread health problems and little infrastructure. The largest expen-
diture in its budget was for defence and security, far higher than health
and education combined. Tense relations on its northern border offered
an explanation, but much was being paid out to keep its thousands of

soldiers quietly in their camps in the face of a number of areas of unrest, some of which involved local SPLA commanders. A UN peace-keeping mission was scheduled to remain in the south, but its ability to handle the dangerous possibilities of militia fragmentation remained in question, especially after the problems UNMIS had faced in the years from 2005. At the same time there was a lack of qualified personnel to man many posts at all levels in the new government, as well as allegations of corruption against a number of those holding office.

Economically the GoSS has held great hopes for further mineral developments, especially in the oil sector. Yet output was expected to peak in 2012 and decline thereafter, unless exploration revealed new reserves. In addition, the south's agricultural potential has also been recognized. Indeed, with world food prices rising and long-term food security of great concern, a number of land deals involving 9 per cent of the new country were being set up as independence arrived. Such developments have the capacity to contribute to both local food security and export earnings, but if mishandled could involve land clearances or lack of appreciation of local conditions, adding to the security problems the new state already faces with outbreaks of ethnic fighting in seven of its ten states. The GoSS was also keen to reduce reliance on links with the north and look more to East Africa, including membership of the East African Community, but it was clear that it could not turn its back on its new northern neighbour with whom there was much unfinished business to be settled in what had become an increasingly acrimonious atmosphere.

At the same time as both states faced major internal challenges, their own relations remained unresolved in a number of areas that should, according to the CPA, have been settled by the end of 2010. One outstanding issue was the question of oil revenues after the end of the sharing agreement in the CPA. The new basis would be one in which the south would be the recipient of the revenues of its oil exports and would henceforth pay rent for the use of the pipelines through the north to the Red Sea, unless and until an alternative route was established through East Africa to the Indian Ocean. Hard negotiation and threats by Beshir in particular had failed to bring about a resolution by the south's independence day, although it appeared that neither side could afford to see a failure that would deprive both of a major source of revenue – in the case of GoSS, 98 per cent of its revenue. However, with the issue still unresolved, in January 2012 the GoSS halted oil production leaving both governments with a severe loss of revenue. Agreement had also not been concluded on the border, while attention still focused on the three areas subject to special procedures under the CPA – Abyei, South Kordofan and Southern Blue Nile. Citizenship, especially affecting the southerners in the north, was another unresolved issue where the NCP government had ruled out the suggestion of dual citizenship. A further important, unresolved issue was that of Sudan's large external debt of some $38 billion. The south saw little reason to take any responsibility for the debt built up under successive governments in Khartoum, part of it arising from importing arms in trying to defeat the SPLA, while the NCP appealed increasingly desperately for international debt relief. It all pointed to the difficulties ahead for the two states which emerged from the long decades of struggles.

Sudan's division into two states can be interpreted in various ways. From the standpoint of political sociology it can be argued that Africa's largest state was simply too big and too heterogeneous. Given its sheer size, lack of development and diversity of population from many perspectives – once called by Ali Mazrui 'The Multiple Marginality of the Sudan' – it has been said that it could not be held together.[6] In addition, the development that had taken place was so skewed towards the centre that a combination of neglect and structural marginalization in geographically outlying regions provoked resistance, giving rise to Garang's vision of a 'New Sudan'.[7]

That view of the dominance of the politics by the centre–north can also be seen as including a series of errors or missed opportunities by those northern politicians to call an end to the years of conflict in the south. Independence in 1956 was one such opportunity, as southern politicians were offered consideration of federalism in the writing of a permanent constitution that simply never occurred. The Addis Ababa Agreement of 1972 ending the first war included regional autonomy, only for President Nimeiri to effectively tear it up before his downfall in 1985. In 1989 it appeared that northern politicians and the SPLA were close to serious talks, only for an Islamist coup to take place, aborting the possibility of the withdrawal of *sharia*. A final major opportunity had been the CPA of 2005 with its plans for a government of national unity and a pledge 'to make unity attractive' that so clearly failed in the subsequent years. Abel Alier, head of the south's autonomous government after 1972, had subtitled his memoirs 'Too many agreements dishonoured', but why was that so?[8] Was it that the structure of northern Sudanese politics was such that it was simply incapable of accommodating the understandable aspirations of the south? Was it that the societal gaps were simply too wide? Or was it the failure of the northern political leaders to recognize the need to seriously address the views of the southerners if the state was to be maintained?

A long-term historical view can also be made to the effect that Egypt's carving out of the territory to its south in the nineteenth century provoked successive waves of resistance. In northern Sudan resistance took the form of the Mahdist defeat of rule from Egypt in the late nineteenth century, followed by the decision to reject the union Egypt once more sought in the mid-twentieth century. Relations between Egypt and Sudan remained closely linked at many levels and their character is probably unique in the external relations of both countries, but they have remained separate states. South Sudan emerged from the dominance of north-central Sudan and fought for decades before eventually voting for independence. Although independence day, 9 July 2011, was marked by the unveiling of a large statue of John Garang it was not his vision of the 'New Sudan' that had been followed by the

SPLM after his death so much as this historical narrative of resistance to forces from the north. After the referendum Garang's successor, Salva Kiir, invoked the image of the new nation as one born in successive struggles since 1821, the year of the start of Egypt's conquest of Sudan. The first stage, Kiir said, had been southerners' resistance to slavery in the nineteenth century; then in the twentieth century southerners had experienced and sought to resist the policies of imperialism through 'primary resistance'; while finally, after Sudan's independence, they had resisted repression by the north. It remains to be seen if, with independence attained, it will be possible for a discourse of nation-building to emerge that is rather less about victimhood and rather more forward-looking. There is awareness of the problem and efforts are underway to address it, although, as one leading southern intellectual put it, 'At the moment, South Sudan is only slightly more than a geographical expression'.[9]

CHAPTER 6

Eritrea and Djibouti

Eritrea

Throughout the years of conflict in Eritrea the Eritrean People's Liberation Front (EPLF) had been the dominant guerrilla force in what was then Ethiopia, and was arguably one of the most respected liberation movements in Africa. It had defeated its rivals in Eritrea, most notably the Eritrean Liberation Front (ELF), which had first raised the flag of revolt in the territory in the early 1960s, and then gone on to withstand the Soviet-backed might of the Ethiopian army including its own long march to its redoubtable fortress in Nacfa in the north. The neighbouring Tigrean People's Liberation Front (TPLF) was often regarded, rightly or wrongly, as something of an offshoot of the Eritrean highland leadership, with which there were indeed close, if not always friendly, links including those between the respective leaders, Issayas Afwerki of the EPLF and Meles Zenawi of the TPLF.

It was partly out of respect for the EPLF that the then Organisation of African Unity (OAU), with support from the United Nations, was willing to make an exception for its claim to independence. Africa had seen a number of secessionist claims, perhaps most famously that of Biafra as it fought the federal government in Nigeria in the late 1960s, but most members of the OAU supported the organization's charter recognizing the former colonial borders, largely from fear that with any secession a precedent would be set which might be taken up elsewhere on the fragile continent. However, it was agreed that Eritrea would be seen as an exception and not a precedent. It was argued that Eritrea had first been a separate colonial territory under Italian rule and then a UN trusteeship. The UN had then agreed to its incorporation into Ethiopia in 1952 by a vote in parliament. This prevented the Eritreans endorsing the move through a referendum on their future (a measure the UN was prepared to use in Western Sahara). Moreover, Ethiopia had violated the federal arrangement agreed to by the UN and swallowed up Eritrea within a decade.

Nor was there any protest by the new TPLF-led government of Ethiopia to Eritrea's claim for a referendum on separation. The two guerrilla armies in power from 1991 had had their differences, but they had also been mutually supportive for much the period of their respective struggles with Ethiopia. In any case the new government in Ethiopia was hardly in a position to challenge Eritrea, since the latter appeared militarily strong, and its cooperation was believed important at a time when Ethiopia, now a landlocked state, was heavily dependent on it for access to the sea. The referendum in Eritrea took place in 1993 and duly delivered the expected near-unanimous vote for independence. It was the first time that a new state had emerged in this way in independent Africa, but at the same time it was also a period when, partly in the wake of the end of the Cold War, other states elsewhere were in the process of breaking up in central and eastern Europe, central Asia and the Balkans.

At first the EPLF seemed more likely to move easily into government than the TPLF. The latter was drawn from one comparatively small area of the country it now set out to rule, and needed to rapidly build a coalition with others, while the EPLF dominated much of Eritrea which was a far smaller country and appeared more manageable. At the same time the EPLF, led by the powerful and ruthless Issayas Afwerki, seemed itself to be a formidable core around which to build the new government. While it had started out as a guerrilla force, by the time it won power it had evolved into a regular army of around 100,000 men and women. In the course of what many saw as an impressive achievement it had developed a range of capabilities and built a high level of discipline and morale as well as renewing a commitment by its troops to continue to serve without pay for some years after independence.

Although its core leadership was mostly from the Christian and Tigrinya-speaking highlands, the EPLF had also developed links with many other communities during the decades of conflict. The movement's China-trained leaders knew of the value of 'swimming amidst the fishes' and had cultivated support amongst the lowlanders, partly by organizing food relief from Port Sudan, especially in the hungry years of the 1980s, and had also encouraged programmes of land reform. Overall the EPLF appeared to be capable of integrating into the society within which it set out to build its new government. Judging by the rhetoric of the leadership, as it moved from being a group of fighters into a liberation government which looked initially to be genuinely popular, it seemed that there might be an opportunity to build a participatory democracy.

The EPLF had been seen as having an egalitarian culture, albeit with a strong leadership, and in peacetime it might have proved to be an open mass party in practice as well as theory. That was at least the hope of its many Western supporters, who saw the new rulers as high amongst the leaders of the African renaissance that was taking over from the continent's autocratic old guard and establishing better governance, including following the path of democratization. In 1997 a new constitution was announced that looked as if it might go in that direction. Ideologically the emphasis was on nationalism and the building of a distinctive Eritrean identity, complete with national holidays and parades, rather than the Marxist ideologies of the revolutionary years. Throughout most of the 1990s there were still grounds

to think that governance might develop: the small civil society organizations still struggled on; a number of individuals still openly
supported a more pluralistic approach, including some who had participated in the writing of the new constitution; and private newspapers
appeared from time to time. But there were other signs as well: the
EPLF's old rival the ELF, with its support in the southern lowlands,
was not permitted to return and take its chance in participatory politics.
A number of protests by EPLF fighters and wounded veterans, who
felt badly treated in various ways, were afforded a harsh response by
the new rulers. There was a clampdown on indigenous and international NGOs, while in the countryside a start was made on replacing
elected local leaders with others appointed by the emerging national
authorities.

As the decade wore on it was clear that instead of a possible direction of pluralistic democracy the structures for a more authoritarian
future were being put in place. The EPLF's leaders had established
themselves as the Provisional Government of Eritrea (PGE) headed by
the State Council, of which President Issayas Afwerki was Secretary.
The EPLF leadership also sat in the new National Assembly together
with 30 representative drawn from the country's nine (later five) provisional assemblies and a further 30 nominees of the EPLF. There was
briefly lip service given to a multi-party system developing, but,
according to Isayas Afwerki, only if parties emerged without being
based on potentially divisive ethnic, religious or provincial identities,
which he described as making for 'pseudo-multipartyism'. It also
emerged that within the EPLF was a secret inner party, the Eritrean
People's Revolutionary Party (EPRP), which functioned as the real decision making vanguard, a concept of which the leaders, steeped in Marxist
ideology during the war years, approved. Whatever the formal structures of government appeared to be, in practice there were informal
layers of control developing, likened by one well-informed author as
being like a Russian doll in its secretive layers. At the centre was the

President's Office, while other layers of control stretched out through the leaders of the military and security authorities to the party secretariat: the office of a minister did not necessarily mean that the minister was a party to key decisions, not even those relating to that particular ministry. Nor did the inner core act as a collective central committee, as all senior appointments were made by Issayas Afwerki who gained a reputation for moving personnel around, and if necessary making dismissals, entirely on his own. In the two decades after taking power in 1991 the performance of Issayas and other core leaders became subject to growing criticism. At the same time the EPRP was establishing a mass party: the People's Front for Democracy and Justice (PFDJ). By 1996 the PFDJ claimed to have a membership of some 600,000 in a population of about five million, and there seemed little room for another 'national party' in the constrained situation established by the new president.

The 1997 constitution was not implemented, the scheduled elections of 2001 were not held, nor did the existing parliament meet after 2002: Issayas Afwerki and his colleagues, mainly drawn from the highland Tigrinya speakers, remained in power without securing the legitimacy to be derived from an election. Instead all political parties other than the PFDJ were banned as the ruling group steadily tightened its grip on power. The start of the fighting with Ethiopia in 1998 was the beginning of an increasingly brutal era. The war triggered a coming together of critics, including some in the PFDJ itself, who were concerned at the way the situation was being handled by Issayas Afwerki and his colleagues, and grew through further rounds of fighting in 2000 in which Ethiopian forces made significant advances into the country, with some allegedly saying that it was time for the president to stand aside. In October 2000 a letter that became known as the 'Berlin Manifesto' was produced, calling for greater openness in government and recognition of the freedom apparently accorded by the constitution. The letter itself, and the fact that it was signed by 13 prominent figures, was dismissed out of hand. Instead Issayas Afwerki decided to focus on the middle-level cadres of the PFDJ thus seeking to isolate his critics but, in 2001, 15 signed a new letter and publicly criticized the leader in a burst of activity with which it appeared that a real challenge was being mounted. But by the end of the year the government was using the excuse of war to arrest hundreds of opposition figures, incarcerating many for unspecified periods, often in very harsh conditions. This was accompanied by a forcible recruitment sweep of young people for the war. It soon added up to a situation of terror, and became one that was to last for the whole of the next decade. The record of incarceration in prison was reported to be one of the worst in the world, a situation that was not helped by the executive's effective control of the judiciary. Tight control was also exercised over the student body as the quality of educational provision declined, with the staff and students of the national university being increasingly distrusted and largely replaced by smaller, more easily controlled local colleges with lower standards. Independent and international NGOs were more severely restricted and supposedly replaced by government sponsored organizations. At the same time the generally free and relaxed activities of religious organizations were also subject to control, especially in the western lowlands where there were stirrings of radical Islamic opposition. The war with Ethiopia from 1998 also saw a growing prominence of the army alongside the ruling party, providing much of the justification for the growing authoritarianism. Plans that the military would be reduced after independence had been reversed and instead one of Africa's largest armies was built with around 300,000 men and women called up.

A new path had also been expected with regard to the economy, where decades of war and drought had devastated the newly independent country. During the war the EPLF had won the support of some sections of the largely subsistence peasantry, who comprised some 80 per cent of the population, and once in power it announced that all land was now under the control of the state, although peasants could hold land allocated to them on a usufruct basis. The belief was that once a more secure environment had been established local agricultural production would rise, as indeed for a while it did, but not to levels of self sufficiency and so food aid was still required to make up a shortfall of 30–40 per cent of the country's needs. In the Italian era there had been a measure of industrialization and the country was generally seen as more advanced than neighbouring Ethiopia. However, following Eritrea's absorption by Ethiopia some of it had gone south across the former border, while what remained had suffered from the impact of the war of liberation. The remaining industrial plants were to be resuscitated using the skills well honed by Eritreans in the years of struggle. Rehabilitation work was also required on the ports of Massawa and Assab which would be necessary not only for Eritrea but also Ethiopia, as her trade passing through Eritrea played a significant part in the Ethiopion economy in the 1990s. Indeed, with few resources of its own the approach adopted was one in which Eritrea would seek to develop as a trading hub at the southern end of the Red Sea, becoming a kind of Singapore by utilizing its overland routes to both Ethiopia and Sudan as well as its proximity to the Arabian peninsula. It was to have an export-led market focus – complete with free-trade zones at the ports – run by the state thus openly making reference to Eritrea becoming a developmental state along Asian lines rather than an isolated and self-contained revolutionary state: more South Korea than North Korea. The ruling party owned a range of businesses, most notably the Red Sea Trading Corporation, the major trading organization, which had been established originally to purchase equipment for the EPLF. The possibility of private sector companies appeared in the 1990s, but after that they were seriously curtailed unless linked in some way to the ruling group. Industry was short of capital, with the government owning the Bank of Eritrea and other banks, preventing the development of a free market in capital, while even in the optimistic era of the 1990s there were question marks over the strategy of export-oriented industrialization. In practice there was not a significant transformation of peasant production to serve as a base for agricultural industrialization, while other forms of industrial activity were limited in scale, mainly in the public sector, and geared towards Ethiopia, the destination for two-thirds of the country's exports. As a result of the Eritrean–Ethiopian conflict, Eritrea lost that market, as well as the revenue from Ethiopia's trade through Assab, in addition to which many Eritreans in Ethiopia, often working in commerce and trade, were forced to return to their country of origin. In all about a million people were directly affected by the war, either being forced to leave Ethiopia or being displaced by the heavy fighting along the disputed front.

During the years of the struggle for independence, numerous Eritreans had become refugees. Many were in camps in neighbouring Sudan, but some also found their way to Europe and North America from where they sent remittances generally intended for their families, although some income was also garnered by the government. These remittances were to be increasingly important to many families, and pressure was placed on them to encourage those in the diaspora to 'voluntarily' contribute 2 per cent of their incomes. Money could only be remitted through the government-controlled Hidri Trust Fund which handled all foreign exchange transactions. At the same time Eritrean officials overseas also pressured the diaspora of around 150,000 in wealthier countries in the West and the Gulf, saying that it was their duty to support the new state, even though the latter became increasingly disillusioned and critical over the years. By the late 2000s, with the economy declining, overall exports were estimated to be down to only about $20 million, although imports were many times higher at $700 million, showing how reliant Eritrea had become on continuing the flow of remittances. In addition to sending remittances, it was only in exile that opposition groups could be formed, but they were numerous and disunited with one scholar listing 28 groups known to him in 2004.

Although it required food aid for many of the people, Eritrea was determined not to become aid-dependent, especially if the latter carried many strings: on these grounds it even rejected a US aid package not long after independence. Instead of seeing food aid as a humanitarian contribution for desperately poor people, its distribution was seen instead as a means of controlling and, if necessary, disciplining the needy population.

Men between the ages of 18 and 50 could be conscripted into the army as well as the so-called development programme, Warsay-Yikeala, introduced in 2002. Many were kept in camps, the most well known was the Sawa camp, which combined the final year of schooling with military training in what has been described as 'the national finishing school'. Here there was indoctrination, while links to families were kept to a minimum as the students and soldiers were prepared for their life of service. The veterans of the war had been prepared to sacrifice their lives for the independence of the country and the young should be prepared to show a similar level of self-sacrifice when called upon. They could remain in these militarized camps for an indefinite period during which they were subject to nationalistic, especially anti-Ethiopian, indoctrination for little or no pay for what was in effect forced labour to be used in infrastructure and construction projects in particular. At the same time an estimated figure of over 300,000 men and women were kept in the army, many near the Ethiopian border, a huge drain in a population of five million.

Many of the young sought to evade conscription by going underground or escaping as refugees to neighbouring countries or further abroad, especially if they had family members abroad from whom they were receiving remittances which spoke of a better life: Eritrea was becoming an increasingly unattractive place for young people in particular. From 1998 onwards life was increasingly harsh with conscription, shortages, rationing, unemployment, surveillance and check points as well as continuing malnutrition in many rural areas. Additionally, for those seeking to escape the power of the state there were round-ups to catch draft dodgers and escapees; punishments were harsh and included extra-judicial killings. Nevertheless, many made it, often paying dearly for their passage. Sudan was the easiest destination for many, with reports that up to 100 Eritreans were arriving daily, while in 2009 UNHCR recorded an average of 1,800 per month registering with its refugee camps. In Ethiopia some refugees joined the various opposition movements which mushroomed with the onset of war and the active encouragement of their new hosts. In December 2009 the Eritrean national football team all sought refugee status in Kenya. However, opposition within the country remained severely restricted, although there were some activities by Islamic Jihad, especially in the 1990s. Historically the Muslim community had been peaceable and existed alongside the Coptic Christians with their stronghold in the highlands, but while the regime was resolutely secular in character it was increasingly perceived as having a core from the Tigrinya highland area asserting increasing control over the various other communities. In addition, the western lowlands had been the area of the ELF which had started the revolt against Haile Selassie's rule and which the EPLF had defeated militarily on its path to power. It was contained not only locally but regionally by the management of relations with Sudan, whose policies were significant for Eritrea's western lowlands, just as Eritrea's were for eastern Sudan. But, in spite of the difficulties of escape from the country, the continuing exodus of young refugees, many not understanding or accepting the traditions of struggle of the older ruling liberation generation, suggested widespread discontent. With repression in the country, and many leaving if they could, it was predictable that amongst the exiles opposition movements would develop and that some would try to infiltrate back. From time to time there were reports of attacks being mounted inside Eritrea by various groups, but with reporting so restricted it was difficult to verify the scale of attacks or the numbers involved in the opposition.

The government was increasingly run from the president's office where Issayas Afwerki was depicted as ever more dictatorial and unbalanced; nevertheless, he also had a ruthless survival instinct. From time to time rumours circulated of assassination attempts on him. Ministers were regularly rotated, but their powers were often limited, and a shadow network of his trusted colleagues, many of them ex-fighters, was believed to exercise the real power at the president's behest. This was also apparent outside Asmara. The plans for regional devolution were never implemented: under a 1996 proclamation traditional village and area level councils were disbanded and replaced by a top-down process that effectively took decisions from the president's office to the villages. The slogan 'unity in diversity' clearly put the emphasis on the former, increasingly at the expense of the latter. Afwerki also appointed the province governors who were all army generals. With the situation on the Ethiopian border unresolved the regime became increasingly militaristic in character at all levels, to such a degree that Eritrea has been called the second most-militarized state in the world after North Korea. Indeed, the army appeared to be an intrinsic component of the government, in close cooperation with the national security service which had numerous spies and informers across the country.

At the same time the economic situation declined, especially once the wars with Ethiopia commenced. The conflict had a devastating effect on the country, far more than that on Ethiopia. In war-affected areas there was serious disruption, with as many as one million people displaced. Bank borrowing to finance the war drove up inflation. The export trade to Ethiopia dried up, as did the revenues on goods to and from Ethiopia through the port of Assab. The war brought expansion of the military, many of whom remained after 2000 rather than being demobilized since there was no peace agreement and tension on the border remained high, which in turn led to some labour shortages in rural areas. Some commercial agriculture continued in the lowland areas, in some areas to the detriment of local pastoralists, while for most of the peasants poverty and malnutrition remained high with intermittent shortages and high prices for goods of all kinds, due in part to the war. In addition there were shortages of skilled labour, while the projects to rehabilitate the infrastructure were generally of poor quality often being carried out under the highly inefficient Warsay-Yikeala programme. These activities included working on farms controlled by the military and on PFDJ-owned construction companies. In spite of all this some international aid still reached Eritrea. Perhaps there were thoughts that aid might still be some kind of restraint on the country's aggressive foreign policy adventures, although more likely it was out of humanitarian concern with the growing poverty of so much of the population. Insofar as there was any light at the end of the tunnel for the economy, hopes lay with minerals, especially gold, potash, zinc and copper; by 2010 there was growing interest in the international business world, in spite of Eritrea's reputation as being a difficult place to work.

Many supporters of Eritrea's successful fight for independence felt disappointed or worse at the direction Eritrea took once the war of liberation was completed. Yet ideologically and organizationally there was always at least a possibility that it would be thus. The EPLF had been a powerful mobilizing force, but at the same time it had always had a strong leadership. While Mao and Lenin were literally discussed by the fighters in the trenches – as ideologists they always required discipline alongside commitment – there was to be no deviation towards a more liberal interpretation of the ideological wellsprings of the movement once power had been attained. Indeed, some even argued that the pursuit of enemies abroad and the maintenance of a large army helped to provide continuing justification for the holding of power by the PFDJ. It all added up to one of the outstanding examples of an Orwellian world.

Djibouti

For much of the post-Cold War era Djibouti, with a population of less than one million, was the forgotten state in the Horn, though it was to become increasingly drawn into the picture particularly through the situation in neighbouring Somalia. That tiny Djibouti existed at all was largely down to a combination of French ambition and frustration. In the late nineteenth century that ambition was similar to that of Britain and Italy: to play a part in the protection of French interests in the international shipping through the Red Sea, and if possible to build a line of connected territories across Africa linking French Equatorial Africa to East Africa. But just as Britain had frustrated France in Egypt by taking effective control there in 1882, so in 1898 it was once more to frustrate France on the Upper Nile during the Fashoda Crisis. And while France did make diplomatic advances in Ethiopia, having defeated the Italians at Adowa in 1896 Emperor Menelik was not about to become over-dependent on the French. However, one lasting legacy of French engagement was its building of the railway from Djibouti to Ethiopia's new capital in Addis Ababa.

During the era of European imperialism Djibouti was known as French Somaliland. However, a significant part of its population were not Somalis but Afars, a people also to be found in Ethiopia and Eritrea, and in 1967 it was renamed the French Territory of the Afars and Issas (the main Somali clan). Ten years later its colonial status seemed somewhat anachronistic, and it became independent as Djibouti, although France continued to have a military base and play a large part in its internal affairs. Politically as well there was considerable continuity. France did not retreat in the face of nationalist pressure and the reliable Gouled Aptidon, an Issa who was already in place at independence, simply continued thereafter without even the creation of an independence constitution until 1992, when, under pressure from France with its new concern for democracy in francophone Africa, a limited form of multi-partyism was introduced. Nevertheless, the Rassemblement Populaire pour le Progrès (RPP) retained all the seats in the legislature in the elections of 1992, while in the following year Gouled won a comfortable victory to begin his third term as president. As president, Gouled was politically cautious and endeavoured to distribute positions proportionately amongst all sections of the population, including appointing Afar ministers. At the same time he ruled patrimonially, expecting loyalty in return for his largesse, and headed the country's only political party, the RPP. With conflict spreading in the Horn, Djibouti became known as a place of comparative calm in the eye of the storm, but it was not entirely immune from troubles. The Issa and Afar communities were linked to their respective ethnic neighbours, and when war broke out between Somalia and Ethiopia in 1977 there were tensions and some clashes before calm was restored. However, community tensions rose again in the 1980s and, in 1991, an Afar resistance movement was formed known as the Front pour la Restauration de l'Unité et la Démocratie (FRUD), partly inspired by the general expectations that the post-Cold War era would be one of re-democratization in Africa. FRUD was also inspired by claims of anti-Afar discrimination by Gouled, the success of guerrilla movements in Eritrea and Tigray and the ready availability of arms as Mengistu's regime in Ethiopia fell.

With French encouragement, in 1992 constitutional changes were made which were intended to pave the way for a more competitive democratic system, although FRUD was initially excluded from national politics, and Gouled sought with some success to defeat it militarily. Meanwhile, the RPP continued to dominate, winning all the seats in the 1992 legislative elections, while the following year Gouled won a comfortable victory to secure his term as president. In 1994, after military setbacks, FRUD made a power-sharing deal and joined the government, although a faction continued the struggle on a small scale until 2000 when a further peace deal was signed. During his third term Gouled continued with his very personal style of rule until, in 1999, he finally stepped down. In a somewhat dynastic move he handed over power to his nephew, Ismail Omar Guelleh, who was already a well-established political force in his own right, and generally just known as 'IOG'. While Guelleh continued the tradition of ruling in a highly personalized manner, there were political moves to give at least the appearance of greater inclusiveness. The RPP continued to wield effective power but now within a coalition called the Union pour la Majorité Presidentielle (UMP) in which there were four other parties, one of which was FRUD. There was also a legally recognized opposition movement, the Union pour une Alternance Démocratique (UAD), but in practice its activities were severely curtailed. The maintenance of a high degree of government control was at least partially legitimized by tension with Eritrea over its border claim, which produced a sharp clash between the two countries in 2008. However, there was still a degree of unrest when Guelleh sought a constitutional change that would enable him to run for a third term in the presidency in the elections of 2011. There was also unrest amongst dissident FRUD supporters in the north amidst fears that conflict might erupt once more in that area.

Economically Djibouti relied on the military and commercial significance of its key strategic position at the southern end of the Red Sea. Its value as a base was illustrated during the first Gulf War in 1991 when France used it in its operations, and continued to use it thereafter. Following 9/11 the USA established its only base on the African mainland, occupying a former French base at Camp Lemonier from which it undertook counter-terrorism operations across the region, including Yemen. Camp Lemonier built up to some 2,000 men including elite Special Operations Forces which were engaged in a variety of activities. Djibouti was also used by various contributors to the multi-national naval operations against the growing threat of the Somali pirates, including Russia, China, India and Japan. All these activities brought not only direct revenues and local spending by international forces, but also various forms of additional aid, including food aid, to the barren country.

Traditionally local communities had had to rely heavily on pastoralism, but survival was often precarious and significant numbers required intermittent supplies of food aid. The port also served as an important commercial centre. Following the war between Ethiopia and Eritrea the importance of Djibouti to the former's trade picked up once more, with plans to modernize the old railway link to Addis Ababa. In addition, other landlocked African countries also made use of Djibouti for trading and thus there was a steady income from handling charges and taxes on the transit of goods through the city state. To aid this role a large new container terminal was inaugurated in 2010 with investment from Dubai. The management of the business sector was closely watched by the RPP, with several leading businessmen having links with Guelleh and his family.

It appears somewhat paradoxical that the Horn's smallest and most vulnerable state should also be the most stable, with no major political turmoil since its independence in 1977. But perhaps its growing importance as a trading centre, coupled with its strategic significance for international security concerns in the region, have done much to shelter it. In addition to this, it has contrived never to behave in a manner that is perceived as threatening to any of its neighbours, which certainly makes it unique in the Horn. Instead Djibouti endeavoured to capitalize on its vulnerability to play what part it could in a peacemaking role.

The regions two smallest states, Eritrea and Djibouti were in many ways contrasted. Though both had strong presidential leaders, Djibouti was more inclusive and less repressive, as well as having a better economic record. In relations with their neighbours they were also contrasting, for while Eritrea was seen as assertive and willing to deploy force, Djibouti sought a more conciliatory involvement with both its neighbours and the wider international community.

CHAPTER 7

Regional Relations

Regionalism has become one of the most discussed themes of international relations since the end of the Cold War, including the significance within those relations of specific regional organizations. Following the end of the Cold War it was thought that a new era could open up in the Horn. At the regional level the old protagonists had largely fallen with the upheavals in Ethiopia, Somalia, Sudan and the creation of independent Eritrea, while globally the end of the Cold War had removed the need for rival superpowers to compete through local proxies. However, it soon became apparent that a new era of peace and tranquillity was not about to dawn, and that somewhat unpredictable fresh themes of regional rivalry and conflict were to emerge.

One of the themes common to the major changes in the early 1990s was the extent of ideology in driving the new rulers in Ethiopia, Eritrea and Sudan; but while the former pair had been heavily influenced by strands of Marxism and Maoism, Sudan was of an Islamist character. The regime was soon to indicate that Islamism was not just about the building of a new Islamist state, it was also about projecting Islamism outwardly, much like other ideologies of an international character and potential application. At the core of the ideology and organizational success of Islamism in Sudan was Hasan al-Turabi.

The Muslim world, Turabi felt, had a tradition of pursuing the community of the faithful, right down to the Ottoman empire – the last great manifestation of pan-Islamic society – and with its collapse the position of Caliph had also ended. There had been signs of a new awakening. In the 1960s the growth of radical secularist pan-Arabism had been partly countered by the creation of the Organisation of the Islamic Conference (OIC), but that had been set up by Saudi Arabia and supported by other allies of the West. And it was the West that had not only ended Ottoman power but divided much of the Muslim world into nation-states which Turabi saw as a manifestation of divide and rule: one that had failed in its proclaimed agenda of viable state-building. But there were more radical Islamic successes, notably in the Iranian revolution and then the success of the *mujahidin* in Afghanistan, both of which had shown the limitations of the then-dominant superpowers. Now Sudan could become a 'beacon' for the large *sunni* Muslim world.

Always a man of action as well as ideology, Turabi established the Popular Arab and Islamic Conference (PAIC) in Khartoum in 1991, and representatives from 45 countries attended his installation as its Secretary-General. While Turabi travelled widely and sought to project himself in the West as a man of peace, the new regime was also hosting men with a more violent approach to the task of leading an Islamist movement, and there were many more to join in. In secret training camps men were trained by Hezbollah, Hamas, the Popular Front for the Liberation of Palestine (PFLP) and several other groups. One of the then-lesser-known groups was al-Qaeda, headed by Osama bin Laden. He arrived in Sudan in 1991 and he used his share of the family fortune in business as well as in building his movement, later to be described as a 'hybrid capitalist–terrorist network'.[1] Sudan's particular contribution with regard to the promotion of Islamism should be amongst its African neighbours, especially those on its eastern flank with large Muslim populations which hitherto had not been mobilized for the cause: Turabi's dream was of linking Muslim communities stretching from North Africa to the Indian Ocean.

Aiding insurgents in neighbouring Ethiopia and Eritrea was nothing new to Sudan, it had been vital for both the Eritrean People's Liberation Front (EPLF) and the Tigrean People's Liberation Front (TPLF), but the regime in power in Khartoum had changed, and with it came a harder attitude to those secularist and Marxist organizations whose ideologies had long been key targets of the growing Islamist movement. Eritrea in particular was an early target, with the lowland Jihad Islamiyya Eritrea just across Sudan's border. In sharp response, by 1994 Eritrea had broken diplomatic relations with Sudan as well as calling publicly for the overthrow of the regime in Khartoum and availing the Sudanese opposition movement, the umbrella National Democratic Alliance (NDA), of the empty embassy building in Asmara. There was also support for Sudan's eastern opposition movement, the Beja Congress, at bases across the border near Haikota, Tessenei and Sawa where there was support, training and arms available. Ethiopia was in a more delicate situation since the TPLF had cooperated in driving the Sudan People's Liberation Army (SPLA) out of its Ethiopian bases in 1991, and then facilitated Sudan's forces with access to the SPLA's eastern positions. But relations with Ethiopia were also to deteriorate, as support from Sudan went to a group called Oromiyyah Islamiyya which was alleged to have been linked to a number of bombings in Addis Ababa. Even worse, in 1995 Sudan was implicated in an attack in Addis Ababa on Egypt's President Mubarak which came close to assassinating him.

Sudan also undertook an excursion into the Somali imbroglio of the early 1990s. At the time US troops led the UN operations there in 1992–93 there were those in Sudan who saw it not only as an opportunity to attack the world's only superpower, but were fearful that, if unchallenged and successful in Somalia, the USA, which listed Sudan as a terrorism-supporting state in 1993, might turn its attentions on them. Thus Sudan became involved in supporting Mohammed Farah Aideed and his branch of the Habre Gidr clan with arms and training, while recognizing that Aideed himself was no friend of Islamism. In the end the US/UN mission in Somalia was terminated by Clinton, leaving an ambiguous outcome in which, in the short term at least, there was little mark left by Sudan's Islamist involvement.

However, by the mid-1990s, Sudan's overall record was such that it was under growing suspicion by its neighbours, some of whose governments were well regarded by the USA, leading to renewed fears that the latter was supporting the neighbours with help to the SPLA which increasingly threatened the Islamist regime. In consequence the government was quick to retreat on its ideological foreign policy agenda: Osama bin Laden and al-Qaeda were hurried out of the country to Afghanistan in 1996, and the PAIC was quietly discontinued. Nevertheless, by 1997 the pressure on Sudan's Islamists from inside and outside was growing, with the SPLA receiving more support from Eritrea, Ethiopia and the USA, but just when it appeared that the government might be genuinely vulnerable they were saved by an unexpected clash between its two eastern neighbours: Eritrea and Ethiopia.

The EPLF and the TPLF had not always seen eye to eye in the years of struggle, but they seemed intimately connected nonetheless, with the relationship apparently underpinned by Ethiopia's readiness to accept Eritrea's independence, coupled with the economic links which seemed so significant for the world's largest landlocked country. There was therefore surprise at the escalation of an apparently minor dispute on the border, which had not been negotiated fully at the time of Eritrea's independence. It centred on the town of Badme, a poor area of little obvious strategic significance, and was to result in one of the two bloodiest inter-state wars in Africa since World War II (the other having been the Somalia–Ethiopia war 20 years previously) which led to the deaths of 70,000–100,000 soldiers on the two sides. Yet Eritrea had already shown a degree of belligerence towards its eastern neighbours:

Yemen, where it had launched sharp attacks in support of its claim to the Hanish Islands in 1996; and clashes with Djibouti over another border issue that had already led to discussion of the basis of its foreign policy. Many felt that it was seeking out enemies in an apparent attempt to 'punch above its weight' in the troubled region. Others suggested further underlying characteristics revealed in the first years of independence: suspicion and the use of force. Eritrea's leadership appeared to view its best interests as being served not by seeking to win regional friends but by regarding all its neighbours as actual or potential enemies of one kind or another, and that the answer was to meddle in their politics to obtain degrees of containment and leverage and to deploy force at the first opportunity if that also seemed a useful instrument in weakening them. As a basis of foreign policy it appeared also to reflect trends in the domestic political management of Issayas Afwerki. Ideologically it reflected the primacy of nationalism over the Marxism (with its internationalist class perspectives) that had been so apparent during the liberation struggle. The turn towards aggressive nationalism was also reflected in the powerful and inflammatory rhetoric regularly deployed by Afwerki for both foreign and domestic consumption.

Nevertheless, the strike against Ethiopia was on a different scale entirely. It was soon being suggested that, in addition to the immediate border dispute, there had been differences over economic relations which had soured the atmosphere between the two for some time. The Addis Abba–Djibouti rail link had long been in decline, and following Eritrea's independence its port of Assab was particularly important for Ethiopia with 80 per cent of its foreign trade passing through it, a fact that led to differences over the tax Eritrea sought to levy. In addition, Eritrea expected that its new currency introduced in 1997, the *nacfa*, would be on a par with the Ethiopian *birr*; when Ethiopia refused, the *nacfa* fell significantly, at which point Ethiopia demanded that trade between the two countries be conducted in hard currency, of which Eritrea had little.

Eritrea's use of force on the undemarcated border in 1998 unleashed a fresh outburst of nationalism in both countries. Eritrea appeared to feel that as the EPLF had been the larger factor in the overall struggle against Mengistu it should continue to be a powerful voice with regard to all its neighbours, and that the Ethiopian People's Revolutionary Democratic Front (EPRDF) should be reminded of its past debt. As for the EPRDF, some had felt that too much had been given away with the independence of Eritrea and it was therefore necessary for Meles Zenawi and his allies to take a strong stand, perhaps even to retake Eritrea or at least the area to the port of Assab. Whatever the thinking, both sides appeared determined for war despite desperate efforts by the USA in particular to call a halt. There were to be two major rounds of bloody fighting, and in 2000 Ethiopia came off the better on the battlefield, occupying a swathe of Eritrea's land, although still without a resolution of the border dispute itself.

Under international pressure an agreement was reached in Algiers in late 2000 by which the two parties agreed to an international boundary commission whose ruling both would accept. But when the commission's conclusions came out, including the return of Badme to Eritrea, Ethiopia rejected it and called for a review which Eritrea then predictably refused. With the war officially ended by the unimplemented Algiers Agreement it was left to the UN to send a peace-keeping force to the still-disputed border where there was now a stalemate. Eritrea's case was that there had been a clear ruling by the internationally established Boundary Commission, but the lack of implementation led to forceful public criticism of the UN and the African Union (AU) by Issayas Afwerki which won him few friends around the world. At least that was what he thought as he withdrew Eritrea from the AU in 2003, not to return until 2010, while in 2008 the UN peacekeeping force on the disputed border was forced out by Eritrea's withdrawal of cooperation.

On the border tension persisted: Eritrea maintained its large force there and kept up its nationalistic media outpourings while Ethiopia, once more administering the disputed town of Badme (as it had before 1998), maintained a significant force. At the same time each side encouraged opposition groups in the other country. With a steady flow of refugees from Eritrea, Ethiopia could encourage their strikes back into their homeland, while Eritrea assisted indigenous movements in Ethiopia, such as those in the Oromo region and Somalis in Region 5. With relations between the two states still poor, Ethiopia also pursued the development of its trade outlets through Djibouti, Kenya, Somaliland and Sudan, maintaining effective relations with all.

The unresolved character of Ethiopia's relations with Eritrea continued to be central to regional relations. The Sudan peace process was an early test since both parties had had their differences with Sudan and had supported the SPLA in the mid 1990s. But their own war and the long borders both had with Sudan influenced their outlooks once their conflict had started. Neither wished to provoke Sudan to the point at which it might side with the other, since the long border made both vulnerable. Instead it was the regional organization Inter-Governmental Authority for Development (IGAD) that formally led the peace process, backed regionally by Kenya and with a great deal of support from the Troika of the USA, Britain and Norway. Ethiopia and Eritrea kept on the fringes of the process while watching developments carefully, especially the growing possibility of the separation of South Sudan. However, both were building their direct relations with Sudan. For Ethiopia this involved growing economic ties between the two countries. General trade between them grew as both economies expanded, and there were also significant developments in the field of power. As an oil producer Sudan became increasingly important for Ethiopia, by the end of the decade supplying over 80 per cent of Ethiopia's needs, while Ethiopia was developing its hydro-electricity production with a view to selling to Sudan's expanding power network.

Eritrea could not match that trade development with regard to Sudan, but did become politically involved in Sudan's two other conflicts amongst its 'marginalized' communities in Darfur in the west, and in the east. In Darfur Eritrea continued its policy of supporting and arming Sudan's opposition groups, now including the Justice and Equality Movement (JEM) and the Sudan Liberation Army (SLA). It was a reminder to Sudan that Eritrea was still a regional player despite the unresolved conflict with Ethiopia. At the same time Eritrea also gained leverage by helping the Sudanese government with regard to the east. The east was far more strategically important for Sudan than Darfur since it contained the routes from the growing central areas to Port Sudan, as well as the oil pipelines from the south. At the same time as the Darfur conflict was erupting there was a smaller one developing in the east where two local opposition groups, the Beja Congress and the Rashaida Free Lions, came together in 2005 to form the Eastern Front. Like Sudan's other opposition groups the eastern groups had long had links to Eritrea, indeed they were particularly strong with cross-border social and religious ties. Eritrea actively promoted the Eastern Sudan Peace Agreement (ESPA) in 2006, just one year after the Comprehensive Peace Agreement (CPA). It was not so much a change of approach by Eritrea as a reminder to the region of its continuing importance, and to Sudan that peace in the east was linked to relations with Eritrea. In return, Sudan quietly banned Eritrea's opposition groups from acting on its territory.

Eritrea also renewed its border dispute with tiny Djibouti. It had rumbled on in the 1990s, but did not amount to a significant clash until 2008 when Djibouti accused Eritrea of sending its troops into a border area. Djibouti took the dispute to the UN but the matter remained unresolved. It appeared to be another example of Eritrea using its army as an instrument of regional assertiveness. In response militarily weak Djibouti was encouraged to cooperate with Ethiopia to counter the common enemy, and in 2011 they acted jointly against an Oromo group, which had been supported by Eritrea, trying to operate through Djibouti territory.

However, the major regional impact of the Ethiopia–Eritrea war was on Somalia. While the rise of the Islamic Courts Union in the mid-2000s was essentially down to developments within Somalia itself, the movement also received support from Eritrea. It involved logistics and military advice and, according to some claims, Eritrean troops as well, once more indicating Eritrea's ideological flexibility. In the 1990s it had turned against Sudan because of its threat of exporting its brand of Islamism, but now Eritrea would support similar ideological strands in Somalia. Some saw it as Eritrea opening up another front in the proxy war with Ethiopia, others as solidarity with Somalis in resisting Ethiopian attempts at hegemonic domination of the Horn, but whatever the reasoning it contributed to Ethiopia's decision – with US support – to send its troops into Mogadishu to bring down the ICU and attempt to clear the way for the Transitional Federal Government (TFG) to become more of a reality. In time it was to contribute to further conflict in Somalia, with neither those backed by Eritrea nor those backed by Ethiopia able to hold and sustain a dominant position, leading to the development of further fragmentation.

Somalia's other neighbour in the Horn, Djibouti, also continued to play a role in the country, endeavouring to act as broker. In 2000 Djibouti had hosted yet another initiative to bring the Somali factions together, this one known as the Arta Process, which produced the Transitional National Government (TNG). However, the TNG's endeavour to project itself into Mogadishu proved unsuccessful. Nevertheless, Djibouti continued to play a role with regard to the later TFG. In 2008 it facilitated the eventual signing of the Djibouti Agreement, while the following year it hosted the elections for the new expanded TFG parliament. The growth of the Somali pirates also projected Djibouti port as an important regional centre used by several of the navies deployed in anti-piracy operations as well as the anti-terrorism activities of the USA from its new base at Camp Lemonier.

Although there had been new 'revolutionary' regimes in the Horn in the 1990s, they had not brought a significant improvement in regional relations which continued to combine mutual suspicion and conflict. However, there was to be an attempt to create a regional organization engaged in major peace efforts. Sub-Saharan Africa had a significant if mixed record of regional organizations purporting to work for regional developments of various kinds. The Economic Community of West African States (ECOWAS) was largely Nigerian-inspired, though how far it had achieved the cooperation intended was questionable. In southern Africa the fall of apartheid brought a new era in regional relations through the Southern African Development Community (SADC). Meanwhile, in East Africa the ambitious plans for integration of the 1960s had seen the failure of the East African Community, although more realistic efforts to revive it developed in the new millennium. The Horn, however, had not had its own regional organization until the emergence of the IGADD. Its initial formation in 1986 owed much to the promptings of the international community and especially the response to the famine that swept the region in the earlier years of that decade. At the time the region's international relations were largely divided by the Cold War, with Ethiopia firmly in the grip of a Marxist–Leninist regime closely supported by the USSR, while neighbouring Sudan and Somalia were in turn backed by the USA: an exact reversal of a period in the previous decade.

The Cold War division meant that any attempt at a regional organization should be as 'non-political' as possible, and in theory IGADD's founding approach, based on environmental and other measures to address drought and its consequences, appeared to abide by that. Thus it was that, in spite of different alignments with competing superpowers, Ethiopia was able to join the new organization along with then clear Western allies Sudan, Somalia, Djibouti, Uganda and Kenya, brought together in part at least by the allure of foreign development aid and reflecting the major aid donors' view of a 'Greater Horn' facing common developmental challenges. However, in practice little was achieved for, although IGADD came up with a number of project proposals, the international donors generally found them less than convincing and IGADD appeared in danger of withering on the vine in its remote 'neutral' headquarters in Djibouti.

The end of the Cold War allowed IGADD to move from unconvincing project proposals and focus instead on conflicts, on the understandable grounds that development would inevitably be limited unless and until the region had proved itself capable of peace. IGADD thus had an opportunity to reinvent itself and was encouraged to do so by its international supporters. To this end it took its first major step in 1994 by involving itself in an attempt at peacemaking in southern Sudan. Down the years there had been numerous failed peace talks, but the end of the Cold War, and the end of the conflicts in Eritrea and Ethiopia that swiftly followed, seemed to offer the opportunity for a new chapter of attempts. With the international community initially somewhat reluctant to start the ball rolling, it was former US president Jimmy Carter who made an early effort which proved unsuccessful, as did a further US attempt by Herman Cohen, the Assistant Secretary of State for Africa. That was followed by efforts from the Nigerian government backed by the Organisation of African Unity (OAU) which led to further failures known as Abuja I and Abuja II. It was after that that Ethiopia, Eritrea (independent in 1993 and a new member of IGADD), Uganda and Kenya – all IGADD members directly affected by Sudan's wars in the south – offered, with the agreement of the Sudanese government, to make a fresh attempt under the auspices of IGADD with encouragement from the OAU and the West.

The attempts in successive talks in 1994 in Nairobi failed, but during and after the talks the IGADD leaders, especially Isayas Afwerki and Meles Zenawi, formulated what became known as the Declaration of Principles (DoP). The DoP recognized that, in theory at least, a major factor in the failure of the talks had been the Sudanese government's determination to preserve the Islamic state that it had established after the 1989 coup, while the SPLA had sought a secular state for Sudan such as there had been before Nimeiri's introduction of *sharia* in 1983. The way out proposed by the DoP was that if the government side would not accept peace based on a secular state, then the south would have the right to a referendum to determine its future, including separation. It was probably a solution that could only have come from the Horn, for ever since the foundation of the OAU in 1963 African states had rejected separation and wars had been fought to prevent it, as in Nigeria, Congo Kinshasa and Ethiopia itself. But, after the fall of Mengistu in Ethiopia in 1991, the idea of a referendum determining separation had been adopted in the case of Eritrea, with the agreement of the new government in Ethiopia from which it was expecting to secede. The same principle was now being put forward by IGADD and accepted by its members, with the exception of Sudan itself where the government still hoped for outright victory in the south. IGADD had taken its first step into the conflict in southern Sudan. Partly in recognition of its more wide ranging role, in 1996 it dropped 'Drought' from its official title becoming simply IGAD.

Although the Sudanese government had rejected the DoP proposed by IGAD, it was to find itself prepared to adopt a similar position in a different context. In an attempt to escape from dealing with either the SPLA or IGAD, the government was pushing for what it liked to call 'peace from within' with a breakaway movement from the SPLA led by Riek Machar in 1997. In the course of arriving at a settlement, known as the Khartoum peace agreement, there was a statement that the southerners would be able to 'determine their political aspirations' through a referendum. This was the least that Riek Machar would agree to if he was to retain any credibility, rather than a real acceptance of the possibility of separation for the south by the government at that stage. In the event, Machar was later to abandon his rapprochement with the government and return to the SPLA, but it did leave the government on record as being prepared to countenance a referendum along the lines that IGAD had proposed.

In the years immediately following, IGAD sought to restart Sudan's talks but without success. However, following 9/11 the Sudanese government was more fearful of the USA and possible action against it as part of the 'War on Terror', and responded positively when the new US administration – led by George W. Bush, who had personal sympathy for the war-torn south – appointed former senator John Danforth as his special representative to Sudan. This wider internationalization of the IGAD efforts, with the USA joined by Britain and Norway in the Troika, was to be a vital additional dimension to the search for peace. At the same time Kenya, a close US ally in the region and keen to develop a role as a 'neutral' peacemaker, announced that it was setting up a permanent office to facilitate mediation on behalf of IGAD, to be led by Lieutenant-General Lazarus Sumbeiywo. Other IGAD members, as well as the wider international community, were strongly supportive of the move and continued to be so throughout the process. It was to start with the Machakos Protocol of 2002, which included a ceasefire based on the DoP formula by which the maintenance of *sharia* in the north would trigger the right of the south to a referendum on separation. Sumbeiywo was to continue to preside over a series of protocols which eventually led to the Comprehensive Peace Agreement (CPA) three years later.

It seemed like a considerable achievement, however, subsequently the Sudanese government, nominally a Government of National Unity (GNU) but in practice largely dominated by the ruling National Congress Party (NCP), proved resistant to attempts by IGAD to be significantly involved in the implementation of the CPA. Nevertheless, IGAD showed persistence in its wish to be active in at least monitoring the implementation of the CPA, and in March 2010 it called a special meeting in Nairobi to discuss the upcoming elections and the various problems that were occurring. It was encouraged in this by the new Government of South Sudan (GoSS) which had put considerable store by IGAD in view of its own establishment by the IGAD-brokered CPA (in contrast to the AU where only Sudan's national government was recognized). The complex elections across Sudan went ahead in the following month in controversial circumstances. However, the express intention of the parties to the CPA, that the manner of its implementation would make unity attractive for the southerners, was not to be borne out in the intervening five years: IGAD members were left to address the implications of the increasingly likely decision by the southerners in January 2011 to secede. The Sudan People's Liberation Movement (SPLM) in particular wanted IGAD to remain involved in post-referendum developments because of its role in the CPA, and in June 2010 it was announced that IGAD and the AU's High Implementation Panel for Sudan, led by former South African President Thabo Mbeki, would play a continuing role.

At the same time as IGAD was convening the negotiations that resulted in the CPA, the organization was also playing host to another set of talks in Kenya, this time focused on Somalia. It was the 15th time that there had been efforts to negotiate a solution to the collapse of the internationally recognized Somali state since Siad Barre's downfall in 1991. These new talks were supported by the European Union (EU) but proved much less focused than the Sudan talks. Over 1,000 Somalis descended on the venue claiming to be representatives of one group or another, and talks seemed set to drag on more or less indefinitely until October 2004 when Uganda's President Museveni, as then chair of IGAD, intervened to call time. A Transitional Federal Government (TFG) was then cobbled together but was unable to claim its capital in Mogadishu and instead was forced to wait in Kenya before seeking to assume its place in Somalia.

Having committed itself to the TFG, IGAD responded positively when the TFG's choice of president, Abdulahi Yusuf, called for peacekeepers to assist him in the establishment of his authority in Somalia.

It agreed to an IGAD Peace Support Mission in January 2005,
followed a period of uncertainty including concern amongst t
Somali supporters as to the likely source of forces for such a mission,
especially as it was feared that they would in practice come largely
from the traditional foe: Ethiopia. Shortly thereafter Ethiopia made
clear its concern over developments in Somalia by sending its forces
in to bring down the ICU. The contrast between the impact of IGAD's
involvement in peacemaking in Somalia and Sudan could hardly have
been more stark. IGAD's support for the TFG and accusations against
Eritrea also resulted in the latter suspending its membership of the
organization in 2007.

The Eritrean–Ethiopian dispute has become the outstanding inter-
state conflict of the Horn in the post-Cold War era, but it has been far
from the only dispute involving borders. As seen earlier, the Somali–
Ethiopia war of 1977–78 was also a border dispute, in that case Somalia's
irredentist claim, and means that Ethiopia has been at the centre of the
two largest inter-state wars in Africa since World War II. Eritrea also
disputed its border with Djibouti, which even involved border skirmishes
in 2008. The independence of South Sudan in 2011 raised further concern
over border problems, as after years of sometimes bitterly contested
border negotiations the task of agreeing it had still not been finalized,
while the future of the three disputed areas – Abyei, Blue Nile and South
Kordofan – was also in doubt with conflicts on both sides of the borders.
The border disputes of the Horn have all been about much more than
simply the borders. Often they reflect more complex relations between
the states involved, such as the wider struggle between Eritrea and
Ethiopia. But they often also reflect the domestic tensions within those
states which contribute much to the approach to border issues, as for
Sudan and South Sudan as separation raised new issues in the former.

Much of the discussion of regionalism embraces economic relations,
and especially the hope that regional economic cooperation will help
to improve political relations. However, where there is widespread

conflict within the states of a region the prospects for economic co-operation become complex. For some time work on conflict in Africa has pointed to the economic dimensions of civil wars, including throwing up phrases such as 'greed or grievance' and 'resource curse' to suggest that these are underlying factors in what may often be presented as ethnic or cultural conflicts. The many cases of conflict in the Horn have all involved cross-border dimensions that embraced the economic as well as the political, not just as a necessary supply route for the continuation of conflict, but as a dimension of the economic benefits that may accrue to some combatants by sustaining their wars. Most if not all of this, of course, will not appear in the formal economic data on the countries involved, but will often be well-known aspects of the informal economies which are so ubiquitous in Africa.

In addition, within the formal sector itself, economic arrangements between neighbouring states may contribute to deteriorating relations, perhaps even to the point of inter-state conflict as the Horn has experienced. The Ethiopia–Eritrea war has been ostensibly about a border, but any analysis of the causes of that conflict must also include the continuing deterioration in economic relations between the two states following Eritrea's independence. The secession of South Sudan was also to threaten economic relations between the two new states, in that case the rent the Sudan sought for the south's use of the oil pipelines; a matter unresolved when independence came.

While politics may present obstacles to regional economic integration, there are areas in which there has been a growing need for at least the exploration of issues of integration. In the Horn infrastructure has been one of those areas, for while infrastructure is largely very poor it has also needed attention with some requirement of cooperation. The most obvious example is Ethiopia which, following the independence of Eritrea in 1993, has become the largest landlocked state in the world, and for which the closure of the border with Eritrea has meant the need for new or improved alternatives. Communications have consequently improved, with Ethiopian trade making more use of ports such as Djibouti, Berbera in Somaliland, Port Sudan and those on the Kenyan coast, where there are plans for a deep water port at Lamu in addition to Mombasa.

Infrastructure has to be for a purpose, and historically Africa's rail and road networks have run down to the coast rather than linking regions within or across the continent. The major reason has been that throughout Africa there has been a lack of complementary production. In colonial times territories produced raw materials for metropolitan markets rather than encouraging regional cooperation, while bodies such as the World Bank have persisted with doctrines of comparative advantage in world markets, which did little to encourage regional cooperation, and produced competition within Africa, driving down prices, especially when compared with long-term trends in the costs of imported manufactured goods. One area of cooperation in the Horn thus far has been with regard to Sudan's oil. Since 1999 Sudan has become the supplier of over 80 per cent of Ethiopia's oil, which has brought the two countries closer and given Ethiopia a stake in Sudan's stability, in stark contrast to the Cold War role of both countries in encouraging instability. However, the independence of South Sudan has 'regionalized' the output of that oil, which mostly comes from South Sudan via pipelines through what is now the separate Sudan. The delay in resolving the rent for that flow by the time of independence led to tensions and mutual threats which affect not only the treasuries of the two states directly involved, but vital oil supplies to Ethiopia.

This illustrates the problems of interdependence in unstable regions, a lesson which Sudan appears to recognize in another area of power: electricity. Ethiopia has a large and controversial programme of dam construction with the aim of becoming a regional exporter of hydroelectricity. Sudan imports some power, but also has its own programme of dam building with similar intent, which will at least prevent

Telecoms

dependence on Ethiopia. A more straightforward and fast-growing area of cooperation across the region has also been in the field of telecoms.

The 'informal' sector is also significant in regional economic relations. One traditional sector has been pastoralists, who are more numerous in the Horn than anywhere else in the world. Scarcely respecters of state boundaries, their cross-border movements are a dimension of local and regional economies that will not go away with 'modernizing' settlement, as once assumed in some quarters, and which are relevant in social and political as well as economic terms, as the growth of conflict in Darfur over some 25 years has shown. The border area of southern Somalia–Kenya–Ethiopia, where there are issues of land ownership and riverine agriculture as well as cross-border livestock trade, has shown the regional dimensions associated with traditional livelihoods. This is also the drought area to which the world was alerted in 2011 when an estimated 13 million people were reported to be under threat. The drought has done much to sharpen these issues, ranging from the impact of Somalia's conflicts on famine relief through to the area's future, with some questioning its long-term carrying capacity in the face of rising populations, environmental degradation in many areas, the absence of a functioning government in much of Somalia and neglect of marginal areas in Kenya and Ethiopia, as well as climate change.

At least some of these issues reflect the original intentions behind the establishment of IGADD following the famines of the 1980s, but apart from recognizing the problems and undertaking research into the potential for cross- border economic cooperation, which has some intrinsic value, there has been little that IGAD has been able to accomplish. It has found itself in something of a Catch-22 situation. IGAD lacks the resources or the capabilities to achieve anything on its own in the area of economic cooperation, and has to turn instead to the international community and especially the IGAD Partner's Forum (IPF), often known as the 'Friends' of IGAD. Consisting of 16 states, and four international organizations, IPF was established to give a boost to IGAD in 1997, but the Friends appear unconvinced of the organization's abilities in this field. Insofar as the states of the Horn do become involved in the issues of sustainability raised, they generally look towards their own governments or other international agencies, with the outcome that IGAD itself is seen as largely irrelevant in the field of economic development. However, economic regionalism has been growing with the emergence of the neighbouring East African Community (EAC) aiming to develop a common market. This is attracting interest from the states of the Horn and could be significant for regional economic integration more widely.

The need for the planned expansion of agriculture for both local and international consumption with rising populations almost everywhere has intensified water issues. The Nile has long been both the most discussed and most contentious water source in the region, and the growing difficulties between upstream and downstream states show the urgency of the subject. The most dependent country of all, Egypt, did not join IGADD, although it did acquire observer status. Many put its exclusion down to the perceived long-running regional rivalry with Ethiopia. While Egypt and Sudan, the only countries with a treaty on the Nile waters (signed in very different circumstances in 1959), appeared to work for the status quo, Ethiopia brought together the upstream states, comprising the members of the Nile Basin Initiative (NBI) established in 1999, as the pressures on the river became more intense. However, by late 2011 Ethiopia was engaging with Egypt, perhaps indicating that the NBI was concerned more with leverage than a potential threat to the downstream state. Sudan is placed in a tricky position caught as it is between Egypt and Ethiopia and their long-running tensions over the Nile. It has strong connections to Egypt both through the 1959 treaty and a range of cultural and commercial links, as well as its growing economic links to Ethiopia, though it is also a position that can be exploited diplomatically with both its neighbours. The situation became more complex when South Sudan became a separate state in 2011 and joined the NBI, which has been a major reason why Egypt and others in the Arab world were actively courting the south's political leadership from the signing of the CPA. In March 2011 Egypt announced its interest in seeing the completion of the Jonglei Canal. With Ethiopia, Sudan and South Sudan looking to develop their commercial agricultural sectors (with foreign investment), the whole question of Nile waters can be expected to grow, although there are signs of the post-Mubarak government in Egypt seeking greater engagement with Ethiopia on the question. While the Nile may be the most obvious river with regard to cooperation, it is far from being the only cross-border water issue in the region. For instance, the relations between Ethiopia and Somalia can also be influenced by issues relating to river basins in the eastern Horn.

Terrorism has also become a regional factor. It has been around in the region since the early 1990s when Sudan welcomed Osama bin Laden in 1991 and sheltered him as he grew al-Qaeda's network. From there it was involved in the confrontation with the US-led UN intervention in Somalia in 1993 as well as later attacks on the US embassies in Kenya and Tanzania in 1998. Islamist terrorism also operated in Ethiopia, especially in connection with opposition to the new regime established in 1991. Developments in Somalia, especially the rise of the ICU in the mid 2000s and its destruction by Ethiopian forces with US backing at the end of 2006, served to enhance a sense of a growing threat from al-Shabaab and others, particularly by Ethiopia and then Kenya. In 2010 these fears were heightened by terrorist attacks in Kampala because of Uganda's willingness to commit troops to support the TFG in Mogadishu. While the states of the Horn have concerns over Islamist terrorism, and IGAD set up a unit to encourage cooperation, in reality it has been the USA that took the lead, linking its intelligence cooperation and military support to governments across the region. In particular it has moved to bolster the security forces of

[handwritten margin note:] River

[handwritten margin note:] Terrorism

[handwritten note at bottom:] It is not surprising that you don't mention Islamic jihad in Eritrea

Uganda and Kenya in the face of perceived dangers from al-Shabaab and its al-Qaeda associates in Somalia. Kenya and Uganda appear to have been drawn in further to the security issues across the region, expanding the area of interconnected conflicts. With apparent US approval, if not encouragement, in October 2011 Kenya announced that it would be sending troops into southern Somalia apparently to set up a security zone inside the country, while Ethiopia also expanded its military activities there. By the end of the year there were reports of successes against al-Shabaab, but military intervention in Somalia still carried high risks. Would there be sustainable reduction of the movement in the light of the impact of the Ethiopian invasion of 2006? Or would these 'outsiders', with the threat they posed to local communities, lead to a resurgence of resistance? In addition, both Ethiopia and Kenya had substantial Somali and other Muslim communities raising the possibility that al-Shabaab could once more use terror tactics in those countries.

Given the levels of conflict across the Horn, and the interconnectedness of those conflicts, it is easy to see that there are, viewed internationally, common security issues. Indeed, it is possible to see them in classic Buzan terms as forming a security complex: 'A group of states whose primary security concerns link together sufficiently closely that their national securities cannot realistically be considered apart from one another'.[2] The logic of that is that they cooperate to reduce the security concerns. But suppose those concerns at the level of the respective regimes work against each other, reflecting their limitations as nation states? Not only have Eritrea and Ethiopia gone from being bedfellows against Mengistu (even if they occasionally kicked each other), they are now facing each other in hostile camps on either side of the still-disputed border, with at least one of them prepared to withstand the international mediation of the supposed cause of their dispute. And it is suggested that, in the classic ways of finding external enemies to justify domestic coercion, nationalism is being manipulated by both

External enemy to justify extreme domestic coercion

regimes to strengthen their domestic control. Meanwhile, Ethiopia judged it in its interest to fight for the imposition of the IGAD-backed TFG in Somalia rather than seeking an accommodation with the ICU, the most successful effort at the restoration of government in Somalia since the fall of Siad Barre. In Sudan the unfolding of 'marginalization' on all its border areas under successive governments over half a century has enriched the ruling elites of the centre even though it has created issues for its neighbours resulting from impoverishment, refugees and the overflow of domestic conflict. The independence of South Sudan ended one conflict but contributed to new conflicts in both states. IGAD, as a regional organization was important in the process that produced the CPA, but would it have been possible without wider internationalization, especially the involvement of the USA? And would it even have taken the shape it did without the USA? It was the USA that checked the Egyptian–Libyan initiative of 2000 for a broader form of political participation than just the two armed camps of the NCP and the southern SPLA, an omission which continued through to the decision by other major political parties to boycott the 2010 elections.

The suspicion has been that improving regional relations has not been a necessary step for the regimes of the Horn, so much as the fulfilment of an agenda encouraged from outside at several levels of the international community. There has been a dependency in IGAD that has encouraged it to trim its activities to the winds of its international backers as much as coordinated thinking by its member states. Its concern with terrorism is an obvious example, for while there appear to be some links between Somali Islamists and international Islamism (i.e. al-Qaeda) these are small compared with the overwhelmingly domestic agendas of all armed actors in the Horn, at least since Osama bin Laden quit Sudan in 1996. Yet waving the threat of Islamist terrorism becomes a card in international politics and brings responses, especially from the USA, as a number of recent studies have recounted.

This perception of the region's international organization, IGAD, as a body heavily influenced from outside, has given it a low priority and little public perception, with a lower profile than the AU and of course the UN. At the same time such reputation as it has acquired is often associated with hegemonic ambitions of Ethiopia, rather in the way that South Africa is perceived in SADC and Nigeria in ECOWAS. As such it has limited institutionalization and, while it has become a part of the region's international furniture and unlikely to go away, it has hardly proved capable of making a sustained mark in its own right, rather than as the partner of other international and/or regional actors.

To add to the problems of the region the areas they affect have been expanding to the east and west. It has been the whole question of Somalia's statehood, or lack of it, that has been central to the emergence of the issue of piracy now stretching hundreds of miles off its shore, while the evolution of the conflict in Darfur has its roots not only in western Sudan but in national politics, as well as having a regional input. When added to the outcomes of the 'Arab Spring' as they emerge in Libya and Egypt, it leaves great uncertainty and potential instability from the eastern Mediterranean to the Indian Ocean.

CHAPTER 8

International Politics

As the 'victor' at the end of the Cold War it was expected that the USA would play a role in the strategic region of the Horn. It had already been involved since the end of World War II, especially with its use of Ethiopia's strategic position to set up an important communications base in Eritrea, and the Cold War extended its involvement to proxy engagement with the USSR as both sought allies in the unstable region. While the USA was involved in Ethiopia, the USSR took its chance to move into Egypt in the mid 1950s, Somalia after 1969 and briefly Sudan from 1969 to 1971. The USA countered by a new relationship with Sudan in the 1970s only for it to reluctantly lose its position in Ethiopia following the revolution of 1974, instead of which it moved to Somalia as the latter's war with Ethiopia in 1977–78 cost it Soviet support. These moves resembled a game of dominoes in which the countries of north-east Africa were all on both sides in the Cold War at different times. However, the roots of change lay less with the superpowers themselves than with the domestic instability across the region, although the USA and the USSR contributed to that instability through their machinations.

With the end of the Cold War there seemed less for the USA to be concerned about in the region. The Horn was still of strategic impor-tance and therefore significant, but with no obvious challenge to the

USA there, initially at least. There were few direct economic interests for the USA in the region, especially after Chevron had been pushed out of Sudan's oilfields in 1983, but there were humanitarian concerns which from time to time surfaced and engaged the attention of the US public. This had been the case in the mid 1980s in particular with the widespread famine in northern Ethiopia and western Sudan which had produced not just an American but a global response, especially as it linked into the youthful pop culture of the time. Humanitarian concern at that time had focused on themes such as drought and environmental issues more than the role of conflict, although that was very relevant in Ethiopia in particular. There was then a realization that with widespread poverty and environmental decay there was a continuing risk of humanitarian crises and expectations that the USA would become involved in calls for relief. There was also an awareness that in 1989 no less a body than the World Bank had laid out its belief that there was a connection between continuing poverty and the quality of government to which the answer should be the promotion of 'good governance'. This was widely perceived in the West as something approximating its own broad approach to government, including liberal democracy. That in turn would provide an 'enabling environment' for economic development based around the implementation of free-market principles that would lift poor states out of the endless cycles of poverty and conflict in which they all too often appeared to be trapped. The Horn seemed as much in need as anywhere for the application of such medicine, with the USA as the leading dispenser.

As seen, the first major US involvement had come in Somalia with the deployment of American forces to lead the UN intervention to deliver famine relief, and in the eyes of some to engage in statebuilding. It was, in principle, an easy decision for President George Bush, and accepted by his successor, Bill Clinton, although he was ready to pull out when confronted by unexpected local resistance led mainly by Mohammed Farah Aideed. At the time of its initial engagement the

USA had little awareness that Aideed received encouragement and support from fighters trained in Islamist camps in Sudan. Following the coup of 1989, Sudan offered facilities to a number of groups employing terror tactics, who it referred to as 'Brothers in Islam', with Sudan itself looking to promote the rise of Islamism across the Horn and down to the Indian Ocean in East Africa. This hosting of Islamist groups – including al-Qaeda – did come into America's sights during 1993, and Sudan was added to the select group of countries on the US terrorism-supporting list. This led to the imposition of US sanctions, but links between the two countries were comparatively few and thus had little effect. Sudan was later also placed under UN sanctions after the attempted assassination of President Mubarak in 1995, but these too were quite light since Egypt in particular argued against punitive sanctions, while Sudan took steps to lower its profile as a terrorism-supporting state, although it remained on the US list.

However, the USA was still keen to pursue the regime in Sudan, but now through a new strategy of building stabilization in the Horn around those perceived as bringing a new broom, not just to the region but to Africa. Those revolutionary figures who had led fights for the freedom of their countries against old-style tyrants were lauded in the State Department under Madeleine Albright as 'renaissance' leaders. And when the issue of Islamist terrorism turned Issayas Afwerki of Eritrea, Meles Zenawi of Ethiopia and Youeri Museveni of Uganda (where Islamist Sudan paradoxically backed the 'Christian' Lord's Resistance Army (LRA) of Joseph Kony) against Sudan they were encouraged to back the SPLA as its fight in South Sudan was extended to the east of the country. In late 1996 the USA gave $20 million to the three neighbouring countries for 'defensive' and non-lethal equipment and there was talk of John Garang and the SPLA also overthrowing a despotic government, if not by direct military victory then by triggering a successful uprising in Khartoum of the kinds that had taken place in 1964 and 1985. In the growing evangelical circles across

America, particularly in the south where there was growing support for South Sudan, it was also seen as a struggle of 'frontline states' against Islamist expansion.

US hopes for a change of government in Sudan were to be dashed, not just by the failure of either an outright SPLA victory or a popular uprising, but by the unexpected war in 1998 between two of its supposed close allies, Eritrea and Ethiopia. It horrified the State Department, where it was seen as such an unnecessary conflict. The young, forceful Under-Secretary of State for African Affairs, Susan Rice (a protégée of Albright's) was despatched to pour water on the flames but to no effect. Rice was followed by several visits from national security adviser turned special envoy, Anthony Lake, but also without success. The continuation of conflict and tension between Ethiopia and Eritrea showed the limitations of conducting US operations (in this case against Sudan) through proxies, since the latter may have overriding agendas of their own. For Sudan the unexpected war was a godsend.

There was, though, to be one last direct use of force against Sudan in 1998. In response to the bombings of the US embassies in Kenya and Tanzania, and a narrowly averted attempt on the embassy in Uganda, Clinton approved missile attacks on Afghanistan and Sudan. Neither attack was successful as Osama bin Laden, the target in Afghanistan, escaped, while a factory destroyed in Khartoum North turned out to be peaceful pharmaceutical plant rather than manufacturing ingredients for chemical weapons as was alleged. By 2000 the USA had done an about turn as it sought intelligence on Islamist terrorism from Sudan's security services while still leaving the country on the terrorism list.

This change of direction by the USA was to be even more marked during the presidency of Clinton's successor, George W. Bush, for instead of encouraging an SPLA victory over the Islamist regime in Sudan, Bush proved an active proponent of peacemaking. Bush had a particular concern for Sudan largely through a genuine commitment to the evangelical Christian movement in the USA that saw southern Sudan as a frontier region threatened by expansionist Islamism, over and beyond the more cynical electoral plans for that constituency displayed by his close advisor Karl Rove. Bush was twice sworn in as president by his personal friend Franklin Graham, who ran the largest American NGO in southern Sudan, Samaritan's Purse International, while senior Republican senators Bill Frist and Sam Brownback were also involved with the Freedom House Coalition which campaigned for South Sudan. Sudan's long conflicts in the south were also judged 'ripe for resolution'. Military deadlock on the battlefields was one propitious circumstance. Another was that Sudan had become an oil exporter in 1999, but with most of the new-found oil in the south it was at continued risk while war persisted, and thus elites in both north and south stood to benefit from peace bringing greater security of supply. Neighbouring states were either in agreement with a peace effort or at least not likely to seek to abort it, and US diplomacy led by Bush's special envoy, retired senator John Danforth, sought to ensure support for the US-led Troika with Britain and Norway. Danforth also warned off an effort by Egypt and Libya to promote their own significantly different peace plan. The peace talks under the auspices of IGAD lasted from 2002 until the eventual CPA three years later, and gave US foreign policy a real sense of achievement at a time when policies in Afghanistan and Iraq were under constant criticism.

Following the signing of the CPA the USA remained supportive of the implementation of the agreement into the Obama administration, which also aimed at ending conflict and mass crimes in Darfur as well as preventing Sudan from becoming a haven for terrorism (a concern that received added impetus when Israel appeared to twice destroy weapons moving overland in Sudan, apparently destined for Hamas in Gaza and emanating from Iran). When the CPA process concluded in 2011 with the decision of southern Sudan to separate, the USA expressed its readiness to accept the outcome.

However, one limitation of the CPA was that it involved almost exclusively the two main warring parties: the NCP government in the north and the SPLA in the south. The very success of the process that began with the Machakos protocol of 2002 encouraged a new revolt in Darfur in the west. By 2004 the conflict there was giving rise to widespread international demands for action, especially in the USA where the Save Darfur Coalition soon emerged, and rapidly became too loud for Bush to ignore. Darfur was depicted as the biggest humanitarian crisis in the world, and in the year of the tenth anniversary of the Rwanda genocide First Secretary of State Colin Powell and then Bush himself used the 'G word' to describe what was taking place in the region. Action was required and the USA pushed for talks between the government and the rebel factions in Abuja in 2005–06 under the auspices of the African Union (AU). However, the success of the CPA was not to be repeated. The rebels were split into competing factions; the government was reluctant to offer major concessions having already accepted the possibility of losing the south in the CPA; while the international community, led by the USA, showed its frustration, presenting terms to the rebels on a take it or leave it manner that led to rejection by two factions and agreement by only one. Conflict in Darfur dragged on, while protest in the USA declined and with it active US involvement on the scale that had been deployed in the making of the CPA and the run up to the failed Abuja talks. Darfur showed that, despite the success of the CPA, peacemaking in Sudan remained difficult. Indeed, the success with regard to the south contributed to the scale of the Darfur crisis from 2003. Peacemaking requires informed judgement with regard to all aspects of the conflict involved and careful assessment of how 'ripe for resolution' it actually may be, including not only the immediate situation but the wider national and regional context. It also involves patience, flexibility and engagement in support of direct negotiations between the parties and, if successful, there is likely to be a need for continuing support for peace implementation in the evolving post-conflict situation.

After its experience of Somalia in the early 1990s the USA was reluctant to become involved there once more, and it was not seriously involved in the numerous unsuccessful attempts to restore peace. However, the apparent growth of Islamism in southern Somalia in particular in the mid-2000s, coupled with the spreading of al-Qaeda from Afghanistan to Iraq and Yemen, led to fears of a link to Somalia. Fears were also fanned by Ethiopia's worries not only with regard to Somalia but also threats from activities amongst its large Muslim community and memories of terrorist attacks in Addis Ababa in the 1990s. Following 9/11 these concerns intensified and Ethiopia was regarded as one of America's 'anchor states' in Africa in its response to the threat. In late 2006 the USA actively encouraged Ethiopia in its decision to attack the ICU in Somalia with American air support, the first overt use of US military power in sub-Saharan Africa since the involvement in Somalia over a decade earlier. In addition, both Ethiopian and US covert operations continued in Somalia following the withdrawal of regular Ethiopian forces in 2009, including the use of US drones to target leading figures in al-Shabaab. In 2011 the USA announced an agreement that Ethiopia would host a new base for drones.

The growing concern in Washington at the growth of Islamist terrorism, especially in the wake of 9/11, contributed to the militarization of its approach to sub-Saharan Africa, and especially the Greater Horn area. A Joint Task Force, Horn of Africa (JTF-HOA) was established at an old French site, Camp Lemonier, in Djibouti. Camp Lemonier was also used in actions in Yemen, the home of al-Qaeda in the Arabian Peninsula, and seen by some in Washington as more of a threat than al-Qaeda in Pakistan or Afghanistan. JTF-HOA was not to be seen in isolation, but as an important part of a wider body known as AFRICOM which was to be engaged in anti-terrorist operations across Africa. It was not intended to engage in purely military operations but work with diplomatic and NGO activities: as *The Economist* wrote it was 'To win hearts and minds and so deny terrorists havens from which to operate'.[1] There is though an obvious danger that AFRICOM's centrality in combined hard and soft power activities could prove damaging to perceptions of the latter.

Diplomacy is difficult enough without appearing to be overtly linked to security objectives. It primarily involves seeking out and working with local partners in pursuit of a range of common objectives, but already it appears that US relations with its key strategic partner in the Horn, Ethiopia, is compromising its broader interests. Within governmental and non-governmental organizations in the USA involved with Ethiopia there has been growing awareness of its authoritarian character, even described by some as creeping totalitarianism: yet US perceptions of Ethiopia's importance in counter-terrorism appear to trump other concerns, and it remains the largest aid donor to the country. In part because of fears of terrorism, US diplomats are in danger of becoming restricted by the dominance of security concerns, including their own, to the detriment of direct engagement with societies in which they are supposed to operate, leaving them vulnerable to the views host governments wish to put across. Writing in 2005, an experienced senior American academic wrote, 'The greater Horn of Africa (Yemen excepted) is in too many respects a terra incognita to Washington . . . Washington lacks any coherent vision for integrating and advancing diplomatic and security initiatives in the region'.[2]

US aid has sometimes been seen as an arm of diplomacy, and a case for this could be made in the era of the Cold War at least: it was noticeable that aid to the Horn was cut back after it ended. Nevertheless, the USA was to be central to food aid. It was the delivery of food aid that took the USA into Somalia in 1992–93, and it was mainly US food supplies that were delivered for years by the large-scale UN Operation Lifeline Sudan (OLS) that provided support to the peoples of the war torn south. USAID was also active in southern Sudan and was a significant voice in Washington for the SPLA. And when the crisis in Darfur exploded in 2003, it was largely food grown in the USA that was handed out to the Internally Displaced People (IDPs). The USA also kept up a major aid programme in Ethiopia, and even a smaller programme in Eritrea. Yet aid also brought dilemmas. For example, OLS fed people of South Sudan, but supplies were also expropriated by the parties to conflict leading some to point to aid's contribution to a cycle of violence. Nor did aid appear to do much to influence the behaviour of the governments of the recipient countries, at least as far as encouraging the wider objectives of political, social and economic development that successive US administrations espoused. These governments continued to be driven more by their own agendas and domestic politics, as they had been for much of the Cold War. The dilemma was brought into even sharper relief by the famine in 2011 in which the USA would not provide relief to the large areas of south-central Somalia under al-Shabaab's control, lest it be used by the latter to consolidate its position and thus the rise of aggressive Islamism.

From 1993 the USA also sought to use sanctions as an instrument of policy. The sanctions put in place following Sudan's placement on the US terrorism list were supplemented by UN sanctions following the attempted assassination of Mubarak in 1995, and in 2002 the USA placed additional restrictions under the Sudan Peace Act. The Darfur crisis also brought possible new UN sanctions, but China and Russia led the opposition in the Security Council. US sanctions did have an effect, especially with regard to financial transactions by the Sudan government, and many major Western companies that were traded on Wall Street were prevented from investing in the country at a time when its oil industry was growing fast. Sanctions also had the effect of leading the Sudanese government to think that peace would be swiftly followed by their being lifted, only for frustration to grow when that did not occur due to the US response to the conflicts in Darfur and elsewhere. UN sanctions proved less effective. As noted, to the annoyance of the USA, Egypt in particular did not want punitive sanctions in the 1990s, while there were no sanctions over Darfur.

US policy in the Horn has shifted over the years. Military failure in Somalia was followed by retreat, before returning to military engagement again over Islamism and the threat of terrorism, while Ethiopia's role in relation to combating terrorism overcame any American disillusionment at the country's political direction with regard to liberal democracy and human rights. In Sudan the USA moved from support for attempted destabilization in the 1990s to successful involvement in peacemaking in the following decade.

In comparison with the USA, the other major international actor in the region, China, appeared to be a model of consistency from the early 1990s onwards. China's engagement with the Horn was part of its wider involvement with Africa. With the era of African independence in the 1960s China had embarked on its first large-scale engagement with the continent, but it was a very different China and a very different Africa to that of 30 years later. In the 1960s China was the land of Mao Zedong and economic experiments with highly collectivized forms of economic activity. There was some appeal to African states, but mainly the few with a collectivized agricultural emphasis, most notably Julius Nyerere's Tanzania of *ujama'a* villages. Tanzania was also central to China's best-known project of that era, the Tan–Zam railway from Dar es Salaam to Lusaka. But towards the end of the decade Mao embarked on the Great Cultural Revolution which was to consume China, reducing its engagement with Africa. By the 1990s, however, China was on the road to socialism with Chinese characteristics, which in reality meant state-backed capitalism, and was a rising power that was to have the second largest economy in the world by 2011. In the process it had identified Africa as a continent of huge potential: a largely undeveloped area of the world rich in resources, which was seeking development and eager for a major new international partner.

When it came to the Horn, Sudan stood out as particularly enticing. Something was known about its oil as a result of Chevron's unsuccessful foray, and with sanctions in place there was no chance of imminent competition from major Western companies. China's relations with the country had been quite good for much of the period since independence: it had offered military training and equipment to Nimeiri in the 1970s, and business had continued to grow thereafter. China even liked to remind Sudan that General Gordon had been known as 'Chinese' Gordon for his role in repressing the Taiping rebels before meeting his death at the hands of the Mahdi's more successful rebellion in Khartoum (being more widely known thereafter as 'Gordon of Khartoum'). For its part the Sudanese government was eager for Chinese involvement and in 1994 invited the state-owned Chinese National Petroleum Company (CNPC) to begin activities, and with its own fields in China diminishing the opportunity was too good to be missed. It was CNPC's first major overseas operation and thus a breakthrough in China's pursuit of resources in Africa. The process was to lead to oil exports starting in 1999, by which time China had been joined by other foreign oil companies. Over the next few years China was to expand its operations, holding its place as the leading country in Sudan's oil sector, by 2006 investing over $15 billion in a range of infrastructure and arms deals in return for oil. Much of the oil was in the south, and China was involved in constructing the pipelines carrying the oil north to the Red Sea, as well as building a refinery for local requirements near Khartoum, which had been a major attraction for Sudan. Operating in these remote fields involved clearances of some local communities, and Chinese workers were killed in related incidents, but the work continued regardless. For a short while Sudan was China's largest supplier of oil in Africa and, although overtaken by Angola, it remained important.

China was also involved in other aspects of Sudan's infrastructure including the building of new bridges and roads, telecommunications, agriculture, textiles and improving the long neglected railway system. Its most contentious project was the building of a large new dam on the main Nile near the site of the ancient city of Meroe, where it ran into local opposition from farmers claiming to have lost their lands, and from international environmentalists opposed to such projects on principle. China was also involved in trade and business development: by 2008 Chinese companies comprised 13 of the 15 largest international companies operating in the country.

Prominent in the field of trade was Sudan's sale of arms at a time when civil war still raged in the south. In addition to selling arms, China assisted with the establishment of new arms-manufacturing facilities which also supplied Sudanese forces in the ongoing conflicts. Particular attention was paid to this involvement in arms when the Darfur revolt exploded in 2003, with the UN imposing an arms embargo on Sudan. While there was no evidence that China actively broke the embargo, arms from China were used but may have been sold prior to the embargo: China maintained that it received end user certificates for later arms sales that excluded the use of those sales in Darfur. One of the attractions for African countries in engaging with China has been the proclaimed absence of any political strings. Yet while China may profess its hands off approach to politics in Africa, it is also clear that its economic engagement has major political implications, and on occasions China has been forced to recognize this. One such development occurred with the Darfur crisis. The Sudanese government's arming of the *janjaweed* in Darfur with weapons of Chinese provenance led to the Save Darfur Coalition and other campaigners proclaiming that the Olympic games in Beijing in 2008 should be labelled the 'genocide Olympics' and be internationally boycotted. China's special envoy on Sudan, the experienced Liu Guijin who was appointed in 2007, made a number of international calls to head off this possibility, and was also reported to have expressed concern over the situation in Darfur to the Sudanese government, while reporting that President Hu Jintao had also spoken to his counterpart Beshir about the region. In 2007 China also encouraged the Sudanese government to accept the conversion of the AU's African Mission in Sudan (AMIS) into UN African Mission in Darfur (UNAMID) under UNSCR 1769, and sent 315 military engineers to give support in Darfur. China also found itself engaged politically when the International Criminal Court (ICC) brought indictments against President al-Beshir and two others over alleged war crimes and crimes against humanity in Darfur (the charge of genocide was also later added). China endeavoured to use its seat on the Security Council to propose a temporary halt to possible ICC prosecution in order to facilitate negotiations with the rebels. It also registered its regret, along with a number of African countries, when an arrest warrant against President al-Beshir was issued in 2009. As well as having been central to Sudan's recovery from virtual bankruptcy in the early 1990s and becoming its major economic partner within a decade, it had become the country's most powerful friend on the international political scene. In 2011 South Sudan's independence also saw China step in to try to play a mediatory role between the two states, which it needed to work together to deliver the oil in which China had invested so heavily.

While Sudan was both a breakthrough for China in the Horn, and in Africa more broadly, it was soon seeking new opportunities, with Ethiopia becoming its other main partner in the region. Ethiopia did not immediately offer mineral prospects comparable to Sudan's, although China was involved in exploring possibilities in Region 5 in the east, but the country had obvious needs and a very large population with which to trade. Once again China became heavily involved in much-needed infrastructure projects: the transport sector and information technology. Trade also grew rapidly, reaching over US$1.3 billion by 2009, with China's exports vastly greater than its imports from Ethiopia. China also made substantial soft loans to Ethiopia, with the majority of the money going to businesses with close party and state links, while numerous private Chinese companies also operated in the country. From Ethiopia's point of view there was no criticism from

China over its political, economic and social policies, which seemed in many ways similar, although Ethiopia's economy was not as free-market in practice as China's had become. For China there was an additional attraction in that, with the AU's headquarters in Addis Ababa, it was a good place for the diplomatic networking across the continent which was a necessary part of its expanding activities. Indeed, China built new headquarters for the AU in the city. In addition, Ethiopia's growing importance as a regional power was also helpful to China, as it was able to broaden its perspectives on the security it required for its economic operations. China's connections with Ethiopia have not, however, prevented it from developing economic links with Eritrea, including starting mining in 2007.

China's growing presence in the Horn was to be accompanied by similar criticisms to those it attracted elsewhere in Africa, such as its use of cheap labour (often from China itself and rumoured sometimes to include convicts), poor employment practices, environmental damage and a lack of transparency that included corrupt practices as well as unfair competition, with the support given to its companies by the Chinese state itself. There was also concern as to whether China was joining in Africa's 'land grab', with both Sudan and Ethiopia opening up to foreign investment in agriculture. China's 'Going Out' policy of 2004 encouraged such investment for commercial enterprise, although for profit rather than as a part of China's own domestic food security since it was deemed too much of a political risk to become reliant on external sources. It was also accused of being unconcerned about the political context in which it operated, leading the Director of China's Export–Import Bank to comment that, 'Transparency and good governance are good terminologies, but achieving them is not a pre-condition of development, it is a result of it'.[3] The rise of Somali piracy was, however, a reminder to China that all would not be plain sailing in its growing involvement with the Horn, and *inter alia* threatens China's own oil exports from Sudan.

In the Middle East the country with the longest connections to the Horn has been Egypt. Its links with the upper regions of the Nile go back to antiquity and included pharaonic connections with northern Sudan and Coptic Christian ties with Ethiopia. In the modern era nineteenth-century Egypt had designs on an African empire that would reach the Indian Ocean and include the conquest of much of Sudan and coastal acquisitions extending to Massawa and beyond. In the twentieth century its concerns were mainly with Sudan as it sought to regain the territories it claimed to have earlier won by conquest. Even though that failed Egypt sought to build links with post-independence Sudan, including steps towards a proposed union put forward by Presidents Sadat and Nimeiri in the 1970s. The end of the Cold War involved little adjustment for Egypt, instead its major concern was with Sudan and the implications of the Islamist coup there. It soon led to Egypt's own radical Islamists operating from Sudan, including the attempted assassination of Mubarak in Addis Ababa in 1995. Egypt resurrected its longstanding border dispute with Sudan over Halayeb: since Sudan's independence the dispute has served as a temperature gauge of relations between the two countries, and Egypt decided to send troops to occupy it, a move to which Sudan had no effective response. Angered though Egypt was, it still acted softly, encouraging the USA in particular to impose comparatively light sanctions on Sudan, and thereafter continued to be tolerant of Sudan in international arenas. Behind this lay not only historic, cultural and growing trade links, but also concern to maintain Sudan's agreement with Egypt that their treaty dividing the Nile Waters should remain in place in the face of Ethiopia's growing objections, and success in winning other upriver riparian states to its cause. It was primarily for this reason that Egypt was openly opposed to the separation of South Sudan, and went out of its way to woo the new government to support unity. Although ultimately unsuccessful, Egypt will continue to seek to embrace South Sudan in this vital cause.

Relations between Ethiopia and Egypt were becoming increasingly tense as both countries have fast-rising populations and consequent needs for more of the waters: pessimistic estimates with regard to Egypt suggested that serious shortages might be encountered as early as 2017. With water remaining Egypt's prime concern and Ethiopia perceived as its main threat, relations between the two remained at best guarded and at worst strained, at least until the downfall of Mubarak. It is, however, well remembered that Boutros Boutros-Ghali, former Egyptian deputy foreign minister as well as UN Secretary-General, once prophesied that the next war in the Middle East would be over water, not oil. Egypt has also directed belligerent noises in Ethiopia's direction on occasions.

The narrow waters dividing the Horn from the Arabian peninsula have ensured close links historically, many of which continue. Yemen has social, cultural and trading links in many fields, including the issue of piracy, as well as having had a clash with Eritrea in the 1990s over the Hanish islands. There are also fears in many quarters that the strength of al-Qaeda in Yemen could lead to closer ties with the Islamist militias in Somalia. Saudi Arabia keeps a close watch, concerned at the possible growth of radical Islamism, often paradoxically connected to Wahabist influences in the kingdom itself. It has also found itself with a growing number of Somalis, perhaps as many as 600,000. In the Gulf states there is also concern, although there is a readiness to pursue business opportunities in Ethiopia and Sudan, while some allege that there are links with the increasingly businesslike professionalism developed by the Somali pirates. Somalia aside, the main concern for the governments of the peninsula has been political stability and thus most have been wary at the separation of South Sudan, although at the same time trying to establish good relations with the new state and seeking to help it economically. Qatar has been to the fore in economic and political developments in Sudan, including facilitating and hosting lengthy talks on Darfur. As well as the Arab countries, Iran also played a role for a while. The Islamist takeover in Sudan in 1989 was followed in the early 1990s by military links with Iran, and it was frequently alleged that Iranians trained various terrorist groups in the camps that had sprung up. However, as Sudan retreated from its international adventurism relations became more distant. Also in the Middle East, Israel kept a watching brief: in the early 1990s relations with Eritrea briefly flowered as part of its traditional desire to find non-Muslim allies in the Horn and seek to prevent the Red Sea becoming an 'Arab lake'. In 2009 and 2010 Israel again became concerned that Iran was shipping arms to Gaza via Sudan, and it was widely believed that it was responsible for strikes on arms convoys in eastern Sudan.

Libya too has been active in the Horn, although more marginally than most of the states of the periphery. When sidelined by much of the Arab world, Colonel Qaddafi became a born-again African and sought to play a leading role in, first, the OAU and, after 2002, the AU. He had particular concern for Darfur, a region of Sudan bordering Libya in which the latter had an interest throughout Qaddafi's years in power. Its close links to Chad had long been exploited by him, and once the rebellion in Darfur broke out it was clear that he had connections with at least one of the rebel groups while also seeking to put himself forward as a peacemaker. In the end it amounted to comparatively little in the long search for peace in Darfur, and his efforts were in any case overtaken by his downfall in 2011 resulting initially from the 'Arab Spring'.

Across the Mediterranean the European states were largely reflective of their imperial histories in their continuing engagement with the Horn. Britain had ruled Sudan, manoeuvred Egypt out as Sudan chose independence, administered Somaliland, fought Italy in Ethiopia, and briefly administered Eritrea on behalf of the UN after World War II. After independence it kept quite close relations with Sudan and, though these were strained by Sudan's Islamist turn in the 1990s, Britain played an important role in the Troika that supported the making of the CPA. In Ethiopia Haile Sellasie had looked to the USA more than Britain, while the Mengistu years saw relations weaken further, but during Tony Blair's premiership he and Meles Zenawi forged quite a close relationship as the former sought to save Africa from being a 'blot on the conscience of the world'. Somaliland and Eritrea featured less obviously on the British agenda, but Italy endeavoured to play a role in the region. It saw itself as having a special responsibility for Somalia, though in practice what it could do was limited. It also recognized the wrongs of Mussolini's cruel campaign in Ethiopia in the 1930s, and business links were built with the country after the Cold War, especially in the field of infrastructure construction which had earlier been the best legacy of the brief Italian occupation. Concern continued for the former colony of Eritrea, although it amounted to little in practice. France maintained its small force in Djibouti where it was joined by the US base, while various other foreign navies availed themselves of its facilities in the course of patrolling the pirate-infested waters. Russia was far less conspicuous following the end of the Cold War, especially with Ethiopia demonizing its relationship with Mengistu's regime, but was ready to sell arms when the opportunity arose, as it did to Sudan with its internal conflicts.

The European countries were also represented in the Horn by the European Union (EU), although as always they pursued their own policies outside its purview thus limiting its impact. Nevertheless, the EU did endeavour to play a role. In Somalia it underwrote the long negotiations in Kenya that resulted in the setting up of the TFG, although in practice the EU could do little to facilitate its actual establishment in the country. In Ethiopia the EU also sought to press its human rights agenda, especially through its encouragement of democratic elections in 2005, at a time when the European Commission and the European Parliament were producing the European Union Strategy for Africa, which was seen as a considerable breakthrough. The EU deployed some 200 election monitors who produced a report which was more open in its criticisms than many expected, and was duly denounced by the Ethiopian government. In spite of growing disillusionment with the direction of Ethiopia during and after the 2005 elections, the EU continued to be a major provider of aid and development assistance to the largest recipient of international aid in Africa. As well as humanitarian concerns it was clear that the EU shared the general international concern with terrorism and instability, and that the Ethiopian government had substantial leeway to follow its own agenda under the experienced and manipulative leadership of Meles Zenawi. In neighbouring Sudan the EU did appoint its own special envoy and had monitors at the elections of 2010 and South Sudan's referendum in the following year, but it was generally following the line of the USA and the AU rather than promoting a distinctive policy of its own. As a result of the influx of Darfur refugees into Chad and the Central African Republic, as well as instability in both countries, the EU established in 2007 a peacekeeping force with UN backing, European Force Tchad/RCA (EUFOR) on their borders with Darfur. It grew to 3,700 troops, mostly from France, and in 2009 its role was taken over by the UN.

The UN has had a wide range of activities across the Horn for decades, especially with regard to relief and development programmes of various kinds. One of the largest and most discussed has been OLS which began following the droughts of the 1980s. It was aimed at delivering relief during the conflict in the south, and as such its establishment was the first occasion that the UN had to work with both a national government and a rebel movement: always a difficult political balance. Indeed, almost as soon as OLS was established, the 1989 coup in Sudan appeared to indicate that it would be shut down by the new government. In the end it survived, but relations with both parties were always difficult. Both were concerned about the extent to which the other side could access food supplies that would sustain its enemies, and there were frequent accusations and counter-accusations. In an attempt to get around the suspicions over leakages from relief deliveries

OLS was divided into two sectors, one of which was supplied via the north and the other via the south. In 1996, as the conflicts in the south dragged on and various peace efforts had proved unsuccessful, a major review was conducted that concluded that on balance OLS should continue. At the heart of the problem was the assessment of the balance between suffering caused by the failure to provide aid in a conflict situation and the cost in human suffering by knowing that some leakage was also contributing to supplying the major combatants. Given the circumstances a precise calculation is unreachable, but on balance most examinations of OLS thought it had been justified by the time it was wound down after the signing of the CPA.

While the UN was working in an established context of conflict in South Sudan, in Somalia the situation was very different. The rapid disintegration of the state at the end of the 1980s and start of the 1990s called for increased relief, especially with drought threatening, but the increasingly violent and chaotic situation led to armed groups intercepting many of the supplies. There was growing awareness in the UN that something should be done, but to what end? The recognition by Presidents Bush and then Clinton that action was required made available a substantial US force to head a UN intervention, and inevitably the operations on the military side were led by the USA. However, the new self-confident and ambitious UN Secretary-General, Boutros Boutros-Ghali, believed that intervention to safeguard relief was insufficient and that the aim should be statebuilding. In practice the UN operations ran into sufficient problems with regard to the former question to ensure that the latter would be held over for several years in Somalia's case, though statebuilding became a frequent issue in various parts of the world in the post Cold War years.

The next major chapter for the UN was to come with Ethiopian–Eritrean wars at the end of the century which then left the border issue unresolved, but in the UN's view requiring a peacekeeping force to be stationed along it. The UN Mission to Ethiopia and Eritrea (UNMEE) was thus established in June 2000 amidst hopes that it would stabilize the situation and contribute to an atmosphere of peace-seeking, which was pursued though with no agreed outcome. When its mandate expired in 2008 there was no agreement on its extension in the face of the conditions being demanded by Eritrea and it was effectively forced to close down.

The UN was also to become extensively involved in peacekeeping in Sudan, but in more difficult circumstances than being interposed between two standing armies. The CPA of 2005 recognized three indigenous forces in Sudan: the Sudan Armed Forces (SAF), now effectively the army of the north; the SPLA in the south; and new Joint Integrated Units (JIUs) drawn from the former two forces and the possible basis for a future national army in the event that the respective politicians were successful in 'making unity attractive'. Not only did that fail to happen, but the contentious border area became the centre for repeated clashes involving militias as well as the established forces, leaving the new UN Mission in Sudan (UNMIS) with a complex and difficult task. It had some impact, but it was also clear that operating over a vast area with a restricted mandate of peacekeeping rather than peacemaking it had a daunting task. In addition, the border tensions and local instability in a number of areas meant that fatalities were growing rather than diminishing, as the south moved to first the referendum and then independence. With the end of the CPA transitional period in July 2011 the UNMIS mandate came to an end, and while the GoSS made it clear that it welcomed a post-independence role for UNMIS, the government in the north was equally clear that it had no further use for it.

The other area where a UN force became involved was Darfur. With intense concern about the Darfur conflict, especially amongst the US public where there was a high profile Save Darfur Coalition calling for action, the UN even took the unusual step of leaving New York for a special Security Council meeting in Nairobi on Sudan in

2004. With the UN already heavily involved in southern Sudan, it was hoped that the AU would become the lead international organization on Darfur.

The old OAU had had a poor record in this field with only one unsuccessful attempt to put a peacekeeping force into the field in Chad in the early 1980s. Failure with regard to fulfilling an effective role in conflict in Africa was one of the several charges levelled regularly at the OAU, and contributed to its replacement by the new AU, finally established as its successor in 2002 with international backing through the New Partnership for African Development (NEPAD). The AU had ambitions to be more successfully involved in addressing conflict in Africa than its predecessor, and the eruption of Darfur presented it with an early opportunity to act. At the same time, from a wider international perspective, the involvement of the UN in South Sudan and the wish not to complicate the peace process there by linking it to Darfur encouraged the view that the AU, which was not directly involved in the south, could play a leading role in new conflict. Thus it was that in 2004 the AU became involved in peacekeeping in Darfur when, following the signing of a supposed ceasefire, a small AU observer team drawn from African armies was sent in. The African Mission in Sudan (AMIS) was not long in indicating that it had bitten off more than it could chew. With the agreed ceasefire it was supposed to monitor being violated by all parties, and with limited and inexperienced forces, as well as a similar restricted mandate to that of UNMIS, it was judged necessary to have more direct support from the UN, and AMIS morphed into the UN African Mission in Darfur (UNAMID) in 2007, with its numbers rising slowly towards the intended 26,000 soldiers and police. In spite of the continuing failure to achieve a negotiated peace, overall the level of conflict did fall by the end of the decade, although fighting still continued. UNAMID was stronger operationally than AMIS had been, but, in the absence of a negotiated peace, achieving its intended objectives remained challenging. At the same time, an AU–UN chief mediator, Djibril Bassole from Burkina Faso, was also appointed, although he too struggled to make an impact.

Darfur also became a testing ground for two other developments that centred on the UN, the international right to intervene to provide protection to citizens when governments were either failing to do so or quite possibly were the source of the threat: it became known as the 'Right to Protect' (R2P). R2P reflected an evolutionary process in the post-Cold War world, seeking to encourage a sense that the established acceptance of international sovereignty should not mean that all rulers are free to do whatever they wish to their peoples. Instead, in certain circumstances, the international community should exercise a right to intervene to protect people from the state. In its opening pages it wrote that, 'Where a population is suffering serious harm, as a result of internal war, insurgency, repression or state failure, and the state in question is unwilling or unable to halt or avert it, the principle of non-intervention yields to the international responsibility to protect'. The expected circumstances for exercising R2P were similar to those of traditional just war theory: it should be initiated through a proper authority, most obviously the UN; it should be a just intervention; it should be undertaken with clear intentions; the means should be proportionate; the prospects of success should be reasonable; and it should only be undertaken as a last resort. The R2P report appeared in 2001 and was followed by predictable disagreements over it before the principle was adopted by the UN in 2006, although Secretary-General Ban Ki-Moon's report emphasized measures to limit the necessity for direct intervention. Some of the impetus for R2P came from the international failure to intervene to stop the Rwanda genocide of 1994 and it was just a decade later that Darfur appeared to suggest a repeat, especially when in the USA both President Bush and Secretary of State Colin Powell used the 'G word'. Other international leaders avoided the term, but nevertheless felt compelled to wring their hands and support AMIS and then UNAMID, including some support from China.

The kind of human rights thinking involved in R2P also involved the bringing of perpetrators of violence to account, whether the rulers or the ruled, and this became the task of the UN-established International Criminal Court (ICC). The ICC was an attempt to take over from the growth of a number of separate efforts to bring alleged perpetrators to justice such as had been used over the Balkan conflicts of the 1990s and the Rwanda genocide. From early in its life the ICC focused on Africa, including Joseph Kony, the leader of the Lord's Resistance Army (LRA) operating in northern Uganda and neighbouring countries, including southern Sudan. The ICC also decided to pursue a serving head of government for the first time, announcing charges in 2008 against Sudan's President al-Beshir and two others. This was to place considerable restrictions on Beshir, though in practice some African states that were signatories to the ICC (which Sudan was not) failed to apprehend him on their soil. However, some felt that the issuing of the warrant against Beshir added to the complications of endeavouring to negotiate peace in Darfur, while the Sudanese government predictably continued to protest against it.

At the same time the AU also tried to pursue its own separate involvement in Sudan through the AU High Level Implementation Panel (AUHIP) under former South African president Thabo Mbeki. Mbeki's panel produced a report on Darfur which suggested that alleged criminals connected with Darfur should be tried by joint Sudanese and international hybrid courts, thus by implication sidelining the ICC, an idea that gained little traction. There were also tensions between the panel and Bassole, the AU–UN chief mediator, over their respective roles in the protracted Darfur talks. The panel later moved to Addis Ababa to seek to facilitate negotiations between the northern and southern governments after South Sudan had voted for separation in 2011.

The AU, with the agreement of the UN, also took on a growing security role in Somalia in support of the TFG. The Ethiopian intervention to destroy the ICU was followed by withdrawal in 2008–09 and the African Union Mission in Somalia (AMISOM) force was established in 2007 to try to act as some form of replacement. Intended to rise to 8,000 troops, it took time to reach even 5,000, mostly from Uganda and Burundi. At first AMISOM protected only some key points in Mogadishu, including the presidential compound, government buildings, the port and airport, and some other parts of the divided city, although with al-Shabaab's withdrawal from the city in 2011 AMISOM's area was extended. Its mandate did not allow it to use force to further expand the areas under TFG control, and in practice it had limited impact on the overall military situation outside the capital where Ethiopia and Kenya became more involved.

With its headquarters in Addis Ababa, and Meles Zenawi an active figure in African diplomacy, it was to be expected that the new AU would seek to play a significant role in the Horn. But while it had a higher profile than the old OAU it was clear that it had inherited some of the old limitations, including differences among the member states, which inevitably reduced it to something of a lowest common denominator in its actual operations, as well as limited capabilities especially in the light of its lack of funds.

The end of the Cold War had not left the USA as the single major international power in the Horn, but with a major new entrant in China. However, they have not opposed one another in the way the USA and the USSR once did for they are not strategic military rivals, and the USA has thus far had few commercial interests to clash with China's main driving force of extracting economic resources and exploiting local opportunities. Indeed, both favoured political stability, but for China achieving that was purely a pragmatic issue and did not involve the encouragement of agendas of good governance or the pursuit of counter-terrorism. Instead for governments, especially in Ethiopia and Sudan, the growth of their economies, achieved largely through their alignment with China, reduced the leverage of the USA and the

West more generally in the encouragement of reform. However, in the pursuit of stability both major powers endeavoured to contribute to peace, the USA in southern Sudan in particular, and China in pressure over Darfur. Yet, as in the Cold War, the major powers also acted in ways that promoted conflict, however inadvertently. The US intervention in Somalia in the early 1990s contributed to the entrenchment of warlordism, while it was to seek warlord allies to prevent the rise of the ICU a decade later. When that failed the USA encouraged and gave air support to Ethiopia's invasion to overthrow the ICU in 2006, which was followed by an upsurge of conflict as the more militant al-Shabaab emerged to dominate in much of south-central Somalia. Meanwhile, China's pursuit of oil in southern Sudan increased violent land clearances in and around the oilfields, while weapons it had supplied were deployed by both *janjaweed* and government forces in Darfur.

CHAPTER 9

Conclusion

The end of the Cold War appeared to create a challenge for the USA and the West more generally. Victors always aim to shape the peace, and something as globalized as the Cold War naturally led some to think of the apparently wide range of opportunities, as well as responsibilities, that might be addressed. The Horn of Africa appeared to contain both, but for the West it was perhaps responsibilities that stood out most clearly in view of the turmoil of the region. The most common theme across the states of the region appeared to be conflict, and right across the region the prevalence of conflict had been exacerbated by the Cold War. Once over, the first responsibility of the victorious West appeared to be engagement in ending conflict.

The origins of conflict were essentially internal, but all had cross-border dimensions that contributed both to their virulence and to the character of regional relations. At the same time the strategic significance and fragility of the region had drawn both superpowers into a rivalry that served to fuel conflicts and increase instability. With the Cold War ended, that element of conflict had at least diminished and with it had come the possibility to stabilize the region. That was certainly a thought in Washington as the State Department and the Carter Center in particular embarked on peacemaking efforts. Trying to bring about a peaceful transition in Ethiopia as Mengistu's former Soviet-backed regime collapsed was a high priority and was generally successful, although largely for local reasons with the major insurgent forces in Eritrea and Ethiopia in agreement, and Mengistu's forces routed. The new peace even included international recognition of the separation of Ethiopia and Eritrea. The end of the Cold War was one of those transforming periods that allowed for the change of numerous states, especially the old socialist hegemonies in the Soviet Union and Eastern Europe, and in the former Yugoslavia. Eritrea's recognition was out of line with the norms of the OAU, but seemed acceptable in the exceptional circumstances, and with agreement between the two parties directly involved. But halting conflict in neighbouring Sudan was more difficult as a new and obdurate regime was more intent on war while paying only lip service to peace, and at the same time its enemies in the south experienced a major factional split. Nevertheless, the subsequent unsuccessful pursuit of peace by the regional international organization IGADD did lead to the latter's introducing the possibility of separation of southern Sudan, although it seemed very distant in 1994.

However, the most challenging situation in the Horn in the early 1990s was to be Somalia. In one sense Somalia was not a proper 'conflict' at all, since there were no clearly recognizable 'sides' struggling for power so much as a collapsed state in the environs of which a humanitarian crisis was unfolding, but where aid was impeded by pillaging bands generally depicted as being led by 'warlords'. What was to be the purpose of intervention and at what cost? The purpose was soon disputed and the question of statebuilding was to crop up with open disagreement between the American president, who was prepared to send substantial troops to the crisis, and the new Secretary-General of the UN who saw the humanitarian crisis as his organization's opportunity to push for statebuilding. In the end the failure in Somalia came down to cost – US soldiers' lives were not to be publicly sacrificed in the name of a humanitarian operation in which the USA had no strategic or commercial interest. Leaving Somalia without 'statebuilding' also left Somaliland in the north to continue to self-build, and then to seek recognition as an independent state, although a combination of OAU/AU opposition and a lack of a functioning government in the centre and south of the country able and willing to agree was to prevent the claim being recognized.

It has been remarked in the past that there appeared something of a paradox in the Horn, with African states throwing off their imperial powers yet identifying so much with their colonially inherited frontiers and identities. Eritrea had little collective identity beyond a few *Rubbish* decades of Italian rule; Somaliland appeared part of a greater Somali identity but was clinging to its British-created territory; while southern Sudan had little collective identity apart from anti-northern perspectives which had been accentuated by the country's period of British rule. Yet that may be to underestimate the effects of the longevity of the struggles themselves, beginning with the imperial experience and the lack of resolution of issues as they ended. Many in Eritrea came to the view that a betrayal occurred in 1952 when it was in effect handed over to Ethiopia; Somaliland too was to claim that it was cheated in 1960; while as South Sudan became independent in 2011 its government proclaimed nearly 200 years of struggle against Egyptian and British imperialism and then northern repression. The circumstances of Western decolonization in the Horn exacerbated the claims of the identities created by outsiders.

The continuation of the Horn as a region of conflict also meant that conflict resolution remained high on the international agenda, especially in the West. Domestic conflicts continued in Somalia and Sudan and demonstrated how hard it was for them to be brought to a halt. Somalia was the most obvious example, initially because it appeared so fragmented and in later years because of the complication of the rise of Islamist movements: first the ICU and then its overthrow of al-Shabaab. This had produced the paradox that while structures had emerged which might have sufficient solidity to make negotiation possible, if one or more of those structures was seen as at least suspect if not worse, especially in relation to the 'war on terror', it would be viewed as a target rather than a participant by international sponsors of peacemaking processes. At the same time, the experience of the international backing of the TFG in Somalia showed how seeking to impose one party in a conflict over another could backfire. Darfur was another situation in which the number of groups involved contributed to the difficulty of arriving at peace through negotiation, including the changing character of the parties themselves.

South Sudan, however, appeared to be a great success insofar as two parties with considerable experience of having negotiated with each other in the past did finally bring an end to their major conflict for long enough for the CPA of 2005 to be more or less implemented. But a large part of the outcome was not that for which the international supporters of the negotiating process had hoped. They hoped that the non-military political groups that had felt excluded by the process of the CPA would benefit from the expanded political space as Sudan progressed towards competitive elections: instead the power accumu-lated by the NCP and SPLM in their respective areas left a dominant party in each region and limited space for other parties or civil society organizations. At the same time the exclusiveness from the outset of the negotiations of the CPA also contributed to the upsurge of violence by emerging movements in Darfur. Another agreed aim of the CPA had been to 'make unity attractive' when instead that failed entirely with each party to the CPA consolidating its position in its own region, leading to the vote for separation: the Sudan of competing parties had become instead two separate states, each with a dominant party system. The two developments were not unconnected. The Darfur crisis had partly arisen as a result of the progress of the exclusive NCP–SPLM talks, and the failure of the DPA contributed to the SPLM's growing alienation from the Government of National Unity and its move towards separation. Some even argued that the whole process of international pressure towards the CPA had made the democratic reconciliatory intentions of it appear to the parties as something of an imposition, and that while signing, their first concern would be to their interests as separate signatories. The CPA has been the major achievement of peacemaking in the Horn and has ended Africa's longest running civil war, but the circumstances that made it possible, both domestically and regionally, were particular and unusual. Moreover, the outcome was not that which the international partners had sought, and it also produced a two-state outcome in which there were new questions of conflict both within both states and between them.

The CPA lived up to its name in that the road map it laid down was complex and quite comprehensive. However, while pointing the way it left the most important decision of all – self-determination by southerners – to the end of the process. Thus issues of post-conflict statebuilding were all in part at least provisional. It appeared in 2005 that Sudan had achieved a pacted transition between two parties who had been unable to achieve military victory over each other and had instead come to an agreement about the path to the future rather than the future itself: everything, or almost everything, was transitional. In the end the southerners opted for independence and transitional arrangements north and south now became open to resolution. In Ethiopia, in contrast, the EPLF and the EPRDF had achieved outright destruction of Mengistu's regime and were in a position to move towards their 'victors' peace' from the outset, including state division with the independence of Eritrea. The domination of the question of South Sudan's future status had delayed the emerging picture of the post-conflict state: in Ethiopia it was significantly resolved almost as soon as the fighting was over. Meanwhile, in Somaliland the international community avoided its strong claim for separation while being unable to contribute effectively to the reunification and rebuilding of Somalia.

Peacemaking frequently requires subsequent peacekeeping, often involving the UN, and the Horn has been no exception. Together with the Democratic Republic of Congo, Sudan has seen the largest UN forces in Africa both in relation to South Sudan and then, in conjunction with the AU, in Darfur. However, a major problem has been the extent to which there is a peace to keep, and the effectiveness of the UN peacekeeping force's mandate in such a situation. It can lead to peacekeepers being little more than observers of conflict. In part this may be because peace agreements do not necessarily lead to peace, especially if political fundamentals have perhaps shifted but not fully changed. Thus in the case of what has become the two Sudans, the separation of the south has changed political relations between the major contending parties, but not halted the cross-border manifestations of the ways in which the long years of war involving allies and proxies were conducted. As conflicts mutate in this way it becomes hard for the UN to disengage and involvement can seem endless. In theory the politics of the peace settlement should involve an exit. Kofi Annan, when Secretary-General of the UN, suggested key steps for an exit strategy: consolidating security; strengthening and improving political institutions; and improving socio-economic conditions. All are hard tasks and involve not only the problem of post-conflict situations but also the cooperation of sovereign governments involved, which cannot be taken for granted. The UN has had to withdraw its peacekeepers from the tense standoff on the Eritrean–Ethiopian border, while in contrasting decisions the government in former north Sudan has told UNMIS to leave whereas the GoSS has asked for its mandate to be extended.

Concern with peacemaking leads on to post-conflict statebuilding which in turn elides easily into the fashionable concern in the post-Cold War era of 'good governance'. This concept had sprung into life from its often-forgotten historical origins in the seventeenth and eighteenth centuries through its adoption by the World Bank in particular, and has become a central part of Western policies towards the 'developing' world. It had been backed both by international financial organizations and by governments, sometimes linking it to aid conditionality of various kinds. One of its central themes had been liberal democracy, although there were other interconnected themes associated with it such as constitutionalism and the division of power. Since the end of the Cold War liberal democracy has encountered considerable restrictions by the states of the Horn with a variety of explanations, most of which have some degree of relevance. Perhaps the oldest argument has been of a socio-political character, going back at least to J. S. Mill in the nineteenth century, which has queried the appropriateness of liberal democracy for societies with high levels of poverty as well as low levels of literacy. This view has not gone away, and appears in Chinese comments about Africa just as readily as Western donors propose liberal democracy.

Much has been written about contention or coordination between democracy and development, ranging from their intrinsic compatibility to the actual or potential conflict between the two, while yet others have looked for common ground perhaps through some sequencing of socio-economic development and an evolutionary path to liberal democracy. But whatever theories may be put forward by proponents of 'good governance', local power holders may have their own ideological and pragmatic approaches to pursue. Ideologically some may be committed to paths other than immediate liberal democracy. In Ethiopia in particular Prime Minister Meles Zenawi was long seen as a theorist and ideologist as well as a political leader. As seen, he took a developmentalist view with regard to liberal democracy which sees it as at best relevant to more advanced 'stages' of development, and at worst as contrary to more collectivist approaches to democracy centred around what has become a dominant party state. Eritrea has gone in a similar direction, albeit under a less persuasive leader. In neighbouring Sudan there has also been an ideological question mark about liberal democracy, especially in the writings of the original inspiration behind the rise of Islamism to power, Hasan al-Turabi. Turabi may have been seen as a relatively liberal and pro-democracy Islamist, but it was to be set within his vision of Islamic society. When that society had not evolved as he had previously thought necessary, his movement organized a coup as a shortcut which it followed up with a repressive attempt to impose its ideology in both the north and south. Turabi himself may have been sidelined in 1999, but nonetheless when it came to a choice between liberal democratic secularism as the price of peace in one country or the NCP's version of an Islamic state in the north and the separation of South Sudan, the NCP chose the latter. Pragmatically, power-holding elites may feel that there is more to be lost than gained, and that a combination of patronage and selective coercion is a realistic choice, especially if there are the resources both to deliver to clients and at the same time to resist pressures from within and without to reform. Ironically, the place that appeared most attached to liberal democracy was the one that has not been recognized as a state: Somaliland. It appeared to have a real bottom-up dimension to its democracy not least because clan elders were important to the SNM from the movement's early days: but, while passing the test of changing leaders at the ballot box won it sympathy in Western capitals, it did not bring its goal of international recognition.

However, collectivist ideologies also have their limitations in terms of statebuilding. The ideologies may be seeking to build a new hegemonic order for the state, but it may be that resistance to them continues to exist: Islam, for instance, has been a heterogeneous religion and, from the NCP in Sudan to al-Shabaab in Somalia, there has been resistance from within Muslim societies to the more doctrinaire interpretations seeking to be imposed. More secular ideologies have been pursued in Ethiopia, most recently advancing a developmental state model. It may take root, but it is also possible that it can become another form of elite entrenchment as in the former USSR and China;

while there has been rapid growth in Ethiopia, for most of the population it remains one of the poorest countries on earth. Moreover, in relatively weak states, often with ethnic divisions and uneven economic development, the attempt to impose any ideological form of rule may enhance resistance and perhaps sustained conflict.

Concern about liberal democracy has to be related to the character of post-liberation rule. There may have been hopes of 'renaissance leaders' who carried out cathartic armed struggle for a new and perhaps more real liberation than that of the era of the 1950s and early 1960s, but that route to power itself may have implications. (It was ironic that such Fanonist thinking should come from liberal democrats around the Clinton administration.) However, after taking power through armed struggle the subsequent 'renaissance' did not always follow the script of those who coined the term. There was a tendency to put the struggle at the centre of the legitimacy of such new regimes. As well as being expressed in terms of what could become a rather backward-looking ideology, it also could suggest that opposition, especially from those who had not participated actively in the struggle, lacked an appropriate legitimacy and did not carry the same weight or status as armed service in the liberation movement. Moreover, success in the struggle was associated with unity around the leader and, as in several parts of Africa, those who led the struggle kept the power they had assumed. Such traits have been clearly seen in Eritrea and Ethiopia, and there are those who believe South Sudan could follow the pattern. The carry-over from the period of struggle also related to the figures around the leader whose positions were frequently connected to roles during the conflict and feelings of entitlement thereafter.

Questions about liberal democracy have also been related to the international environment. The first foreign power to raise its position significantly in the Horn after the Cold War was China as it built up its economic position in first Sudan and then Ethiopia. In proclaiming its intention to stay out of politics China was indicating at least its unconcern with moves in an undemocratic direction, but it has also appeared that Chinese officials believe that Africa is not a suitable environment for liberal democracy and that forms of authoritarianism are more appropriate in relation to providing the necessary stability within which development can occur. Indeed, some indicated the view that any Western efforts to introduce liberal democracy by forms of aid conditionality amounted to attempts at a new form of Western hegemony. However, in the case of the USA it appears that post-9/11 the concern with anti-terrorism trumps major pressure for liberal democracy in the Horn, above all in respect of its close ally Ethiopia. As for Sudan, although US sanctions continued after the CPA, it is clear that cooperation on anti-terrorism with the governments there, both north and south, were of high priority. With neighbouring states also relatively unconcerned about the character of government, it was clear that in spite of Darfur and other conflict areas it would broadly be business as usual.

In the more immediate international environment, it was notable how limited the impact of the 'Arab Spring' of 2011 proved with regard to democratization. Sudan's response to events in neighbouring Egypt and Libya was concern, but the country was not directly affected. Instead the ruling NCP pronounced common cause with the reform movements while claiming that it had already brought change, most recently in the moves to ostensibly open the political system by implementing the CPA, including national elections and the building of a 'moderate' Islamic state. In Ethiopia Meles Zenawi made mention of the 'Arab Spring' only to point to its irrelevance for his country. In neither country were there developments within opposition groups to mount an effective challenge to their government's position in spite of the major changes on their doorsteps.

The limited progress on liberal democracy was matched by similar shortcomings in respect of other areas of 'good governance'. Human rights abuses were regularly reported from the region; media freedoms were restricted; judiciaries rarely appeared fully independent; administrative shortcomings continued; and corruption was widespread. The establishment of federal structures appeared to offer devolution of power but in practice was frequently influenced if not controlled by the centre, not least through the dominant party systems.

While governments have often appeared authoritarian in the Horn, there has also been much talk of 'failing states', with additions such as 'the coming anarchy' or throwbacks such as the eighteenth-century world view of 'civilized' states amidst a sea of despotisms and statelessness. Perhaps the lessons of the Horn are that one needs to unpack individual states to try to perceive degrees of 'stateness'. If one still thinks in Weberian terms of 'monopolies on the use of force' then it is clear that no state is more than a partial state, for all at least have areas where weapons abound and their use against the state takes place. Perhaps it is the small scale of Eritrea and Djibouti that makes violence against the state less prevalent. Eritrea is clearly the state most actively enforcing repressive government over much of its territory; while Djibouti largely maintains authority through the use of clientelism, with the neighbouring threats of piracy and Islamist terrorism adding to its resources from outside to enable it to maintain the neo-patrimonial system. Ethiopia's state appears dominant in much of the northern highland areas, but under greater challenge in areas across its southern and eastern regions. Sudan's division into two states indicates the weakness of the repressive state in the face of resistance in the south, and continuing challenges in all its 'marginalized' areas. Challenges have already been seen in areas of both the new states created by South Sudan's secession. Somalia is often cited as the most collapsed state in the world, and the extremely limited authority of the TFG in Mogadishu bears this out for the south-central areas of the country. But Somaliland appears closer to statehood in terms of security, while Puntland makes claims.

Softer views of the state often focus on administration, its scale and effectiveness. In terms of scale, bureaucracies have often been an easy touch for political patronage and nepotism, usually at the cost of efficiency and socially beneficial outputs. International pressure from donors, financial exigencies and the desire to attract inward investment, have all added to calls for reform. Probably the clearest outcome has been the endeavour to promote the power of dominant parties over the state apparatus, directly or indirectly. After all if there is no inclination to surrender power through the ballot box then the need for administrative structures with any significant differentiation from political leadership can be deemed unnecessary if not counterproductive. Much has also been written about decentralization of power, with federal constitutions often seeming attractive. However, unless there is a significant local tax base – rare in poor rural areas – the dependence on central funding often undermines the autonomy of local authorities, while the influence of the dominant party can be a further control from the centre: features of both of the largest states of the Horn – Ethiopia and Sudan – as well as South Sudan latterly.

States may also be assessed in terms of effective policies of service delivery, especially health and education. Here the states of the Horn have seen some efforts to extend the scale and reach of services, though often at the price of quality. Schooling has been extended, but teacher training and the provision of facilities has generally left much to be desired. Higher education is often suspect in the eyes of governments for, while better qualified cadres are needed for development, the sector is also noted for political opposition. Eritrea went as far as breaking up its national university; Ethiopia has used considerable force on its campuses; while Sudan moved resources to Islamic institutions, while also encouraging private provision. Health services are often sketchy or exiguous in practice especially in outlying areas, and payment may in reality be the only way to access sources. Unsurprisingly, at South Sudan's independence in 2011 President Kiir called for higher priority to be given to service provision: hitherto Sudan's governments had spent far more on military and security services than health and education combined.

A frequent focus on political institutions in defining states has encouraged a return to emphasis on looking beyond them towards community and identity. But here the state in the Horn is often difficult to assess. It is easy, if not too easy, to focus political analysis on what may be loosely defined as 'tribalism', often perceived as some kind of primordialism. Ethnic groups, from extended families and clans through to 'peoples' who can be counted in their millions, may continue to have great relevance. But it may not be a relic of the past so much as a highly understandable basis for identity in the vulnerable circumstances in which so many live, not only in relation to people of other ethnic identities but to the state itself. Both Ethiopia and Sudan have been seen as states which advantage those from more central areas of the country, to the perceived disadvantage of people from less favoured regions in outlying areas. The state may even move to seek to build ethnic identities from above, as in Ethiopia, with the 'nationalities' designated in relation to the federal system, or Sudan's endeavours to use its federalism to undermine local ethnic solidarities in the 'marginalized' areas such as Darfur. In contrast Somaliland stabilized and grew after 1991, largely by building on local community identities as expressed through local clan leaders. Where does that leave 'national' identities at the state level? Eritrea and South Sudan appear to emphasize historic struggles, which can also be seen to continue through tensions and conflicts with the new neighbours from which they have chosen to secede: but can this be constructive for the future? Ethiopia endeavours to project the virtue of 'multi-national' nationalism, while Sudan's NCP government put its project of an Islamic state above that of a secular, pluralist country. Perhaps one of the limitations of the TFG in Somalia has been its failure to create an appealing identity, which some argue may have been emerging in the brief period of the ICU and is most clearly seen in the as-yet unrecognized nationalist calls of Somaliland.

International peacemaking has not just been concerned with domestic conflict. The Horn has also been the region of Africa that has experienced the two largest inter-state wars since World War II. The first in the late 1970s had involved Somalia's irredentist claims. Peacemaking efforts, such as they were, had then involved the USSR in trying to restrain its unruly Somali client, Siad Barre, while promoting socialism embracing Somalia, Ethiopia and Yemen. That had proved a total failure and instead, when Somalia attacked, the USSR swiftly switched to Ethiopia and brought about Somalia's defeat. The second war, between Eritrea and Ethiopia in 1998, was even more difficult to predict since the border dispute that triggered it scarcely appeared to warrant a full-scale conflict. Though taken by surprise it was now the turn of the USA to try to douse the flames of war in the Horn, but it proved unsuccessful. In time the UN took over both with regard to peacekeepers on the border and negotiations between the parties, for while agreement was reached at Algiers it was not fully implemented, and the underlying tension and rivalry between the former guerrilla allies persisted and was to link in to growing conflict in Somalia from 2006 in particular.

At the same time regional problems have been spreading. The picture of regional conflict had centred on Ethiopia as the core of interconnected conflicts: Somalia's irredentist aims with regard to Ethiopia in particular, and Sudan's support for the EPLF and the TPLF, while in return Ethiopia supported rebel movements in Somaliland and southern Sudan. But as conflict changed after the Cold War, so it also expanded in area. The collapse of Somalia facilitated the emergence of piracy, taking the lawlessness from land to sea with new international targets, and Kenya and Uganda have become drawn in to the struggle with al-Shabaab. Meanwhile, in Sudan the NCP government had assisted the LRA in northern Uganda, and peace in the south contributed to the context for a large-scale conflict in Darfur. In addition, there was the conflict between Eritrea and Ethiopia and their part proxy struggle in south-central Somalia. There are signs of economic cooperation, especially between Ethiopia and Sudan, that could lead to improved relations generally, but how much this might spread across the region more broadly is far from clear.

Within the wider international community, and especially the major powers, there was at least not the rivalry in the Horn that there had been during the Cold War. Instead there was generally a coming together of interests. China had emerged as a driver of Sudan's economy in particular, and to a lesser extent Ethiopia's. It had taken advantage of the US government's decision to place sanctions on Sudan affecting especially its potential oil sector, but there was little sign of American companies being seriously disgruntled at the loss. America's major concern, particularly after 9/11, was in confronting Islamist terrorism, and if that meant working with Sudan and Ethiopia on security matters, including using air power against the ICU and then al-Shabaab in Somalia, then that was acceptable. The limited US leverage in regard to sanctions helped the CPA process in Sudan, but failure to deliver by lifting the terrorist-supporting designation and sanctions also reduced its credibility with the NCP. China's main concern appeared to be a secure environment for its economic engagement, and if that included more authoritarianism then that was at least acceptable and apparently seen as necessary. But when that failed China found itself drawn more openly into Sudan's conflicts, first in Darfur and then over relations between Sudan and the new state of South Sudan.

Just as political development across the Horn has offered only limited reflections of theories of liberal democracy, liberal hopes for a market economy have rarely been achieved. The domestic environment has been more in line with the politics of the region. The fastest-growing of the region's economies was Sudan's once oil was being exported in 1999. The new income stream made Sudan into a semi-rentier state and as such the evolving political economy adopted certain charac- teristics of such regimes, with new opportunities for the state's patronage of its followers and a growing group of clients. At one level it looked more like a market economy than hitherto, but behind the facade there were trade-offs that amounted to crony capitalism. However, the sustainability of its rate of growth, and with it its powers of patronage, have been seriously damaged by the secession of the oil-producing South Sudan. In neighbouring Ethiopia the politics of economic growth were, if anything, even more open, with the main Ethiopian companies clearly linked to the state, especially with the consolidation of the dominant party. Eritrea was the most authoritarian of the states, but also had the weakest economy of any of the functioning states. In some ways it was stateless Somalia that had the most unfettered market of all and drew its own specialist literature on livestock trade in particular, while economic opportunity unrestrained by any state provided the context for the rapid growth of piracy, from small beginnings amongst former fishermen into an international business with international connections. At the same time Somalia and Eritrea remained heavily reliant on remittances while their own political and economic woes have been discouraging return and encouraging those who could to flee.

The character of economic development in the case of Sudan and Ethiopia owed a good deal to the involvement of China. When the USA and then the UN imposed sanctions on Sudan they inadvertently provided China with an opportunity which it readily seized, first in Sudan and then in Ethiopia. Just as China sought not to be seen to engage with the politics of its new partners, it also avoided seeking to impose on the character of economic development. Not that it would have been much of an issue for it, for authoritarian political systems seeking to shape the direction of economic growth was fully in line with the thinking of the Chinese policy makers.

As one of the poorest areas of the world the Horn regularly experiences drought, and has expectations that the international community will deliver aid. Since the late 1980s, Sudan has been the world's largest recipient of food aid, mainly in the south and Darfur, while Ethiopia has had regular recourse to WFP, as has Somalia. In some respects there has been improvement since the famines of the 1980s. Monitoring and assessment of need, in which the Food and Agriculture Organisation (of the UN) plays a leading part, has become regular, while the various agencies have become well practised in putting out appeals and arranging relief responses which range from refugee and IDP camps, to which the needy are expected to make their way, to air drops for the most inaccessible communities. Understandably the agencies involved concentrate on maximizing the opportunities to provide relief including de-politicizing situations where possible to avoid issues that could make their work harder. Yet it is also clear that this tends to lead to a glossing over of the role of conflict. Struggles in northern Ethiopia in the 1980s were central to the situation there, though largely omitted from media coverage in particular. More mention was made of the situation in Somalia in 2011, but with the simplification of blaming al-Shabaab rather than seeking to present a more nuanced picture in which international involvement with the transitional government in Mogadishu was included. Politics is clearly central, but it is by no means the only problem in regards to famine. Populations continue to rise, placing ever greater pressures on the carrying capacity of the large, arid and sometimes environmentally challenged areas of the region, while global warming is increasingly recognized as a factor in the making of drought conditions. Drought alleviation may have improved, but there is not yet the implementation of a solution, in particular measures that could help develop the long-term livelihoods of the pastoralists of the region.

Development has been in part linked to issues of aid. Emergency relief has largely been left to UN agencies and International NGOs (INGOs) but they would prefer to be involved in development including the provision of services of various kinds, though that has also excited suspicion in some quarters. Sometimes INGOs have been criticized for compliance with funders, especially as more Western government-funded work has been carried out by INGOs, permitting them to bring substantial sums of money and employ numerous local staff, possibly bringing political leverage as well as allowing the national governments involved to absolve themselves of some responsibilities. But at the same time they can incite political suspicion in the countries in which they operate. Certainly the Horn provides regular examples of governments trying to manage if not control INGOs. Eritrea has been the most outspoken case, regularly falling out with the USA in particular and in 2005 telling USAID to quit. Ethiopia may have been more measured in its utterances, but none the less has sought to have a firm grip on the activities of INGOs to the point where in their home countries their apparent acceptance of restrictions has become a cause for criticism. Sudan has shown the extent to which government suspicions have seen INGOs as seeking to encourage local counterparts, sometimes in the name of helping indigenous 'civil society' to grow, with subversive intentions. Its response has been to encourage alternative international and local Islamic organizations, sometimes deserving of the sobriquet 'GONGOs', government-organized non-governmental organizations. In contrast, in areas of Sudan controlled by the SPLA and its allies INGOs operated with greater freedom, since the liberation movement had little non-military capability, and included extensive activities by often religiously based INGOs such as Norwegian Church Aid and Samaritan's Purse International under the leadership of Franklin Graham. Their sympathy for the rebels' cause was as clear as that of War on Want decades earlier in its sympathy for rebel movements in what was then northern Ethiopia. Clearly relief and development would be less without the activities of INGOs, but equally they are politically involved, even if reluctantly.

However, beyond relief and development there have also arisen questions of possible intervention when conflict has been having a particularly hard effect on indigenous populations. From 2000 in particular the issue of the Right to Protect (R2P) came to the fore, including potential international intervention. The Balkans had helped to raise the issue, and being in Europe had done much to lead to action. In contrast, following the US-led UN operation in Somalia in the early 1990s there was no appetite to see a significant peacemaking force deployed there. When there was international support for the TFG it was the AU that took the lead in raising a comparatively small force, AMIS, which could do little to extend the area under government control beyond Mogadishu. Darfur gave rise to fresh concern about R2P, but in spite of talk in the US government of genocide, with its implication of action under the UN's 1948 convention on human rights, there appeared little prospect of direct Western involvement. Instead there was support for the AU peace-keeping force and, when that was clearly inadequate, for UNAMIS, but its impact in reducing the suffering of the people of Darfur was limited. The ICC's role was an extension of interventionist thinking in the form of holding combatants to account, and it soon produced the first indictment of a serving head of state in the person of President al-Beshir of Sudan; but while it inconvenienced him it has made little difference to the situation in Darfur, and has complicated diplomatic efforts to find a solution to the conflicts there.

Clearly the end of the Cold War did not usher a New World Order into the Horn. But perhaps to think it could was to overrate the power of superpowers during the Cold War itself. The Cold War had had a great impact on the Horn but it had often shown the inability of either superpower to dominate events. Rather, they projected power which had outcomes, but those outcomes were often not what had been expected or desired. Why should it have been different after the Cold War? There was no spontaneous democracy waiting to appear directly autocrats had departed the scene, as appeared to be an assumption in the US government with regard to Iraq and the even more unlikely location of Afghanistan. Nor did the USA and its Western allies have the ability simply to enforce their will, as Somalia was soon to demonstrate. Rather, the concerns and aims with regard to liberal democracy, good governance and human rights had to be handled with realism in the light of circumstances within and between the countries of the Horn, the changing international scene with the growing economic power and political influence of Asia, and other priorities and interests of the Western powers themselves.

Select Bibliography

Horn of Africa

Degu, Wondem, *The State, the Crisis of State Institutions, and Refugee Migration in the Horn of Africa* (Lawrenceville NJ, 2007)

Erlich, Haggai, *Islam and Christianity in the Horn of Africa: Somalia, Ethiopia and Sudan* (Boulder, 2010)

Rotberg, Robert I. (ed), *Battling Terrorism in the Horn of Africa* (Washington, 2005)

de Waal, Alex (ed), *Islamism and Its Enemies in the Horn of Africa* (Addis Ababa, 2003)

Woodward, Peter, *The Horn of Africa: Politics and International Relations* (London, 2003)

Woodward, Peter, *US Foreign Policy and the Horn of Africa* (Aldershot, 2006)

Ethiopia

Aalen, Lovise, *The Politics of Ethnicity in Ethiopia* (Leiden, 2011)

Pankhurst, Alula and Francois Piguet (eds), *Moving People in Ethiopia: Development, Displacement and the State* (Woodbridge, 2009)

Tronvoll, Kjetil, *War and the Politics of Identity in Ethiopia: Making Enemies and Allies in the Horn of Africa* (Woodbridge, 2009)

Vaughan, Sarah and Kjetil Tronvoll, *Structures and Relations of Power in Ethiopia* (Stockholm, 2003)

Vaughan, Sarah and Kjetil Tronvoll, *The Culture of Power in Contemporary Ethiopian Political Life* (Stockholm, 2003)

Somalia

Bahadur, Jay, *Deadly Waters: Inside the Hidden World of Somalia's Pirates* (London, 2011)

Bradbury, Mark, *Becoming Somaliland* (Oxford, 2008)

Bruton, Bronwyn E., *Somalia: A New Approach* (New York, 2010)

Clarke, Walter S. and Jeffrey Herbst, *Learning from Somalia: The Lessons of Armed Humanitarian Intervention* (Boulder, 1997)

Elmi, Afyare Abdi, *Understanding the Somalia Conflagration: Identity, Political Islam and Peacebuilding* (London, 2010)

Hesse, Brian J. (ed), *Somalia: State Collapse, Terrorism and Piracy* (London, 2011)

Jhazbhay, Iqbal D., *Somaliland: An African Struggle for Nationhood and International Recognition* (Braamfontein, 2009)

Lewis, Ioan M., *A Modern History of the Somali: Nation and State in the Horn of Africa 4th rev. ed* (Oxford, 2002)

Lewis, Ioan M., *Understanding Somalia and Somaliland: Culture, History and Society* (London, 2010)

Menkhaus, Kenneth, *Somalia: State Collapse and the Threat of Terrorism* (Oxford, 2004)

Murphy, Martin N., *Somalia, The New Barbary? Piracy and Islam in the Horn of Africa* (New York, 2011)

Sudan

Alier, Abel, *Southern Sudan: Too Many Agreements Dishonoured* (Exeter, 1990)

Cockett, Richard, *Sudan: Darfur and the Failure of an African State* (New Haven, 2010)

Collins, Robert O., *A History of Modern Sudan* (Cambridge, 2008)

Daly, M.W., *Darfur's Sorrow: A History of Destruction and Genocide* (Cambridge, 2007)

Elnur, Ibrahim, *Contested Sudan: The Political Economy of War and Reconstruction* (London, 2009)

Gallab, Abdullahi A., *The First Islamist Republic: Development and Disintegration of Islamism in the Sudan* (Aldershot, 2008)

Grawert, Elke (ed), *After the Comprehensive Peace Agreement in Sudan* (Woodbridge, 2010)

Johnson, Douglas H., *The Root Causes of Sudan's Civil Wars* (Oxford, 2003)

Jok, Jok Madut, *Sudan: Race, Religion and Violence* (Oxford, 2007)

Ryle, John and Justin Willis, Suliman Baldo and Jok Madut Jok (eds), *The Sudan Handbook* (Woodbridge, 2010)

Eritrea

Bereketeab, Redie, *State-building in Post-Liberation Eritrea: Challenges, Achievement and Potentials* (London, 2009)

Kibreab, Gaim, *Eritrea: A Dream Deferred* (Woodbridge, 2009)

Negash, Tekeste and Kjetil Tronvoll, *Brothers at War: Making Sense of the Eritrean-Ethiopian War* (Oxford, 2002)

Djibouti

Houmed, Ismail Ibrahim, *Indépendance, Démocratisation, Enjeux Stratégiques à Djibouti* (Paris, 2009)

Saint-Prot, Charles and Zeina el-Tibi, *Djibouti: au Coeur de la géopolitique de la Corne de l'Afrique* (Paris, 2006)

Other Sources

Several leading academic journals have published regularly on the region, including: *Africa, African Affairs, African History, Journal of Modern African Studies* and *Review of African Political Economy.*

As well as the books and journals listed above, think tanks and research organizations have produced numerous studies and reports. These include Human Rights Watch, International Crisis Group, Justice Africa, Rift Valley Institute, Royal Institute of International Affairs (Chatham House) and Geneva Small Arms Survey.

Notes

Chapter 1: Introduction

1. 'Dangers and dilemmas in the Horn of Africa', *Africa Confidential* (September 2009) 50/18, pp. 1–3
2. de Waal, Alex, *Famine that Kills: Darfur, Sudan, 1984–1985* (Oxford, 1989)
3. Rienert, Erik S., *How Rich Countries Got Rich . . . and Poor Countries Stay Poor* (London, 2007)
4. Duffield, Mark, *Development, Security and Unending War* (Cambridge, 2007)
5. Clayton, Anthony, *Frontiersmen: Warfare in Africa since 1950* (London, 1999)
6. Berman, Bruce, Eyoh Dickson and Will Kymlicka (eds), *Ethnicity and Democracy in Africa* (Oxford, 2004)
7. Karadawi, Ahmed, *Refugee Policy in Sudan, 1967–1984* (Oxford, 1999)
8. Zartman, I. William, *Ripe for Resolution: Conflict and Intervention in Africa* (Oxford, 1989)
9. Buzan, Barry and Ole Waever, *Regions and Powers: The Structure of International Security* (Cambridge, 2003)
10. Rotberg, Robert I. (ed), *Battling Terrorism in the Horn of Africa* (Washington, 2005)
11. Kaldor, Mary, *New and Old Wars: Organized Violence in a Global Era 2nd ed* (Cambridge, 2006)

11. Keen, David, *Useful Enemies: When Waging Wars is More Important Than Winning Them* (New Haven, 2012)

Chapter 2: The Evolution of the Horn

1. Best known are the numerous works of E. Evans-Pritchard
2. Laitin, D. and Samatar, S., *Somalia: Nations in Search of a State* (Boulder, 1987), p. 70
3. Samatar, S., *Somalia: A Nation in Turmoil* (London, 1991), p. 13
4. Lewis, Ioan M., *A Pastoral Democracy: a Study of Pastoralism and Politics Amongst the Northern Somali of the Horn of Africa* (London, 1961)
5. Laitin: *Somalia*, p. 70

Chapter 3: Ethiopia

1. Vaughan, Sarah and Kjetil Tronvoll, *Structures and Relations of Power in Ethiopia* (Stockholm, 2003), p. 117
2. Vaughan: *Structures and Relations*, p. 133
3. LeFort, R., 'Powers – *mengiste* – and peasants in rural Ethiopia: The May 2005 elections', *Journal of Modern African Studies* (2007) 45/2
4. Gill, P., *Famine and Foreigners: Ethiopia since Live Aid* (Oxford, 2010) pp. 153, 183
5. 'A leading Ethiopian scholar' quoted by Tronvoll, Kjetil, *Ethiopia: A New Start?* (London, 2000)

Chapter 4: Somalia

1. Hempstone, Smith, *Rogue Ambassador: An African Memoir* (Tennessee, 1997), p. 230
2. Lewis, Ioan M., *A Modern History of the Somali: Nation and State in the Horn of Africa 4th rev. ed* (Oxford, 2002), p. 275

3. Woodward, Peter, *The Horn of Africa: Politics and International Relations* (London, 2003), p. 84

4. *Washington Post*, 25 November 2011

Chapter 5: Sudan

1. Markakis, John, *National and Class Conflict in the Horn of Africa* (Cambridge, 1987)

2. El-Affendi, Abdelwahab, *Turabi's Revolution: Islam and Power in Sudan* (London, 1991)

3. The following draws on the report by Laurie Nathan who was in Abuja for the talks. Crisis States Research Centre, London School of Economics, 13 June 2006; later published as 'No dialogue, no commitment: the perils of deadline diplomacy for Darfur', *Geneva Small Arms Survey* (December 2006)

4. The DPA 'rejectionists' did then come together to form the National Redemption Front (NRF) but it did not make negotiations any more successful

5. Efforts at peacemaking continued, with Qatar becoming a leading centre by 2009

6. Mazrui, Ali Al'Amin, 'The Multiple Marginality of the Sudan', in Hasan, Y.F. (ed), *Sudan in Africa* (Khartoum, 1969)

7. Khalid, Mansour (ed), *John Garang Speaks* (London, 1987)

8. Alier, Abel, *Southern Sudan: Too Many Agreements Dishonoured* (Exeter, 1990)

9. Jok, Jok Madut, *Diversity, Unity and Nation-Building in South Sudan* (Washington, 2011)

Chapter 7: Regional Relations

1. Benjamin, Daniel and Steven Simon, *The Age of Sacred Terror* (New York, 2003)

2. Buzan, Barry, *People, States and Fear: The National Security Problem in International Relations* (Brighton, 1983)

Chapter 8: International Politics

1. *The Economist,* 16 June 2007
2. Rotberg: *Battling Terrorism*, pp. 7–8
3. Raine, S., *China's African Challenges* (London, 2009), p. 113

Index